Walter Lindrum

Walter Lindrum

Billiards Phenomenon

Andrew Ricketts

Brian Clouston
Canberra 1982

First published for the Walter Lindrum Publishing Syndicate by Brian Clouston
P.O. Box 391, Manuka, A.C.T., 2603 Australia

ISBN 0 949742 48 1

Typeset in 10/11pt Times New Roman
by Canberra Times Print

Printed in Hong Kong
Cover design by Gaye Paterson

Foreword

I am honoured to write a foreword for this long-overdue tribute to the life of Walter Lindrum, unquestionably the greatest cueist the world has known.

At the time of Lindrum's visits to England I was a dedicated young player approaching the top flight of English amateur billiards. It was my very good fortune then that the great master took an interest in me and we were thereafter to become very close friends. In those early days of our association I was so pre-occupied with his company I became somewhat neglectful of my girl friend, who however displayed commendable understanding and we later married.

Despite his colossal stature as a player Lindrum was a very human character who indulged his friends, and asked nothing of them but their friendship. In 1931 Laurie Steeples and myself were to represent England in the World Amateur Championship in Australia and we sailed in company with Lindrum and Newman. I fondly recall the friendship and encouragement extended to us by Lindrum, and that he gave a party for my 21st birthday on board.

On the billiard table Lindrum was without peer, a position he had earned. He expected to be acknowledged accordingly, particularly in exhibition matches where he normally conceded handsome starts. On one such occasion I played him at a London Club and received 250 start in 500 up. Whatever was expected of me, I had privately resolved to try and win and at one stage I potted the white and double-baulked. Walter missed and I went on to win. Lindrum then expressed himself in no uncertain terms and suggested the result would have been quite different if he'd known my intentions. I had no doubt of it and knew I had made a mistake in seeking to upstage him. Nevertheless, it was Lindrum who rang me the next morning, apologising for his outburst and hoping it would not affect our friendship.

As referee of the 'Pot Black' series of recent times, I feel I am in a position to make some pertinent observations. Since the early thirties snooker has become more popular than billiards. However, I say without reservation that the standard of professionals in Lindrum's era was vastly superior to that of modern counterparts, and in these days Lindrum was far superior to the toughest bunch of professionals that has ever been. It has been claimed that Joe Davis was, at snooker, capable of giving Walter two blacks start, and a beating. Walter said to me that if he had taken snooker seriously, he would have done with it as he had done with billiards. Who would dare doubt this?

I commend the youthful author for his inspired dedication and painstaking research in compiling this authoritative work. It is stange indeed that a biography of the great Walter Lindrum should have awaited the attentions of a man who never knew him. I believe he has rendered a signal service to the game and I am grateful for it.

SYDNEY LEE
27 February 1980
'Pot Black' Referee
Former World Amateur
Billiards Champion

Contents

List of Illustrations

ix

Introduction

Anyone who sets out to write a biography obviously has a strong motive. My motives were two fold — to satisfy my thirst for more knowledge of Walter Lindrum and try to rectify a gross oversight in the history of Australian sport, while there were still some people available who could provide first-hand accounts of Lindrum, the man. The records of Lindrum, the billiard player, would have survived in the various newpapers and magazines scattered around the world and also in the small number of books where Lindrum has been given some mention. However, there seemed to be a definite need to collect and collate the material and place it in book form, so making the Lindrum story readily accessible to those who have worshipped him from near and afar and to those who are simply curious about the man behind the Lindrum legend. I have not endeavoured to prove that Walter Lindrum was the greatest billiard player of all time. I have always believed that Lindrum was the greatest and my research has only served to strengthen this belief. Rather, my object has been to illustrate the immensity of the gulf which existed between Lindrum and all other billiard players. Billiards is one of the few games where comparisons can be made between players of different generations. No other champion of billiards has a record which remotely approaches the Lindrum record. It would be a brave man indeed who would attempt to argue differently.

There were a number of controversies during Lindrum's career which, I believe, previously have not been explored thoroughly. I have attempted to rectify this in a balanced way, giving both sides of the situation. Although at times I have gone to some lengths to explain the pro-Lindrum cause it is not an attempt to distort the true circumstances. In all cases the reader is left to form his own opinion on whether Lindrum was justified in his action.

There have been inaccuracies about Lindrum which have accumulated down through the years. The facts and figures have been misconstrued in two distinct ways, either to enhance or detract from Lindrum's performances. With Lindrum's deeds placing him on a pedestal in the public's eye it was inevitable that along with the adulators would come the detractors. Every person who holds a distinguished position in some sphere of life faces such a situation. Walter Lindrum was no exception. The unfortunate consequence of this division of society is that the truth is distorted. With Lindrum's billiards prowess being beyond question the detractors had to turn to his personal affairs for their ammunition. They discovered with delight that Lindrum had his fair share of foibles and human frailties. It does seem rather negative to become pre-occupied with detailing what a person was not, as opposed to what he was.

Walter Lindrum was, when at the billiard table, an absolute perfectionist. He was anything but that when away from the billiard table. On the table he appeared to be a cold, ruthless man, relentless in his single-minded ambition to reach the pinnacle of his chosen field. It was his immense powers of concentration that camouflaged the affable, easy-going, emotional being who was Walter Lindrum. For example, it was Lindrum's impulsively generous nature that led him to promise a billiard cue to a spectator at an exhibition; but with the pressure of his commitments, and his own forgetful nature, Lindrum often broke these promises. Apart from his obsession with billiard greatness Lindrum seemed to have few ambitions in life. He never sought material gain and this led to another contradiction in his career. Despite being a professional sportsman Lindrum was the beau ideal of the amateur spirit. Instead of exploiting his enormous skill for his personal gain Lindrum chose to utilise it for the benefit of his fellow man. His years of work for numerous charities and hospitals was a remarkable, and probably unique, chapter in Australian sporting history. For that reason alone Walter Lindrum surely deserved a biographical tribute.

I am indebted to dozens of people for assistance in the compilation of this biography. Firstly, I must thank Vin Giuliano who, as my early billiard mentor, provided the contact and stimulation that triggered my fascination for the life of Walter Lindrum. Indeed it was his early association with Walter Lindrum that indirectly led to Vin, in 1924, settling in the New South Wales country town of Young, where we were to meet almost fifty years later.

Special mention must be made of the invaluable contributions of Jim Collins A.M., and Walter Sykes for their insight and guidance which helped overcome the various problems that confronted this project. Special thanks to Jim Collins also for the appendix, A General Introduction to Billiards, which should benefit those who have little knowledge of the game of billiards. It is suggested that those who feel they fit this description read this section before reading the actual biography as it will help in a better understanding of the technical aspects of billiards. My sincere thanks to Sydney Lee, former World Amateur Champion, and until recent times the referee of the highly successful *Pot Black*, for writing the Foreword.

My thanks to the following persons, and the organisations they represent: Don Richards of *The Herald and Weekly Times Ltd;* Les Wheeler of *The Sydney Morning Herald;* Ian Mackay, the late Willie Smith, the late Claude Falkiner, the late Clark McConachy, Tom Cleary, Albert Johnson, 'Murt' O'Donohue, Stan Wood, Norman Clare, Sir Hubert Opperman, O.B.E., Jack Chown, O.B.E., Cyril Oswald-Sealy, Stephen Lusher, M.P., Frank Williams, Peter Andrew, Bill Hughes, M.B.E., Bill Mandle, Henry Hsu, Kevin McKay, Walter Heiron, "Scobie" Breasley, Vern Ash, Jack Giuliano, Lois Keenan, Carolyn Dewar and the Melbourne manufacturer, Alcock, Thompson and Taylor. Thanks to Mrs June Davis and Clive Everton for permission to quote from *The Breaks Came My Way* and *The Story of Billiards and Snooker* respectively. Thanks also to the staff of the State Library of Victoria,

Mitchell Library (Sydney), National Library (Canberra), Archives Office of New South Wales, J. S. Battye Library (Perth), the State Library Board of South Australia and the Newspaper Section of the British Museum. Would all others who have been of assistance please accept this as my personal thanks.

Finally, I wish to thank that wonderful lady, Dolly Lindrum, whose generosity and kind-heartedness not only added so much to this book but made the task much more pleasant. I can only hope that the Walter Lindrum that I have portrayed bears some resemblance to the uncle that Dolly knew so closely and loved so dearly.

ANDREW RICKETTS
Young, N.S.W.
1982

1 The Evolution of Billiards

Bit by bit I absorbed everything great masters of the cue had left for
my help, a priceless heritage for which I want to express my gratitude.

Walter Lindrum, in *Billiards*, 1930

Imagine that it is the fourteenth of January 1930. The scene is a crowded
billiard room in Hyde Street, London. The principal characters are Joe Davis,
World Billiard Champion, and Walter Lindrum, a left-handed player from
Australia who is on his first visit to England. Davis is a well-groomed man with
a dimpled chin and slightly pugged nose. More noticeably, his face reveals
unmistakably the character of the man behind it. Davis is a confident, self-
assured man in complete control of his life. Lindrum is a somewhat stocky
man. He has a full, almost chubby face liberally sprinkled with freckles.
Lindrum's prominent ears add to a face which is decidedly boyish for a man
of 31 years. A firmly-set jaw is the one contrasting feature of this youthful
countenance.

Davis is waiting on the player's seat with his eyes fixed on the billiard table.
Davis is having his first experience of the mesmeric control which Lindrum
seems to exert over the balls. He watches in awe as Lindrum scores with his
customary speed and ease and carries his break to the thousand mark. After
a brief pause, when the spectators applaud warmly, Lindrum resumes scoring
with the same consummate ease and uncanny certainty. He moves so quickly
between shots that he is virtually in position for his next stroke before the cue
ball stops rolling. The balls are placed in perfect position at the top of the table
and Davis, realising that he may be on the player's seat for some considerable
time, makes himself more comfortable. As Lindrum continues building his
break the voice of an 85 year old enthusiast, seated in the front row of
spectators, can be heard above the excited silence of the room.

"Pot red, cannon, pot red, cannon, pot red, cannon", he declares.

Lindrum, in the depths of concentration, continues his break, unaware of the
old man who is verbally playing each shot for him. Davis, however, hears the
old man's voice and his attention is distracted from the table by its
monotonous regularity. After listening to the voice for a few minutes Davis
leans over and says to the old man: "Don't you think I'm in enough trouble
without you telling him how to play?"

At least that is how the story goes. Davis, of course, said nothing of the sort.
The anecdote, one of many that has been told about Walter Lindrum, serves
to reflect the sentiments that Davis undoubtedly felt all too frequently in his
matches with Lindrum. Despite being the champion, and playing the best
billiards of his career, Davis could see all too clearly in this first encounter that
he was no match for Lindrum. Despite compiling a personal best tally of
26 172 points for the fortnight's play Davis still lost to Lindrum by almost
3000 points. The combined totals of the two player's scores set a record of

55 228. Breaking records was becoming second nature to Walter Lindrum. He was taking England by storm. Despite having only been on tour for three months he had already smashed the break record with one of 3262. But that is another story.

It was no accident that Walter Lindrum was setting records and making large breaks with ridiculous ease. And it was no accident that he became the greatest billiard player that the world has ever seen. Lindrum's achievements were the fulfilment of a long-range plan that had commenced in his early childhood. Fred Lindrum, Walter's father, was obsessed with the idea of having a world champion billiardist in the family. When Walter started playing billiards at about eight years of age Fred ensured that the boy adopted a professional approach from the very first lesson. Perfection was the sure road to success. This meant practice, and more practice. As Walter toiled over the table, he would straighten up for a brief respite. Fred would ask him: "Does your back hurt son?" Walter would nod and Fred would say, "Then it's time you did a little more."

Fred's obsession for billiards engulfed Walter and intensified in him. Walter's childhood was stunted by this obsession. His personal development and education were pushed aside by Walter's desire to reach the pinnacle of billiards greatness. There are few rewards in life without making some form of sacrifice. Lindrum certainly earnt the right to be billiards champion.

Walter Lindrum was more than the champion billiards player who re-wrote the record books. He represented the high point in the history of the game of billiards, a genius who utilised the wealth of knowledge of stroke-play that was a legacy from the champions who had preceded him. He was able to refine the game of billiards by a combination of foresight and physical execution to an exact science. Lindrum was the nearest thing possible to scoring perfection. His was the ultimate performance that has never been remotely approached by any other. He was capable of a level of performance that was previously beyond comprehension. Even today his records are regarded with an overwhelming awe.

It is little wonder, then, that the exploits of Walter Lindrum re-shaped the history of billiards. It is unquestionably true that billiards has never been the same since the advent of Lindrum. He marks the turning point in the evolution of the game. Lindrum lifted the game to the ultimate degree of refinement, to a level that was only possible while he was there to maintain it. It must be accepted, albeit with regret, that the game of billiards has suffered a marked decline in both popularity and standard of performance since the early 'thirties when Walter Lindrum was in his heyday. This is more than mere coincidence and, while there were many factors that contributed to the decline of billiards, the deeds of Lindrum can be placed at the head of the list.

Because of Lindrum's influence on billiards history it is important to look at his career in terms of both the early establishment of the game of billiards and its early history in Australia. Indeed the Lindrum family plays such an important part in Australian billiards that it is impossible to examine either aspect without considerable mention of the other. If this is not a sufficient reason in itself to devote time and space to the early history of Australian billiards then the fact that there are virtually no records compiled justifies some examination of those embryonic days. Therefore it is hoped that the

*Henry Upton Alcock (1823–1912), 'Father of Australian billiards', whose Melbourne factory commenced operations in 1853 (*Alcock's Sporting Review, *14 August 1912)*

reader will find interest in exploring the early history of the game that was later to be remoulded so devastatingly by Walter Lindrum.

There have been numerous attempts to pinpoint the birth of billiards but the exact origin of the game remains obscure. The most popular theories claim either England or France as the country where the game originated but other suggestions include Spain, Italy and China. Among the advocates of the English and French theories there is general agreement that billiards was derived from earlier games, the basic skill of which was the propulsion of a ball or object.

The games of *shovilla bourde* (shuffleboard) and *paille-maille* (pall-mall) are the likely ancestors of billiards. *Shovilla bourde* involved the shoving of objects by hand or with a stick or other implement so that they came to rest on spaces marked on a table, the floor or an outdoor court. King Henry VIII (1491-1547) was reputed to have lost large sums of money playing *shovilla bourde*. *Paille-maille* was an early ball-and-mallet game played on the ground with hoops and believed to have been the ancestor of Croquet. The existence of a French woodcut, dating from 1460, shows that *paille-maille* was a popular game over 500 years ago. The name Pall Mall marks the site in London where the game was played during the Stuart period. One theory is that some players of *paille-maille* were kept indoors by inclement weather and so prevented from playing their usual game. These enthusiasts decided to play an improvised form of *paille-maille* on the board that was normally used for *shovilla bourde*. The game proved a success and became a regular alternative to *paille-maille* in poor weather. The first adaptation that was made to the board was the addition of a railing around the edge to prevent the balls from running out of play. As is apparent by their names, both *paille-maille* and *shovilla bourde* were of French origin.

The first literary reference to billiards was in a poem by the Frenchman, Clement Marot, who died in 1544. It has been claimed that the French artist Henrique De Vigne, who lived in the reign of Charles IX (1550–1574) was the first to formalise rules for the game. Mary, Queen of Scots, some months before she was beheaded in 1587, complained that her captors had taken her *"table de billiards"* away from her. Born in 1542, Mary was betrothed by her mother to Francis, dauphin of France. Mary was sent to France in 1548 to be prepared for her later life. In 1558 she married the dauphin and in the following year they became king and queen of France. However, Francis died in 1560 as did Mary's mother in Scotland. Mary returned home to rule Scotland in 1561. It seems probable that Mary learnt to play billiards during her time in France and had taken the game with her on her return to Scotland. This would indicate that the game was well established in France by 1560. This supports Marot's writings which indicated the game was being played around 1540.

The first billiard table to appear on the American continent was taken to St Augustine, Florida in 1565 by a family from Spain. This suggests that

Facing page: *World Champion, John Roberts junior, in play at the Athanaeum Hall, Melbourne, 1876. His opponent, the South Australian champion, H. A. Albers, played a guiding role in the early billiards career of Fred Lindrum II. (National Library, Canberra, from* Australasian Sketcher*)*

billiards was established also in Spain by about 1560. In fact, Charles Cotton in *The Compleat Gamester* of 1674, attributes the origin of billiards to Spain and/or Italy.

The first English literary reference to the game was in 1591 by the poet, Spenser. In 'Mother Hubbard's Tale' he says of 'The Ape':

> A thousand wayes he could them entertain
> With all the thriftless games that may be found,
> With mumming and with masking around,
> With dice, with cards, with balliards farre unfit.

There are two points to notice from this verse that may offer a hint on the early development of billiards. The spelling of the word as 'balliards' may be of significance for in 1598 the playwright, George Chapman, has one of his characters say: "Go, Aspasia, send for some ladies who could play with you at chess, at billiards, at other games". Notice that Chapman's spelling of the game is different, yet his writing was done only seven years after that of Spenser. Remember also that Mary, Queen of Scots, had also used the word billiards when referring to the game in 1587. The other important difference to notice between these two references to the game is the contrasting attitudes of the two writers towards billiards. Chapman leaves no doubt that 'billiards' is a game to be enjoyed by ladies and that it is a suitable alternative to chess. Conversely, Spenser openly associates 'balliards' with other dubious activities such as dice and cards and drinking beer (the word 'mum' describes a kind of beer originally brewed in Brunswick.) This game is certainly not a suitable activity for ladies of the Elizabethan period. The question that must be asked is why is there such a direct contrast between the social connotations of the two games? The early establishment of the game at the two extremes of the social scale is puzzling, if we assume that the game of billiards originated from a common source. If, for instance, the game was first played by the aristocracy, it would gradually have been passed down to the commoners by the lesser members of Court or by the house servants. If this was the case would the common game have also been known as 'billiards' and not as 'balliards'? Similarly, if the aristocracy had learnt the game from the commoners would they not have referred to it as 'balliards'? At the time of the writings of Spenser and Chapman, billiards was still in its infancy. It seems unusual that such a young game could become so firmly entrenched at each end of the social scale. This suggests the possibility that there existed, in the late sixteenth century, two forms of billiards, one played by the aristocracy and one by the commoners. It is assumed that, if two such games existed, they were both played in a similar manner but it is quite feasible that they were very different from each other. The French aristocracy may have developed one form of billiards which passed through royal circles to the English aristocrats. Possibly at the same time or a little later the English working class may have developed their game of 'balliards'. Any theory that suggests a dual evolution of billiards is by no means foolproof. It could be dismissed easily for a number of reasons. However, a dual evolution theory does have its strong points. It unites the otherwise contradictory views that billiards had its origin in either England or France. It also accounts for that strange social phenomenon which has existed since the very early days of billiards, why the game has been regarded in two distinct social perspectives. In the private home billiards was long regarded as the ultimate form of after-dinner social activity. Conversely, the game that was played in the public billiard room was looked on with disdain and any proficiency so gained was the 'sign of a misspent youth'. It is arguable that these diverse attitudes still exist today.

William Shakespeare (1564–1616) makes the love-sick Cleopatra say "Let's to billiards". It is surely a wild anachronism and it is probable that billiards was popular in the English Court at the time that 'Anthony and Cleopatra' was written, around 1606–1608. Possibly Shakespeare's oversight was because he had been familiar with billiards for most of his life and simply assumed that the game had existed for thousands of years. Indeed one American textbook states that Cathin More, King of Ireland, who died in A.D. 148, left "fifty billiard balls of brass, with the pools and cues of the same materials". Whatever the game was that More played it would not have resembled the game of billiards that developed over one thousand years later. Apart from the difficulty of imagining a table cluttered with up to fifty balls, 'modern' billiards was first played with only two balls.

The early billiard table had a small hoop, often made of ivory, called the 'port', and a peg or 'king'. The port and king were usually placed at opposite ends of the table and scoring necessitated passing the port or touching the king. Billiards was first played with maces that have been described as a slender rod, with a thick piece of mahogany or other wood affixed to its extremity, and adopted at such an angle as to rest flat upon the table while the stick is held up to the shoulder in the act of striking or pushing. The mace was curved so that the player could execute each stroke from an erect or near-erect position.

It is only in the twentieth century that the practice of 'getting down over the cue' has been established. The thin end, or tail, of the mace was used when a ball was under the cushion rail. Gradually some players developed a preference for playing all shots with the tail of the mace. This eventually led to the making of cues without the curved or the flat end. The cue had thus assumed its modern form. The word 'cue' was derived from the French word *queue* which means tail (of the mace). The word 'billiards' is so named from the French *billard* which originally meant a stick with a curved end and *bille* which means stick.

The universal replacement of the mace by the cue was a very gradual process. According to Beaufort's *Hoyles Games Improved* (1788), "the mace is preferred for its peculiar advantage which some professional players have artfully introduced under the name of trailing (or raking), that is following the ball with the mace to such a convenient distance from the other ball as to make it an easy hazard. The degrees of trailing are various, and undergo different denominations among the connoisseurs at this game, viz., the shove, the sweep, the long-stroke, the trail, and the dead trail or turn-up, all of which secure an advantage to a good player according to their various gradations." In some games trailing was not allowed except by agreement, and a rule was introduced to prevent a player trailing from walking after the ball. The mace was still part of the billiard room equipment as late as 1866, for a Captain Crawley, referring to the mace, said, "It is now very little used, even by ladies. With a mace it is impossible to make high, low, or side strokes; or in fact, to hit the ball in any other than a straight forward manner".

In *The Compleat Gamester* of 1674, Cotton describes the billiard table as having a bed made of oak and the cushions were stuffed with 'fine flox or cotton'. The pockets were either nets or wooden boxes; but these Cotton said, "are nothing near so commendable as the former". Early billiards was played with two white balls only, made of either ivory or wood. In the 1734 edition of *The Compleat Gamester* the game of 'French Billiards' receives its first mention. The game was "so called from their manner of playing the game, which is only with masts (maces) and balls, port and king being now wholly laid aside". It appears from the rules that cue-playing was permitted but, for many years after, only good players were allowed to strike with cues, the proprietors of rooms insisting on the use of the mace for fear of damage to the cloth. In French billiards, otherwise known as the 'winning game' or the 'common game', the leader had to give a miss from the stringing-line (baulkline) beyond the middle pocket. The sole object of play was to hole the adversary's ball, which was known as 'winning two'. If the striker holed his own ball, he lost two points, hence the advent of the terms winning hazard and losing hazard. A miss lost one point, a coup (potting one's own ball) three, with the winner being the first to score twelve points (twelve up). The 'losing game' was the common game nearly reversed. In putting yourself in, you won two; by putting your adversary in, you lost two; but if you pocket both balls you get four. The winning and losing game was a combination of the two former games, all hazards counting towards the striker's score. The first mention of the presence of a red ball was in 1775 in 'Hoyle' when reference was made to the winning and losing game, caramboles and hazards. It was the French who introduced the carambole (cannon) to the game. Curiously, the French decided to entirely discard pockets, playing only cannons, and what was formerly referred to as the French game became known as the English game!

Around 1790 it was discovered that if a cue was cut obliquely or rounded a little on one side, so presenting a broader surface to the ball, it was possible to hit the cue ball below centre. This cue was known as the 'Jeffery' and was used for occasional strokes. Eventually the point of the cue was entirely rounded, so reducing the chance of a miscue. In 1807, a Frenchman, named Mingaud, invented the leather tip which marked the start of the final evolution of modern billiards.

Around 1820 the use of sidespin, or side, was discovered by either John Bartley or John Carr. Bartley was the proprietor of a billiard room at Bath where he employed Carr as a marker. When business was slack Bartley and Carr would amuse themselves by placing the red ball in the middle of the table, and attempting to make a losing hazard into the middle pocket from baulk without bringing the red ball into baulk. This difficult stroke was facilitated by the slow wooden tables with coarse cloth and list (cloth) cushions. Even on these tables, only Bartley was able to make the stroke but he eventually showed Carr that to perform the shot the cue ball had to be struck low and on one side. Carr spent many hours of practice in perfecting the side-stroke. Carr was apparently intent on keeping the advantage of side for his own use and when questioned about his peculiar powers he attributed them to a special 'twisting chalk' which he claimed to have invented. Carr made himself a small fortune by charging half-a-crown for his so-called twisting chalk which was in reality ordinary chalk.

It was in 1826 that the first significant improvement was made to the billiard table when John Thurston introduced the solid slate bed. Thurston, who had originally been a cabinet maker, branched out into the billiard trade in 1799. Initially Thurston made billiard tables as a sideline but by 1814 he was a full-time table-maker. For the next twelve years Thurston made his tables with the traditional oaken bed but despite improvements that were made he could not eliminate the inherent imperfections of the wooden base. A major problem was warping which necessitated the removal of the cloth and subsequent planing and levelling of the bed. The presence of knots in the wooden bed was an additional weakness with which the early table-makers had to contend. The slate bed eliminated these problems although the table had to assume its modern substantial form to support the heavy slate.

In 1835 Thurston introduced the 'Indian Rubber Cushion', made entirely of pure rubber. Edwin Kentfield, the first player to be regarded as champion, found that the ball "rebounds with great rapidity and precision" from these cushions. However, he had one objection to the invention, viz., "that in frosty weather the caoutchouc will lose much of its elasticity". To overcome this problem long metal pans, filled with hot water, were used to warm the cushions in cold weather. It was a common practice for billiard firms to send an employee to a private residence to remove the cushion rails and warm them in front of a fire so as to prepare them for the evening game of billiards. This tedious process was obviated when Thurston was granted a patent, in 1845, for vulcanised rubber cushions which retained their resilience in cold weather. With this innovation Thurston gave the billiard table its modern form. There have been some modifications in the ensuing years such as the reduction in the height of the cushions, increased slate thickness and improved cloth quality but the basic table, developed almost entirely by John Thurston, remains as it was in the mid-nineteenth century.

During the nineteenth century the ivory billiard ball was preferred by all players, if they could afford to own a set of the balls. The making of the ivory balls was an expensive process for it was difficult to obtain a matching set of balls that would run truly. In 1860 a standard set of balls retailed for 18 shillings. The ivory was obtained from elephant tusks with Africa being the chief source of supply. Smaller quantities were imported from Burmah, Siam, Cochin China, Ceylon, Sumatra and Java. In one year the total imports of ivory into England were 11 757 hundredweight (600 tonnes). This was produced from about 30 000 elephants.

The evolution of the modern billiard ball began in 1868 in the United States. John Wesley Hyatt, a printer and co-inventor of celluloid, in his search for a better billiard ball, discovered that a mixture of nitrocellulose, camphor and a small amount of alcohol when properly prepared becomes thermo-plastic (soft when heated) and could be moulded in a hydraulic press. After cooling at ordinary atmospheric pressure the ball became hard and strong. This discovery heralded the beginning not only of the composition billiard ball but also of the plastic industry. In the 1920s a new type of plastic billiard ball, produced from cast phenolic resin, proved to be much more durable and offered a greater brilliance of colours. The name of John Wesley Hyatt is a name that all elephant-lovers (and elephants) should never forget.

No reference to the origin of billiards would be complete without a mention of 'The William Kew Theory', which provides a colourful view of the game's birth. Kew was reputed to be a pawnbroker in London around 1560. During wet weather he would take down the three balls that denoted his business and push them around with a yard measure. 'Bill's yard stick' corrupted into 'billiards' and the 'cannon' was invented by one of the clergy from nearby St Paul's who joined in the recreation. Kew, of course, became 'cue' and the term marker supposedly arose from the duties of one player who kept watch for the approach of a certain wife who disapproved of her husband's continual absence: "Mark her!" The imaginative chap who contrived this story blundered badly for it was not until the eighteenth century that the words cue, cannon and marker became part of the terminology of the game. This delightful theory deserves to be preserved in the folklore of the game, if only to illustrate the difficulty that one person experienced in his endeavours to discover the origin of billiards.

The development of billiards in Australia was largely due to one man, Henry Upton Alcock. Born in Dublin in 1823, Alcock studied cabinet making for seven years before gaining some experience in the manufacture of billiard tables in London. The lure of gold brought Alcock to Australia in 1853 but after a brief period on the Victorian goldfields he settled in Melbourne. He set up a small factory in the suburb of Fitzroy and commenced manufacturing billiard tables. Initially Alcock was faced with an acute shortage of timber but he overcame the problem by use of beautiful local timbers such as blackwood, tulip, maple, Huon pine and musk that previously had been spurned by other manufacturers. Obtaining slate for the table beds proved very difficult until Alcock found that many houses, mainly in Collingwood, were made entirely of slate that had been imported by English settlers. These houses were purchased, pulled down and converted into table slates. Later Alcock imported slate by the shipload and even started his own quarry at Castlemaine. (*Sports*, Keith Dunstan)

There was heavy demand for billiard tables and Alcock established larger premises in Russell Street, Melbourne. The factory was one of the most highly mechanised in the city with machinery that was previously unknown to others in the furniture trade. Alcock used steam seasoning equipment to force the sap and gum out of native timbers. There was a constant demand from other Melbourne manufacturers to have their timber treated with the steam-seasoning equipment. Alcock also installed large break-down saws and canting machines to cant and flute the table legs. The most innovative piece of machinery was a four metre diameter veneer saw which was used to cut veneers for the furniture trade. The significance of this saw was recognised when the *Australasian Sketcher* wrote in 1880:

> The consequence [of Alcock's veneer saw] is that the exquisite silky grain of blackwood, the rich wavy patterns of musk, the speckled beauty of huon pine, the gay zebra stripes of tulip wood, and the rich tint of Western Australian jarrah are now gradually gaining favour in Europe as well as Australia.

In 1862 Alcock & Co. was making three billiard tables a week with an average price of £100. There was the 'Exhibition Prize' with well-fed curvy legs and carved flowers and ferns, 'The Squatter's Favourite' made in blackwood and the standard model in cedar with blackwood cushions. The table bed could be made of up to ten pieces of slate so that it could be carried by pack horses over rugged terrain to the remotest of settlements.

Alcock, being a man of great foresight and industry, realised the importance of proper promotion for the game of billiards. In 1864 he arranged for the World Champion, John Roberts senior, to visit Australia. Roberts played matches and gave exhibitions throughout the country and said of the Alcock tables, "I never played on a better table in all my life". When Roberts returned to England he took with him an Alcock table that was to be erected in his own saloon. Made in figured blackwood, this type of table became known as the 'Roberts' pattern.

In 1867, a youthful Prince Alfred, Duke of Edinburgh, became the first member of royalty to visit Australia. During his tour he inspected the Alcock & Co. factory and was presented with a table plus an assortment of cues. Consequently the 'Duke of Edinburgh table, as selected for H.R.H.', of handsome figured blackwood or tulip wood was added to the range of Alcock tables. The visit by the second son of Queen Victoria was the ultimate seal of approval for Alcock & Co. and orders for tables came from prominent people who previously had questioned the quality of colonial workmanship. Alcock tables found their way into the best hotels: Menzies, Scotts, the Port Phillip, the Bull and Mouth, and to the best clubs: the Melbourne Athenaeum, the University and Yorick. They also went into clubs and hotels throughout Australia and New Zealand and to England, Malaya, Java and even to Foote's Club in Yokohama, Japan. Alcock tables won medals in exhibitions in London, Dublin, Vienna and Philadelphia. (*Sports*, Keith Dunstan)

In 1883 Henry Alcock's eldest son, Alfred Upton Alcock, invented an ingenious electric score marker which the player could operate from buttons under the table. Alfred Alcock had a remarkable inventive talent and established the basic principles of the hovercraft long before they became technically feasible. In the mid-1880's young Alcock saw the potential of supplying electricity to the public and built his first electrical plants. One of the first places lit by electricity was the Alcock & Co. factory.

Henry Upton Alcock died in 1912, having played a major role in the development of both the commercial and playing facets of Australian billiards. He also wrote several books on the game but strangely never played billiards during his lifetime.

The first match for the Professional Billiards Championship of Australia was staged at the Perkin's Exchange Hotel, on the corner of King and George Streets, Sydney, on the eighth of September, 1881. The two contestants were Joseph Byrne of Victoria and Mr J. James of New South Wales. Although no official body existed that controlled the staging of Championship matches, those staging the match undoubtedly saw advantages in describing it as for the Australian Championship. The match was simply a contest between two players, each of who was commonly regarded as the best player in his respective colony. Despite the loose manner in which the title was tagged on the match it can now be regarded as the first Australian Championship.

James, who originally hailed from England, was employed as a marker at the Oxford Hotel, King Street, Sydney. He was described as being adept at the spot stroke, that is at potting the red ball off the billiard spot, a stroke which was not limited at that time. Byrne, born at Ballarat around 1856, was a marker at the Victoria Club, Melbourne. He was a daring and showy player who delighted the spectators with his dashing play. Byrne was a keen competitor and it was not beyond him to indulge in a little gamesmanship such as standing in the line of his opponent's next shot. The match was 1000 up and, typical of the times, was played for a side wager — the not inconsiderable sum of £100. Byrne won the match by 122 points with his best breaks being 66 by all-round play and a 59 break that included 18 spot strokes. There were about 200 spectators who paid ten shillings for the privilege of seeing Byrne become the first Australian Champion.

Less than three months later Byrne was challenged for his title by Mr J. Strich of New South Wales. The match, of 1000-up and £100 aside, was played in St. James Hall, next to Jem Mace's Criterion Hotel, Melbourne. Byrne successfully defended his title with a 52 point victory in a marathon match that did not finish until after 1 a.m. Byrne's highest break was 96 which included 30 pots of the red ball.

It was almost two years before Byrne was next challenged for the Championship. His opponent was Fred Weiss, a New South Welshman who was born at Ward's Mistake, near Glen Innes on 23 June, 1862. The match was played at the Athenaeum Hall in Collins Street, Melbourne before 250 spectators who paid ten shillings admission which had apparently become the standard charge for billiard matches. It certainly was a hefty amount to be charging in the eighties and effectively made these matches the province of the wealthy. The 1000-up match took four hours and twenty minutes to complete with Weiss winning comfortably by 298 points. Weiss probably contributed to the enduring nature of the game for he was described as slow, deliberate and almost provokingly cool, playing his game in total disregard of outside influences. Undoubtedly Weiss unsettled Byrne who, with his brilliancy and dash, preferred to play the game at a faster pace. Weiss took break honours with an 88 break (with 15 spot strokes) and collected the £200 side wager.

The next Championship was staged almost exactly twelve months later — in October 1884. Although this might suggest that contests for the title were becoming more organised and regular, it is far from the truth. The staging of Championship matches was usually dependent on a challenge being issued to the title-holder. These challenges were spasmodic — sometimes there might be two or three challengers in one year, but more often several years would pass by without the champion being called on to defend his crown. This 'system' has continued unabated for virtually the lifetime of the Championship.

The staging of the 1884 event was one of the few exceptions when five players competed for the title. Apart from the Champion, Weiss, and former champion, Byrne, the field included James of New South Wales and Harry Evans and H. Albers, both from South Australia. Evans was an Englishman who had competed in big handicap tournaments at home against players such as John Roberts (senior and junior), William Cook and Joseph Bennett, each of whom was world Champion at some stage of his career. Evans arrived in Adelaide in the early 1880s and quickly established a reputation as a very fine player. He shifted to Melbourne in the mid-1880s and for some years manufactured billiard tables. Albers had been a prominent player for several years and had been pitted against John Roberts junior when the Champion first visited Australia in 1876. Albers received a hefty start in his matches with Roberts, as did all the colonial players, but he was still not able to defeat the indomitable Roberts who seemed to cast a charismatic spell over so many of his opponents.

Albers, although not quite in the ranks of the great players, nonetheless made a significant contribution to the Australian billiards scene. It was Albers who exerted a guiding influence on the billiards career of Fred Lindrum II, the father of Walter Lindrum. It was an influence that was ultimately to result in the domination of the Australian game by the Lindrum family, firstly through the exploits of Fred Lindrum III, then by the incomparable Walter and later by Horace Lindrum. Albers must be regarded as one of the most important names in the history of Australian billiards. It is quite feasible that, without the early encouragement and support that Albers gave to Fred Lindrum II, the name of Lindrum would never have become prominent in the billiards world, a prominence so pronounced that there is an automatic equation of 'Lindrum' with 'Billiards' and vice versa.

The 1884 Championship was played at the Temperance Hall in Russell Street, Melbourne. First prize was a handsome billiard table, of Tasmanian blackwood, valued at £150 and presented by Alcock & Co., together with a sweepstake of £200. The tournament was run on a knockout basis with Evans and Weiss meeting in the final. Before a crowd of 500 spectators Evans completely outclassed the Champion with breaks of 171, 108 and 135 unfinished to take the title by 1000 to 497. Evans' superiority was clearly illustrated by the fact that he won all three matches by at least half the distance. The *Argus* (17 October 1884) made the following comment on Evans' play in the final:

> Evans showed such consummate skill in getting on the spot, and scoring upon it as to crush Weiss's efforts and leave him far behind. It was evident all through that the great difference between the two men lay in the spot stroke, Evans being perfectly at home with it, and Weiss having much to learn before it is of much use to him.

Evans' superiority over the other professionals was so pronounced that he held his title, unchallenged, for several years.

2 The Family Inheritance

Walter Lindrum . . . comes of a very remarkable family. It is remarkable
in the sense that it thinks, talks and dreams billiards.

Table Talk, 27 February 1930

A consequence of the domination of Australian billiards in the 1880s by the
Englishman, Harry Evans, was the holding of a special contest, in 1887, for
the 'Native-born Championship of Australia'. The two contestants, both
newcomers to the professional scene, were Fred Lindrum II and Harry Gray.
The duo were originally from Adelaide but both had by this time settled in
Melbourne. Gray was employed as a marker at the select Bull and Mouth
Hotel. It was an occupation that he undertook for most of his life and it
carried him to hotels and billiard saloons in the larger cities of the three
eastern states of the mainland. It is not known what Fred Lindrum's
employment was at this time. On the various marriage and birth certificates
of this period Fred Lindrum II gave his occupation as a painter or billiards
player. It does seem likely that he would also have been associated with a
billiard room, be it as a marker or as a hustler.

Fred Lindrum II was the son of Frederick William Lindrum who, it is
believed, arrived in Adelaide in 1838 from Plymouth, England. In 1862 Fred
Lindrum I married Clara Wolff, the nineteen-year-old daughter of John
Wolff, a cabinetmaker. Fred I was 34 years of age at the time and the
proprietor of a billiard saloon. There is no information available to indicate
how the Lindrum family first became involved with billiards or billiard
saloons. Fred I, though, must have been a very competent billiards player
for, in 1865, he defeated the World Champion, John Roberts senior, at the
York Hotel, Adelaide. It was a memorable occasion for on that very day, 17
September, Mrs Lindrum gave birth to a son, Fred II. News was brought
into the billiard room of the birth and at the conclusion of the match a
collection was made which, when added to the prizemoney, yielded 63
guineas. This sum was sent to Switzerland for the purchase of a gold, keyless
Geneva watch which was to be kept for the baby.

While Fred Lindrum I's income came from running a billiard saloon he
was, in his spare time, something of a wine buff. He established a productive
vineyard near his home at Norwood. He won awards for colonial wines at the
1873 London International Exhibition. In 1872 Fred I became a hotel-
keeper, taking over the Clarence Hotel in King William Street, Adelaide. It
was in the billiard room at the Clarence Hotel that Fred II had his first
lessons at billiards. Young Fred commenced playing at about six years of
age, standing on a box in order to make his shots. Fred I ran the Clarence
Hotel until 1878. He later took over the Crown Hotel at Port Victor (now
Victor Harbour), where he died in January 1880, aged 52 years. He was

survived by his wife Clara, his son Fred II (fourteen years) and his daughters Clara (eleven) and Alvina Elise (eight years).

It must have been a hard blow for Fred II to lose his father when only fourteen years of age. Young Fred began frequenting Adelaide billiard saloons in the hope of making a few bob by playing money matches. One of the rooms that he visited was the Academy of Music Billiard Saloon, Rundle Street, run by H. A. ('Daddy') Albers. It did not take long for Daddy Albers to recognise Fred II's talent for billiards. He took Fred in hand and began to coach him in the finer points of the game. Albers was so impressed by the youngster's progress that he paid for the installation of a small table in Fred's bedroom. The table was designed specifically for spot-stroke practice. Fred spent a couple of hours on the table each night. In June of 1885, being almost twenty years of age, Fred II made 104 consecutive pots of the red into one pocket.

On 30 September 1886, Fred Lindrum II married Harriet Mary Atkins. The address of the couple was given as Hawke Street, Melbourne. Harriet was 22 years of age, Fred was 21. The fact that the marriage took place just thirteen days after Fred's coming of age suggests that there may have been some parental opposition to an earlier marriage. The couple already had a daughter, Florence Lillian, who was born in Adelaide in late 1884. Fred Lindrum's move to Melbourne was probably prompted by the fact that 'Marvellous Melbourne' was the largest city in Australia, the hub of the nation's commerce, industry and social life. Certainly the prospects for a billiards player appeared brighter in the Victorian capital.

The match between Fred Lindrum II and Harry Gray for the native-born Championship was played at the Athanaeum Hall over three nights, 4-6 May 1887. It was for a side wager of £100 with Lindrum being backed by Joe Thompson, a bookmaker and professional gambler known as 'King of the Ring'. The referee for the match was Billy Midwinter, the celebrated cricketer who holds the distinction of being the only man ever to play Test cricket for both England and Australia. After the first night's play Lindrum led in the 3000-up match by 1001 to 865. Gray made the best break with 142 (42 spot strokes) and Lindrum's best was a lowly 68. It would appear that Lindrum was only running at half-pace on the first night (perhaps until his backer had secured all his side bets) for on the second night his play improved dramatically and with breaks of 173 (54 spot strokes), 182 and 155 he set up a commanding lead of 2000 to 1358. Lindrum continued in similar vein on the third night to complete an easy win by 3000 to 1853 and so secured the £100 side wager and an unknown amount in other bets. His highest break on the third night was 200 (54 spot strokes) which earnt him a special £10 trophy donated by Alcock & Co.

Lindrum's performance so impressed some keen judges that they claimed he could beat the champion, Harry Evans, if given the opportunity. It was not until 1890 that the issue was finally settled when Evans and Lindrum took part in a big tournament at the Athanaeum Hall. There were five other players, Weiss, Gray, H. Power (from Broken Hill), Charles Memmott and Frank Smith. The last three mentioned were all making their first appearance in a major event. Memmott, who was born at McKiver Diggings, Victoria on 14 January, 1858 was described as being a very fast player.

Smith, born in Hobart, Tasmania on 14 July 1867, had moved to Melbourne in 1889 to manage the billiard room at the Menzies Hotel. Two of the players in the event were off handicaps (Power received 15 start, Smith received 50 start) but despite this apparent anomaly the tourney was described as being for the Professional Championship of Australia. The event was run on the American system under which each player is matched against all other players. The favourite was Lindrum who was backed to lift the title from Evans. Therefore the crucial match of the Championship appeared to be the Lindrum-Evans encounter, for whoever won this match would very likely win the event. It was Evans who, with breaks of 104, 99, 189 and 106, scored his 500 points in 42 minutes and thus recorded a devastating victory. Lindrum scored 50 at his first visit to the table but only had three other opportunities in which he added a further 15 points. Evans proceeded to win all his matches and thus retain his title, collecting an Alcock table, valued at £150 and a gold medal as his prizes. Lindrum, despite the severity of his loss to Evans, managed to win his other five matches and so finished in second place. The newcomer, Memmott, finished in third place and with best breaks of 221 and 188 gave an indication of things to come.

It was Memmott who, in 1892, finally wrested the Championship from Evans, scoring a magnificent break of 1238 in the process mainly by use of the spot stroke. It was soon realised by the professionals and the promoters that the spot stroke was taking an unhealthy monopoly on the play. The repetitive nature of the stroke was boring the spectators who yearned for the variety and excitement of open play. When a big tournament was organised in March 1893 it was decided that it would be played under spot-barred conditions which limited potting the red off the spot to two successive strokes after which it was placed on the middle spot. If the red was then potted off the middle spot it would then be placed on the billiard spot. The tournament was played on a handicap basis, the matches being 500-up with each player to meet each of the eleven other contestants. The handicapping seemed puzzling with the champion, Memmott, receiving 5 points start from Evans and Weiss who were co-backmarkers. The other contestants and their handicaps were Lindrum (62), Power (63), Gray (66), Smith (82), Sawkins (152), Gledhill (178), Heslop (185), Nantes (188) and Bragge (203). It is interesting to note the apparent decline of Lindrum from his high rating in the 1890 Championship. Undoubtedly he was not suited by the abolition of spot-stroke play which was the strong point of his game. Whatever the reason/s it is apparent from Lindrum's performances in the event, and in subsequent matches, that his days as a first-flight player were behind him. Lindrum was no longer considered as a threat to Memmott, Weiss or Evans. Even Harry Gray, who only six years previously had been thrashed by Lindrum, was now regarded as at least the equal of Lindrum. The spot-barred rule had a marked effect on the size of the breaks in the Tourney with many matches being played without a solitary century break being recorded. The notable exception was a fine break of 295 made by Weiss which was regarded as a record for the colonies. The winner of the event was Memmott who recorded only one loss (to Evans) in his eleven matches. Second place was secured by Weiss who defeated Evans in a play-off after they had each scored eight wins in earlier matches. Memmott had thus confirmed his position as the leading player in Australia, a position that he was to maintain for most of the next fifteen years.

The staging of matches for the Australian championship was complicated in the period from the mid-1890s until the early 1900s by two factors. With a general consensus of players favouring the restriction of the spot stroke, a spot-barred title was established. The champion, Memmott, was at this stage basically a spot-stroke player so he was reluctant to have the championship played under spot-barred rules. A compromise was reached and for several years there were two Australian titles, the spot-barred championship and the all-in championship. Memmott had a mortgage on the all-in title but Weiss was for a time his superior at the spot-barred title. The holding of championship matches was very spasmodic as Memmott and Weiss were seldom in Australia at the same time. Both players made extensive overseas tours. They made a joint trip to New Zealand, separate trips to England and Weiss also visited South Africa. When the duo were in Australia they seemed reluctant to play matches for the titles. They conducted verbal duels, often through the *Referee,* in which neither was very complimentary to the other. This, however, was probably only by-play, used simply as a means of creating interest in their matches. In 1897 Memmott and Weiss actually played two matches, one for each of the all-in and spot-barred titles. Weiss became the spot-barred champion when he defeated Memmott by 8000 to 7780. By this time Memmott was described as having a lovely, velvety touch necessary for nursery cannons and being a pastmaster at the close-cannon game. Memmott had developed this skill after a trip to England where he had played matches with John Roberts junior who was a very fine exponent of nursery cannons. Despite his skill at these cannons Memmott could not defeat Weiss when his favourite spot-stroke was barred. When the match was played under all-in conditions Memmott was invincible as illustrated by his victory over Weiss in the latter part of 1897 by a margin of 10 000 to 8273, in a title match. In August of 1898 the authorities in England introduced legislation that barred the use of the push stroke and restricted to only two the number of successive spots off the billiard spot. Despite these new rules from the home of billiards it was over two years before the all-in game was finally discontinued in Australia.

The decline in Fred Lindrum's status as a billiards player was followed by a similarly dramatic decline in his professional earnings. The economic climate of Melbourne was very bleak following the bank crash of 1893 which resulted from wild speculation in land and buildings. The impact of this financial disaster when coupled with the depression marked the end of the boom times for Victoria. It was clear to Lindrum that life in Melbourne was not nearly as marvellous as it used to be. He decided it was time to move on to a new town if he was to support his wife and children, who now totalled three following the birth of a son, Fred junior, in 1888 and later by a second daughter, Clara who was born in 1891. The Lindrum family became part of a mass exodus of people that was the greatest in Australia's history . . . between 1891 and 1910 the net emigration from Victoria was a staggering 161 000 people.

The Lindrum's new home was to be in the Western Australian town of Coolgardie, some 570 kilometres east of Perth. The shift from one side of Australia to the other occurred in 1896. The Sands Street Directory (which also listed households, businesses, etc.) for 1896 listed Fred W. Lindrum as living at 188 Station Street, Port Melbourne. However, the *Referee* of 30 September reported that Lindrum was now located in a Coolgardie billiard room.

The paper also reported that Harry Evans, H. Power and Billy Weston (an old New Zealand champion) were also running billiard rooms in Coolgardie. These professionals were part of the population explosion taking place in Western Australia in the 1890's which saw population increase from 48 000 to 180 000. The catalyst for this influx of people was the discovery of gold, a metal which has always had a magnetic power over people, and which played such an important role in the early history of Australia. Although the first significant goldfield in Western Australia was discovered in 1881 (at Kimberley) it was not until the 1890s that the boom occurred. The birth of goldmining in Western Australia was very late compared to that in the eastern states where the goldfields were in full swing in the 1850s and 1860s. The late birth was directly attributable to the vastness of the gold regions, which includes some of the hottest and driest parts of the continent. Several parties of prospectors perished miserably in the desert from scarcity of water and supplies.

The rush to Coolgardie followed the discovery of gold in September, 1892. It was the first of a number of finds in the region, generally described as the Coolgardie goldfields and includes North Coolgardie, Coolgardie, East Coolgardie, Broad Arrow and North-East Coolgardie. The most important of these fields is East Coolgardie which has been by far the most productive of any Australian goldfield. The centre of the East Coolgardie goldfield is Kalgoorlie, 39 kilometres north-east of Coolgardie, where Patrick Hannan made his famous discovery in June of 1893. Kalgoorlie and the nearby town of Boulder are situated near the opposite ends of the renowned 'Golden Mile', a small belt of land so named because of the vast quantity of gold that was produced from it.

A thriving township developed at Kalgoorlie with numerous stores, a post office and various other public services. In 1896 the town could even boast its own stock exchange, the Kalgurli Stock Exchange. There were the inevitable hotels, varying greatly in their size and the quality of service available. Probably the most lavish hotel was the appropriately-named Palace Hotel, a mammoth two-storied building that contained a dining room in which two hundred guests could sit in style beneath the swirling fans for evening dinner. The management of the Palace Hotel was taken over on 11 January 1898 by one Wallace Brownlow, an established resident of the town, who was a highly-regarded vocalist. The hotel contained a billiard room (as did most of the Kalgoorlie Hotels) with two tables. The billiard room was leased to Fred Lindrum who had shifted to Kalgoorlie, now established as the capital of the thriving goldfields region. Apart from running the room Lindrum also conducted a bookmaking business, operating a starting price service on forthcoming events. This was a common procedure at the time for the *Kalgoorlie Miner* later carried advertisements for others who were operating in a similar manner. These included Tod Sloan, "c/- Fred Wells Great Boulder Billiard Room", who advised of his service on events at Adelaide and Perth, and Brandon M. Saunders of the City Billiard Saloon who offered "Doubles and Straight-Out Betting". Fred Lindrum also continued playing money matches at billiards against the best talent on the goldfields (invariably the proprietor of another billiard room).

The enormous wealth of the mining towns allowed the inhabitants to live extravagantly and enjoy an opulent lifestyle that was often atypical of the rest of the country. The miners often worked long hours in the sweltering heat and dusty conditions. If and when they made a worthwhile find they often celebrated with a long, hard session at the local hostelry. There were numerous hotels in the various towns and apart from the obvious function of providing liquid refreshments the most important place in the hotel was the billiard room. In fact it is no exaggeration to claim that some hotels relied heavily on the billiard room for survival. This is clearly shown by the accounts for 1904 of the Government Hotel at Gwalia, a gold-mining town. Although there was a loss of £851 on the House Account the hotel showed an overall profit of £588, resulting from the billiard room providing a staggering profit of £1439 (The *Referee*, 23 November 1904).

The main function of the billiard room was as a venue for gambling which was a noted feature of many mining towns. There were numerous gambling games, some being played without any need for the billiard table to be used as such. Of the games played on the billiard table the various forms of pool proved to be the most popular. At the head of the pool games was 'devil's pool', a very skilful game and conducive to heavy betting. As devil's pool is now a forgotten game it is worthwhile to describe one of the more popular varieties. The game was played with the three billiard balls and as many as ten players. There were ten pins, each worth a set number of points, placed around the table. There were two further pins, the devil's pins, so called because if a player knocked over either of these pins he was out of the game (busted). The pool marbles were placed in a basket and each player was given a marble, the value of which he kept to himself. The game was commenced with the red ball on its spot and a white ball on each of the end spots of the 'D'. One of the scoring pins was placed directly in front of the red ball so that the first player, who was required to hit the red ball, had to do so by hitting a cushion/s first. The object of the game was to play cannons off the red ball or object white so as to knock over pins. The winner was the first player to knock over pins, the value of which, when added to the value of his marble, totalled 31 points. If the player scored more than 31 points he was out of the game along with those who had knocked over a devil pin. However, any of these players could buy back into the game by paying an amount that had been agreed to at the start of the game. The player's right to buy back into the game made devil's pool an ideal gambling game and the kitty was often considerably swelled by these 'burst' payments. The popularity of devil's pool was closely linked with periods of prosperity and economic boom as indicated by the following extract from the *Referee* of 29 May 1901:

> A hot devil's pool took place in a certain Sydney room the other night.
> There were three players at £100 per stick and £10 bursts. One of them

— a well-known backer of gee-gees — left off after nine hours play nearly £2,000 ahead. Play of this character is reminiscent of the good old gold days, when pools of five and ten pounds a cue were quite a common occurrence with from eight to ten players taking part. The largest 'pool' that I ever witnessed was played up North in Queensland, some 25 years ago, just after the great Palmer River rush — the field where 52 tons of alluvial gold was filched from its sandy creek in four years. The contestants were a couple of mining speculators, and a bar barney about their prowess at billiards led to a challenge at 'devil's', the best two of three games for £1,000 a game being the stake. They played without marbles and a Charters Towers rep won the two games straight and the £2,000. No doubt money was more plentiful and the people generally more speculative in the roaring seventies than now; but nevertheless, the spirit of gambling still retains its subtle charm. It has happily departed from the billiard table, but in horse-racing and card-playing the indulgence in it is as great as ever.

Although gambling may have departed, albeit temporarily, from the billiard rooms of New South Wales it was certainly flourishing in the rooms on the Western Australian goldfields. Fred Lindrum senior, with his two tables at the Palace Hotel, for which he paid a weekly rental of £25, often had takings amounting to £125 per week. On one occasion he took as much as much as £1000 on the number of the marbles thrown out. Murrumbidgee Pool was purely a gambling game that was played with the pool marbles. Pool was purely a gambling game that was played with the pool marbles. These marbles, numbered 1 to 15, were placed in a basket, shaken up by the chief gambler who then threw a marble to each shareholder in the pool. The person who held the highest numbered marble won the stake, less a 10 per cent commission to the chief gambler. Another popular game was Racecourse Pool, in which the coloured balls were lined across the baulkline and pushed down the table with a piece of board. The gambler who was on the ball that finished nearest to the baulk-line or bottom cushion (whichever had been agreed) won the pool.

It was into this world of high living and gambling that a fourth child, a son, was born to Fred and Harriet Lindrum on 29 August 1898. On that very night Fred Lindrum played a money match at the Shamrock Hotel against Fred Wells and, after conceding 200 points start, scored an easy win by 1000 to 551. After the match Lindrum had a drink with Wallace Brownlow, to celebrate both his victory and the birth of his son. The question of names for the infant arose and Brownlow suggested that, seeing he was the first Lindrum to be born in Western Australia, his initials would have to be 'W.A.'

Facing page: 'Station Hands at Billiards' was the caption of this fine drawing from the Australasian Sketcher of 21 May 1881. (State Library of Victoria)

Overleaf: A Sydney outing in 1903 in honour of the visiting English professional, H. W. Stevenson. Those who have been identified are: on the extreme left, J.B. Belfield; in the back row, on the left is Charles Memmott, 5th from left is Frank Smith, 7th from left is J. B. Smith (of Heiron & Smith); middle row, seated 2nd from left is H. W. Stevenson (nursing master Stevenson). Seated at the front, left is W. W. Heiron (of Heiron & Smith), next to him is E. A. Boyle — later to be known as the grand old man of Australian billiards. (W. F. Heiron)

Fred Lindrum I (Walter's grandfather), who ran billiard saloons and hotels until his death in 1880. Fred I was a competent player and defeated the world champion, John Roberts senior, at the York Hotel, Adelaide in 1865. (Dolly Lindrum)

Preceding page: *From left: Fred Lindrum junior, Fred Lndrum senior, George Gray and Harry Gray. The photo was taken about 1909, when Fred Lindrum junior and George Gray were the outstanding players in Australia. (Dolly Lindrum)*

So it was that the newest Lindrum was christened 'Walter Albert'. Indeed it was Brownlow who became young Walter's godfather, an indication that the friendship between Brownlow and Fred Lindrum went further than their business arrangement over the billiard room. What transpired, if anything, in the next six months between Brownlow and Lindrum is unknown. It is sufficient to say that by the second of March 1899, Lindrum was no longer in the billiard room at the Palace Hotel. He was now in charge of the billiard room at Mrs Durrant's Australia Hotel and he was still doing business on "forthcoming events". Perhaps the change of rooms was related to an advertisement that Lindrum had run in the *Kalgoorlie Miner* on 25 November 1898, which stated: "On account of the bad times Billiards will be reduced from today to 2s and Is for games of 100, and 50 respectively."

Lindrum may have found that, due to the decline in patronage of the Palace Hotel billiard room, he could no longer afford to pay the weekly rental. It could not be expected that the boom conditions, when fortunes were made overnight (and lost the next night on a drinking and gambling spree) would last forever. When the gold became more difficult to extract the miners were forced to reappraise their lifestyle. When the gold had previously been easily obtained the miners were content to spend their wealth in a carefree, reckless manner. However, when the gold recovery process involved longer hours of tedious labour, the miners had more respect and appreciation for their hard-won reward. Consequently they spent their money more selectively and reduced their extravagant spending on the less-essential activities such as drinking, gambling and billiards. Life on the goldfields took a more sedate form although it never really resembled the orderly demeanour of the large, established cities.

Fred Lindrum's move from the Palace Hotel was probably associated with such a change in the lifestyle of the Kalgoorlie miners. One of the best-known stories about the Lindrum's time at Kalgoorlie concerns the day when the Palace Hotel is supposed to have caught on fire. A group of miners, who were addicted to Devil's pool, ignored Mrs Lindrum's cries for help (from another part of the hotel) until they firstly carried the billiard table out of the hotel and to safety in the middle of Hannan Street. Whenever this fire did occur (if it did in fact take place) it was certainly not in the latter months of 1898 or early 1899. Therefore it was not a fire which precipitated the Lindrum's shift from the Palace Hotel. Indeed it was not very long before the Lindrums shifted from Mrs Durrant's Australia Hotel but this time they moved away from Kalgoorlie and out of the Coolgardie goldfields region. They took up residence in Donnybrook, situated on the Preston River some 200 kilometres south of Perth. Fred Lindrum was continuing to chase the golden rainbow for gold had been discovered in the Donnybrook district in 1898. The field, however, proved to be a disappointment, yielding only about 1000 ounces in the next couple of years. Fred Lindrum had a change of occupations at Donnybrook becoming the publican of a hotel that contained a two-table billiard room.

It was at Donnybrook that young Walter Lindrum caused his parents some worrying moments. When the Lindrum children misbehaved, the usual punishment was for them to be locked in the hotel laundry. They had to copy out exercises from a copybook for the duration of their confinement. On one occasion both Walter and his sister, Violet, were sentenced to the confines of the laundry. Walter was only three at the time so naturally he could not copy out the exercises. Violet, who was several years older, started copying the exercises but soon wearied of the task. Instead she preferred to play with the washing mangle and encouraged Walter to join in the fun. Violet busily turned the handle while Walter fed some old newspapers into the mangle. Somehow Walter managed to get his right index finger caught in the cog wheels of the mangle. Walter's piercing screams brought his mother running and the boy was rushed off to the doctor. The finger was badly mutilated and the doctor had no option but to amputate the top joint.

Walter first showed interest in the game of billiards when about four years old. He would sneak into the billiard room to see his big brother, Fred junior being coached by his father. Fred senior was a serious-minded and thorough coach, a perfectionist who would do anything to ensure that Fred junior became as proficient a player as possible. So absolute was the father's dedication to this end that he made a significant decision in the early days of Fred junior's billiard career. Young Fred had been born left-handed as had his father. Fred senior took the dramatic step of converting Fred junior to playing billiards with his right hand. Fred senior later explained that this was "a result brought about from the fact that when practising, if I were showing him a stroke, his back would be towards me, so I brought him up as a right-handed player more as a matter of convenience than for any other reason, although being a left-hander myself, I have a certain bias in favour of that style." (The *Referee*, 21 December 1904.)

Fred senior was referring to when he was demonstrating stance, bridge and cue grip to Fred junior on the table. Young Fred was required to line up alongside his father and copy his stance, etc. The problem arose that because both father and son were left-handed, young Fred was turned away from his father, making it impossible for either of them to get a satisfactory view of the other's bridge and cue arm. One solution to this problem was to convert young Fred to a right-handed player, a step that was taken at an early stage and that had no detrimental effect on the subsequent development of his game.

The conversion of Fred junior to a right-handed player may have been a radical step but it typified the devotion and single-mindedness that Fred senior applied to the task of guiding his son along the path to billiard greatness. When young Walter ventured into the billiard room he was invariably thrown out for he generally made a nuisance of himself and distracted his father and brother from the serious task at hand. One day, after being expelled from the billiard room, Walter went to play with friends on the bank of the Preston River. The river was in flood at the time and Walter fell in. He clung desperately to some reeds while his young playmates ran off to raise the alarm and return with some men who dragged a weary Walter to safety. As a result of his soaking Walter contracted pneumonia and was given until midnight to live by the family doctor. However, Walter defied the doctor's prognosis and grew into a small, but sturdy, boy.

A year later Walter had a further close brush with death. A giant jarrah tree, which had been struck by lightning, came crashing down on the Lindrum house one night during a fierce storm. Walter's bedroom was right in the path of the tree's fall and his anxious parents rushed in to find Walter sitting up in bed howling with the fallen tree close to his bed. After this close encounter Walter's childhood settled into a more routine and less eventful pattern — much to the relief of his parents. The fallen jarrah tree made an enormous mess in the Lindrum's backyard. The ever-alert Fred organised a woodchopping contest and the best axemen from all around were drawn to Donnybrook to compete for the prizemoney. The axemen also used the occasion to settle any arguments about their relative merits and substantial sums changed hands in a series of challenge matches. Fred Lindrum senior lost heavily on the promotion but could draw some consolation from the enormous pile of firewood that would last for several winters.

In January of 1903 Fred Lindrum senior made the journey from Donnybrook to Perth for the racing carnival. He missed a mammoth collect when Homeward Bound was beaten into second place by Cypher in the Perth Cup. Later in 1903 the Lindrums moved to Perth where Fred senior, finding no suitable billiard room available for lease decided to open a new room. It took some months for premises to be secured and fitted out. The *West Australian* on 4 January, 1904 marked the opening with the following reference:

> Today Mr. Fred Lindrum, the champion billiard player, will open his newly fitted-up saloon, in Empire Buildings, corner of Murray and Barrack Streets. An idea of the dimensions of the place may be gained from the fact that 275 yards of linoleum were required to cover the floors. The furnishings are excellent, and there are four Alcock tables — two of the English standard height and two of the Australian standard. There is also connected with the saloon — which is admittedly equal, if not superior to anything of the kind in Australia — a cafe and lounge. Mr. Lindrum will personally manage the place, with Fred Lindrum junior, the boy champion, assisting.

Fred Lindrum junior in the few short months since his arrival in Perth had gained a reputation as a good billiards player. In the Marker's Tournament, an event restricted to those employed in billiard rooms, he performed well, winning several matches. After one of these matches, in which Fred junior defeated Mr Bastian by 228 with a best break of 39, the *West Australian* (28 October 1903) reported: "Although no large breaks were made the winner played consistently, and with dash and brilliancy. The audience showed some enthusiasm over the boy Champion's clever manipulation of the cue, his long losing hazards being particularly good."

This was one of the first newspaper reports on Fred Lindrum junior and already he was being described as the 'Boy Champion'. This was a totally unofficial title which was loosely thrown about as a means of describing any young player who was showing considerable potential. There is, though, little doubt that Fred junior deserved to be referred to as the boy champion for his game was improving rapidly as a result of regular competition. Fred junior went on a country tour in early 1904 and played matches against the local champions in various country towns. Such was the lad's prowess that he conceded a sizeable start in most of his matches. A typical encounter was played at Northam in July against Mr Letcher who recived 300 start in 750 up. Fred junior scored an easy victory by 750 to 524 with a highest break of 114 — his first century break in public. On 31 July at the Commercial

Travellers Club in Perth Fred junior suffered his first loss in eighteen games when Mr Brown, after receiving 300 start, won by 750 to 623. On 4 August young Fred returned to the winning list when he won the final of the Marker's Tournament from 125 behind, defeating Mr E. Thompson (30 behind) by 250 to 183. This final had been staged at the billiard saloon in the Empire Buildings, the room which Fred Lindrum had opened earlier in the year but which he no longer occupied. Fred senior had apparently sold out his interest in the room for he was now located at the Commonwealth Hotel. He had also become a professional member of Western Australia Tattersall's Club which, of course, meant that he was now operating as a bookmaker at the various race meetings.

In October of 1904 Fred junior undertook his first major tour under the aegis of Alcock & Co. who erected tables especially for his exhibitions. Fred's tour embraced the main eastern States and his opponents were usually the best of the amateur players. The reporter for the *Referee* upon seeing the 'Boy Champion' for the first time gave the folowing verdict on 14 December:

> In style and general comportment round the table young Lindrum has evidently taken H. W. Stevenson for a model. He has the same sailor-like roll when doing his walk round, goes down to the stroke in the same resolute manner, has much the same kind of bridge, with the fingers well extended, and the same working of the little finger as our late visitor from down under had. In selecting the shot the youngster does not hesitate a moment, nor does he saw away time, but executes his stroke instanter. Not only is he likely to be a great billiardist but, just as important, he is sure to be a great showman.

These were prophetic words to apply to a 'Boy Champion', a youth of sixteen years who, while indeed showing enormous potential, was a long way from being a serious threat to the leading Australian professionals such as the Champion, Memmott and the vastly-improved Frank Smith who was ranked now as second only to Memmott. Fred Lindrum junior was to later fulfil every expectation of the *Referee's* reporter for he certainly became a great player, a fact that has been submerged with the passing of time by the overwhelming exploits of his younger brother. Fred junior also became a great showman, an aspect of the profession of which he was acutely aware and which he deliberately cultivated. It was always Fred's intention to play an entertaining style of billiards and he certainly achieved this objective. Fred was a billiards artist, a very pretty player who "could be watched all day without becoming boring". When Walter Lindrum emerged to the pinnacle of billiards greatness he did so in a cool, calculated, mechanical way. Walter was a billiards tradesman who was so intent on being the champion that he overlooked what the paying public wanted to see. In this regard Walter could have possibly taken a page out of Fred junior's book. On the other hand, if Walter had devoted more time to developing a 'showy' type of billiards he would not have reached the same level of proficiency.

Fred Lindrum senior had accompanied Fred Junior on the tour of the eastern States and he was amazed at the extent of the popularity that billiards enjoyed, particularly in Sydney. The first years of the twentieth century saw the start of an incredible billiards boom, which continued until 1914 when the outbreak of war caused a halt. There were many factors that contributed to the billiards boom but two of these were at the heart of the boom. The first was the overall strength of the economy which has always influenced the popularity of recreational activities. If the economy is strong, then the public enjoys a level of affluence that facilitates their indulgence in the various forms of recreation. This is particularly true for billiards which has often proven a sound barometer of the general state of the economy. In the early 1900s the economic situation was strong following the recovery from the depression of the early 1890s. Thus the billiard enthusiast could afford an extra game or two of billiards each week. The second factor that led to the billiards boom was the fact that it had become cheaper to hire a billiard table for a game of 100 up. This situation, strange as it may seem at a time when the economic outlook was one of strength and prosperity, was a consequence of the formation of a large number of social clubs. These 'toney' institutions such as the N.S.W. Sports Club, Commercial Travellers Club, Yacht Club, Sydney Bicycle Club and Professional Musician's Club to mention just a few, provided billiards for their members at a tariff which was much less than it had been in the 'good old days'. Consequently the public billiard rooms suffered a loss in patronage and in order to compete with the clubs they were forced to reduce their charges to a shilling for 100 up and sixpence for 50 up. This made billiards even more accessible to the average man and it had a snowballing effect on the billiards boom. A sure indication of this boom was the fact that in May, 1901 the two Sydney manufacturers, Heiron and Smith, and Beddy and Todd had to introduce double shifts to cope with the demand for their tables and services. (The *Referee* 8 May, 1901.)

Fred Lindrum junior returned by boat to Perth after his Eastern tour which had been an invaluable experience for him. On January 26, 1905 he commenced a match at His Majesty's Hotel against Bert Teague, a left-handed player who was regarded as the Western Australian champion. After a series of four matches of 1200 up, with the scores being added together, Teague won by 4800 to 3229. The heavy loss was a timely reminder to Fred junior that despite the progress that he had made he still had to improve his game before he could be even be regarded as champion of his State. In August of that year Fred junior won the Marker's Tournament for the second successive year. He started from 175 behind and defeated Alex Scott (70 behind) in the final by 250 to 50. The co-backmarkers in the event, on 250 behind, were Bert Teague and Fred Lindrum senior who had returned to the competitive scene after several years in retirement.

The year 1905 had been a successful one for Fred junior and he was gradually edging his way up the billiards ladder. It was in 1906 that he first shaped as a real threat to the leading professionals. In September he had a re-match with Bert Teague at the Kalgoorlie Goldfields Tattersall's Club. The match was to be 3000 up spread over three nights with the Club putting up a purse of £50. There was an estimated £2000 bet on the result of the match. It was Fred Lindrum junior who justified the confidence of his backers with a fine display to win by 3000 to 2416, after having the misfortune to break his cue at 1750. The class of the performance is illustrated by the fact that Fred junior made eight century breaks with a top of 250 unfinished and he averaged 28 per visit to the table. It was young Lindrum's most important win to date and he now became the acknowledged champion of Western Australia.

While Fred junior was pleased with his win over Teague he could not afford to rest on his laurels. News had reached the West of the deeds of one George Gray, the son of Harry Gray who was now running a saloon in Brisbane. Young George had been born in Melbourne on 28 March 1892 in the days when his father ran the billiard room at the Bull and Mouth Hotel. Reports filtered through of some staggering breaks by George including one on 25 June of 513 points compiled by an unbroken sequence of 171 losing hazards. Young Gray's development was remarkable for he had made a relatively late start as a billiards player. He was twelve years of age before he picked up a cue and even then it was more by accident than design. George's parents were strongly opposed to him following in his father's footsteps as a professional billiardist. They thus encouraged him to work hard at school, which George did. He proved a capable student and just missed a valuable scholarship when twelve years old. During the school holidays George suffered a badly broken arm and the family doctor advised that the arm be placed in a box splint. Harry Gray pleaded for a simpler method of treatment, the doctor finally agreeing provided that Gray senior take personal charge of his son. This meant that George had to be taken to his father's billiard room every day. From retrieving the balls for the customers it was a natural progression for George to knock the balls about. The lad showed an aptitude for the game and after some further parental opposition George was put into serious training by his father. On 18 July, 1906 the *Referee* carried its first report on George Gray:

> The youngster is only 14 years old, an age at which it is even doubtful if there was ever a player in Australia his equal. He has been studying the game under his father's tuition for the past couple of years, but it was only in the last few months that the gift (for it really is a gift) came to him. He is quite a phenomenon, with a knowledge of the table and all the tricks with the balls that is most marvellous for one so young. His strongest point now is with the losing hazard stroke.

Perhaps George would not have quite agreed that the 'gift' had only come to him in the last few months. Gray's progress at billiards was the result of a prodigious amount of practice which often amounted to twelve and fourteen hours each day. While Gray undoubtedly had natural ability it was his incessant appetite for practice that was responsible for his emergence as the latest 'prospective champion.' So dramatic was George's arrival on the billiard scene that he was now referred to as 'Boy Champion', a title which had previously been the unchallenged prerogative of Fred Lindrum junior. It may be questioned if Fred Lindrum junior, who was now 18 years of age, was still to be regarded as a 'boy'. There were a number of keen judges prepared to include Fred junior in this category but who considered that George Gray was now the 'Boy Champion'. There was considerable speculation about the relative merits of the two exciting young prospects but it was not until 1909 that they finally met and their ability could be compared.

3 Laying the Foundations

Billiards champions are made, not born.

Walter Lindrum

During the latter part of 1906 the Lindrum family left Perth and returned to the Kalgoorlie district where Fred senior took over the management of the billiard room at the Great Boulder Hotel in Maritana Street. The early boom years of Kalgoorlie were well and truly over and the city had settled into a more organised and sedate existence. It could now boast its own tramway system and a permanent water supply: the water was brought by pipeline from the Mundaring Weir on the Helena River, 570 kilometres away.

Although the really 'golden' days were behind her, Kalgoorlie was still the most important goldfields settlement. Just as all roads had once led to Rome they continued to lead to Kalgoorlie. This fact was clearly illustrated when in December of 1906 the sporting promoter, Rufe Naylor, organised a series of sprint races to be staged in Kalgoorlie between two of the finest sprinters in the world. The world champion, an Irishman by the name of Rochfort Beauchamp Day, was matched against the Australian champion, Arthur B. Postle, or the 'Crimson Flash' as he was popularly known because of his all-red racing colours. Postle, a Queenslander, set world records for 50 yards (5.1 seconds) 60 yards (6 seconds), 75 yards (7.2 seconds), 80 yards (7.75 seconds) and 200 yards (19 secs.). He had arrived in Kalgoorlie in late November to prepare for the match races and also to get set for the betting money which he was carrying. By 30 November, still five days away from the actual race day, Postle had placed £235 on himself, comprised of £200 of his own money and £35 which had been given to him by friends prior to his departure from Queensland. There was an enormous amount of betting on the race and although Day had originally been favourite the weight of money saw Postle shorten and displace the Irishman from favouritism.

The match races were set down for 5 December and some days before the event visitors began to flock into Kalgoorlie. Special trains brought people from the nearby towns and the crowd on race night was estimated at between 15 000 and 20 000. The contest was to be staged in three heats over distances from 75 yards to 300 yards. The first race staged was the 75 yards heat, Postle's favourite distance, and the Crimson Flash duly won in 7.2 seconds. The second heat was over 300 yards which was Day's pet distance but it was Postle who again won. Postle was carried around the ground on the shoulders of numerous delighted fans, but there was one very loyal fan who could not participate in this exaltation of the Crimson Flash. That fan was a boy of eight years of age, a diminutive lad who lacked the physical dimensions to partake in this act of hero worship. His name was Walter Lindrum and it is not known if the youngster was even allowed out to watch his idol defeat the world champion. Maybe Walter had to be content in the knowledge that in the days leading up to the big race he had carried Arthur Postle's gear to the local track for training sessions.

The Lindrum's stay at Kalgoorlie was only brief and they soon moved on to another goldmining town, Broad Arrow. It was at Broad Arrow that Walter was allowed into the billiard room but it was only to pull the balls out of the pockets for brother Fred. Walter spent many tiring hours fielding the balls but it was not without its reward for occasionally he managed to sneak a little practice. All the time Walter was taking in Fred junior's moves, dreaming that maybe someday he could play some of those beautiful shots. Walter pleaded with his father to be allowed to play the game but Fred senior steadfastly refused to teach him and forbade him to play. Fred senior was preoccupied with coaching his first son who was polishing his game in preparation for matches arranged with the English professional, Melbourne Inman. There was simply not enough time for Fred senior to teach Walter about billiards.

Walter was a determined mite and he decided that he was going to play billiards, with or without his father's approval. One day when Fred senior was at the local races Walter sneaked the key to the billiard room from behind the bar. He was having a great time hitting the balls about the table and all went well until he tried to imitate a shot that he had seen brother Fred play, with the cue held vertically! The result was disastrous, a hole in the priceless cloth. A panic-stricken Walter fled from the billiard room, hid behind his bedroom door and cried himself to sleep. When Fred senior returned from the races young Walter was nowhere to be found. The police and black trackers were called in to search for the lad before Walter finally awoke and alerted the family with his crying. He received a thorough spanking for disobeying his father's instructions but it was to prove all worthwhile. Fred senior realised that it was futile to deny the boy and so Walter was allowed to learn the game.

It is hard to imagine a more ideal environment in which to learn to play billiards than that available to Walter. With a father who had ranked among the best players in the land and a brother who was showing enormous potential, Walter's introduction to billiards was made under the most enviable of circumstances. One very important matter was decided before Walter had his first lesson. Although he was naturally right handed Walter had great difficulty holding the cue in his small hand, mainly because he was hampered by the missing joint of his index finger. Fred senior decided that there was no alternative but for Walter to learn to play with his left hand. It is strange to say the least, that both Walter and Fred junior learnt to play billiards with their 'unnatural' hand.

Walter soon learnt, as brother Fred had before him, that his father was a dogmatic teacher who demanded absolute obedience from his pupil. Fred senior believed in the old adage that practice makes perfect and he organised Walter's practice sessions accordingly. Fred senior showed Walter how to hold a cue and how to make a bridge. He chalk-marked the floor to show Walter where he must place his feet and also placed chalk lines on the table to indicate the natural angles that the balls would take. Fred senior would leave Walter in the room to practise as he had instructed. From time to time Fred senior would look in the window and if Walter had wandered from the set routine the balls were taken off him for the rest of the day. The first six months was devoted to practice with only one ball. Once Walter could place the cue ball anywhere on the table that his father desired he was allowed to move on to practice with the red ball. Despite his severe methods Fred senior was careful in those early days to restrict Walter's time on the billiard table. He did not want to force the boy too hard with hours of tedious practice and so destroy Walter's enthusiasm for the game. Harder work would come later once Walter had established a sound knowledge of the basics of the game. Fred senior need not have been concerned. Walter had such a driving passion for the game that instead of spending his leisure time with other children he would slink off to the local Mechanic's Institute for secret practice. Walter could not afford the modest fee that was charged for the use of the table. He made friends with the room attendant and was allowed to use a table, free of charge, whenever one was available.

When the English player, Melbourne Inman, arrived in Western Australia in May 1907 Fred Lindrum junior received his initiation into big-time billiards. Inman conceded a sizeable start to young Lindrum in their early matches but usually recorded a comfortable win. One typical example was a Perth match that finished on 22 May which Inman won by 3000 to 2929 after conceding 1200 start. Inman reached his points with a break of 220 unfinished while Fred junior's best break was a lowly 81. This was well below Lindrum's true form and perhaps an indication that he may have been overwhelmed by the stature of Inman.

Inman and Fred Lindrum junior went on an extensive tour, visiting most states of Australia and the nineteen-year-old gradually grew accustomed to the Englishman's aura. In a match at Melbourne Fred junior, after receiving 4500 start, scored a well-earnt victory by 10 000 to 9630. In Sydney Inman was matched with his fellow-countryman, H. W. Stevenson, who was making his second trip to the Antipodes under contract to Heiron and Smith. The match for a £100 cash trophy was staged at Belfield's Hotel on the corner of George and King Streets. The Hotel was run by J. B. Belfield who declared, when he assumed control of it in 1904, that he would re-establish the billiard room and endeavour to bring back some of its pristine glory. The hotel when known as Perkin's Exchange Hotel had been the venue for the first Australian Championship match in 1881 and earlier for matches by such celebrated visiting players as Cook, Kilkenny, Rudolph and Carme. Belfield was a very fine billiards player, although strictly an amateur, and won the Australian title on several occasions. He was an unlikely-looking fellow for a billiardist being a gross man, weighing in excess of 95 kilograms. However, he possessed a fine touch and had a thorough knowledge of the game and so dominated the amateur scene that he retired in 1909 to 'give others a chance'. So fine a player was Belfield that he was regarded as being in the professional class but it is likely that a highly-strung and sensitive temperament would have prevented his progress in the professional ranks. One example of Belfield's skill was in a friendly match with the Australian champion, Memmott, in 1903 when Belfield averaged 31 per visit in winning by 600 to 429.

In Brisbane a match was arranged between Inman and George Gray. The youngster was conceded 2500 start in 4000 up but Inman won by a margin of 168 points, with a top break of 504. Gray's best breaks were 79 and 159. After the match Inman commented: "Although I had been warned what to expect, it was one of the shocks of my career to see this child, in knickerbockers and a turned-down collar, rattle up a confident 79 break almost at his first visit to the table." (*Australian Encyclopaedia.*)

During his visit to Australia Inman had been impressed by the performances of both Gray and Fred Lindrum junior. H. W. Stevenson was particularly enthused by the style and performances of the Lindrum youngster and wanted him to return with him to England. Fred junior declined Stevenson's invitation and lost an excellent chance to gain experience of the English scene. Instead he chose to undertake an extensive tour with Charles Memmott which carried them into the country districts of New South Wales and Victoria as well the State capitals, Sydney, Melbourne and Adelaide. The most important match of the tour was played at the Globe Hotel, Adelaide where Memmott won by 8000 to 7628. The match carried some suggestion of being for the Championship but it appears as if the word 'championship' was only thrown loosely around for advertising purposes. The result of the match was some indication that Fred Lindrum junior was fast approaching the top flight of the Australian game. The *Referee* made a very interesting comment in regard to the Memmott/Lindrum tour: ". . . but Memmott is so volatile, easy-going and good natured that he is apt to allow the youth too free a rein, and possibly injure a career that is full of the greatest billiard possibilities." (27 November 1907.)

The words may have been regarded at that time as the misgivings of an over-cautious prophet of doom. However, in retrospect they may have been very sound words for as it turned out Fred Lindrum junior later developed a drinking problem which unquestionably thwarted his potential and damaged his billiard career. One can only speculate from this distance on the impact that the tour with Memmott had on Fred Lindrum junior. The short term advantages of the tour for Fred junior were further experience and development of his billiards. But quite posssibly the long-term legacy of the tour was that Fred Lindrum acquired the taste for beer which was later so deleteriously to affect his highly-promising billiard career and tragically dominate his life.

The development of Fred junior's billiards in 1908 was very pronounced. In some of his matches with Inman (who was again in Australia) he recorded impressive victories. One example was Fred junior's win by 9000 to 6692 after Inman had conceded him 3000 start. The merit of Lindrum's performances assume their significance when it is noted that Inman won the World Championship in the following year and was then runner-up to Stevenson in the next three years. During the 1908 tour by Inman there were thirteen occasions on which he was defeated by Fred junior who admittedly received a start in most of the matches.

With Fred Lindrum junior in fine form it was no surprise when he challenged Memmott for the Australian title. Memmott was already committed to a challenge by Frank Smith and it was decided that Fred junior would play the winner of this match. The Memmott/Smith encounter was played in October at the showroom of Heiron and Smith at 214 Castlereagh Street, Sydney, Memmott retained his title and collected the £100 side wager with a narrow win by 15 000 to 14 849. The match between Memmott and

Fred Lindrum junior commenced after a week's recess but proved somewhat of an anti-climax after the closeness of the Memmott/Smith encounter. Fred junior with a break of 316 and five other breaks over 200 ran out the easiest of winners by 14 000 to 8312. Apart from the Australian title he collected the £100 side wager and a trophy which was presented by Mr J. Joynton Smith, a keen follower of professional billiards.

Joynton Smith (later Sir Joynton) was a business and sporting magnate of the highest order. He controlled three newspapers, the *Referee, Smith's Weekly,* and the *Arrow*. The *Referee* must rank as one of the finest sporting newspapers ever to be published, giving a comprehensive coverage of all major Australian sports. Smith amassed a vast fortune in the hotel business and by conducting pony races. In 1918 he offered the Melbourne sporting entrepreneur, John Wren, the sum of £350 000 for two of his racecourses, Albion Park and Kedron Park. The offer was refused. Smith had a strong influence in the establishment of Rugby League football in Sydney. When Rugby League was in its infant days, and locked in a battle with the established code, Rugby Union, for the services of players, Smith (in 1909) made a lucrative offer to the leading Union players who subsequently defected to the professional code. Smith was a keen billiards player and had maintained a billiard saloon in his Arcadia Hotel which was regarded for many years as the best room in Sydney. He was closely associated with the 1910 visit by John Roberts junior. On one occasion he played a match with Roberts and managed to lure the astute Englishman into a shrewdly-laid trap. The stake was £10 bet and, as he had only one eye (the result of an accident in his youth) Joynton Smith suggested that he should bandage one of Roberts' eyes to make the odds more even. The old champion airily agreed only to find that when Smith bandaged his cue eye he could hardly play at all. Smith gleefully recalled in later years how he 'skinned' a tenner off the illustrious 'J. R.'

The long-awaited match between Fred Lindrum junior and George Gray finally took place in the first week of the New Year, 1909. It seemed a most unusual time to be playing such an important match — right in the middle of summer, in the 'off-season'. It had been accepted for many years that the billiard season traditionally opened on May 1. The first match between the billiard prodigies was played at Queen's Hall, Sydney with the champion, Lindrum, conceding 4000 start to his younger opponent. Gray belied the handicaps with a win by 14 000 to 9357, his top break being 388. The ease of Gray's win prompted several keen judges to declare that Gray was the best player in Australia and he was entitled to a match with Fred Lindrum junior with the championship at stake. Mr Joynton Smith, who at this stage had a business arrangement with Fred junior, responded to these claims by declaring that the champion was prepared to play Gray or anyone else for the title. The one stipulation that Smith made was that any such match must carry a side-wager of a minimum of £100 up to a maximum of £500. There was no rush for the Gray camp to put the money down for a crack at Fred junior's title. This lack of response seemed to confirm the underlying belief that Smith's declaration inferred — that Fred Lindrum junior was capable of vastly improving his billiards when the money was down and the pressure was on.

A return match between Lindrum and Gray was staged a few weeks later in Melbourne. Gray's start on this occasion was reduced to 2000 and despite making a fine break of 591 he was soundly thrashed by Lindrum to the tune of 16 000 to 12 954. Although Fred junior's best break was only 253 it was apparent that he was capable of scoring with far greater consistency than Gray which proved to be the telling factor. Lindrum's win had the 'experts', who had jumped on the George Gray bandwaggon, eating humble pie. He had clearly established that he was a worthy champion. The situation, however, was thoroughly confused again in a match played at Melbourne in August/September. Gray, after receiving 1000 start, made a mockery of the handicaps when he defeated Lindrum by 16 000 to 11 874. Gray's best breaks were 836 (831 off the red), 800 and 588 and he averaged a fine 43.48 per visit to the table. It was little wonder that Fred junior was left in the wake of such a deluge of breaks. Gray's win rekindled the arguments about who was really entitled to be the Australian champion. It was an issue that was never conclusively resolved for the duo never played a match for the title. Although George Gray and Fred Lindrum junior dominated the local scene and their matches were good drawcards they played surprisingly few matches together.

Fred Lindrum senior had, in April of 1909, made a trip from Western Australia to Sydney. He was on the look out for a good billiard saloon to rent or manage. The *Referee* of 7 April carried a brief mention of Fred senior's trip and made a reference to Walter Lindrum: "He (Fred senior) had with him a little son, Walter, who, though only ten years old plays a really good game. His record break is 52, and he is a very likely looking youngster." (The *Referee,* 7 April 1909.)

Fred senior managed to secure an upstairs room at Belfield's Hotel, so he was most successful in his search for a good room. He returned to the west and after quickly disposing of his interests there he brought his family to Sydney in June. Fred senior equipped the Belfield's room with three tables which provided a good return under the continuing boom in billiards' popularity. The strength of the boom can be gauged by the number of English professionals who visited Australia during the first decade or so of the twentieth century. Apart from Inman and Stevenson there were visits by Tom Reece and, of course, that most-travelled of professionals, John Roberts junior. Most of these players returned for a second or third visit, a sure indication that Australia was indeed a happy hunting ground. In 1910 the illustrious John Roberts junior, who was by then known as the 'grand old man of billiards' (having entered his 62nd year), made his final trip to our shores. Since his first visit in 1876 Roberts had noticed a vast improvement in the standard of play. Fred Lindrum junior so impressed Roberts on this final tour that he was the Englishman's opponent in virtually every match. Fred junior recorded some fine wins over Roberts. In Melbourne at Alcock's Proprietary Rooms, Elizabeth Street, Fred junior, after receiving 3000 start, won by 18 000 to 12 296. His highest break was 507 which was a personal best. In a later match in Sydney Roberts again conceded 3000 start and Lindrum again won comfortably by 18 000 to 15 693. In all fairness to Roberts it must be remembered that he was approaching his 63rd year and he suffered from fatigue in the long matches spread over a fortnight. This fact was confirmed when Roberts scored a series of wins over Lindrum in short matches of 3000 up.

Roberts was in the twilight of a remarkable career that had seen him completely dominate the professional billiard scene. He was an extremely accomplished player with a strong appreciation of what the public desired from billiard matches. Despite Roberts' skill as a player (of which his break of 1392 made in 1894 under spot-barred conditions was ample evidence) he is best remembered for his contribution to the status of the game. It was largely due to Roberts that billiards became accepted as a respectable form of recreation. He was a dominating personality who commanded the respect of everyone, including that of royalty whose patronage he enjoyed. Probably no one ever saw Roberts taken at a disadvantage. In one of his matches with Fred Lindrum junior he made such a blatant foul at nursery cannons that it was expected he would stop without waiting for the inevitable protest. But while Fred junior was getting up to protest Roberts made two little cannons at lightning pace, and declined to accept the protest: "You know the rules, Mr. Lindrum. You must protest on the shot, not afterwards." (The *Argus,* 2 September 1918.)

Roberts went on with his break without condescending to argue the point, to the great amusement of everybody except Lindrum. This episode occurred in an exhibition match. Roberts would not have resorted to such tactics in a match with money involved. For sheer presence of mind it is hard to surpass an incident that took place on one of Roberts' trips to the Orient. Roberts was playing a game at the palace of a Chinese potentate to be followed by an exhibition of trick shots. One of the trick shots was a 'hat cannon' that required the red ball to be struck with great force. Roberts successfully performed the shot but in doing so he split the red ball in half. The Oriental calm and bejewelled elegance of the select audience was shattered by murmurs of amazement. No one was more amazed than Roberts himself but he stood still, resting on his cue, and received the applause with a stately inclination of his head. Presently an interpreter approached Roberts and said that his Excellency would like to see the shot repeated. "Tell his excellency", replied Roberts, "that I never play that shot more than once in an exhibition." (The *Argus,* 2 September 1918).

Roberts played many matches in England for money. Perhaps his most famous game was the 'Match of the Century' played in 1899 against Charles Dawson. The match was for a comparatively modest side wager of £100 but one of the conditions was that the winner of the match was entitled to the entire gate receipts. It was Roberts who won the match and collected the £100 side wager and the gate receipts of £2154. In his many tours to Australia Roberts played only one money match and that was against Fred Weiss in October, 1900. The match was 21 000 up with half of the points being played in each of Sydney and Melbourne. The side wager was £500 and went to Weiss who, after being conceded 7000 start, won the match by 21 000 to 20 110. When John Roberts junior departed from Australia on 27 September 1910 he was accompanied by Miss Ruby Roberts, a very accomplished cueist. Ruby Roberts was the niece of Charles Memmott but was not related to John Roberts junior. The two Roberts went on an extensive tour which carried them to Ceylon, Java, Burmah, India and England.

During his last Australian tour Roberts' play had been watched on several occasions by Walter Lindrum. Roberts made an indelible impression on the lad who, from a secluded spot in the back corner of the billiard hall, scrutinised every movement of the great player. After watching a session of play Walter would go home and, with the aid of a prodigious memory, attempt to reproduce the best break that he had seen made. He would seldom make the break perfectly, occasionally having to re-set the balls and continue playing. Still that was only to be expected from a boy of almost twelve years of age. The extent of Lindrum's memory powers were exemplified in 1930 when in his first book, *Billiards* he said of Roberts: "He is unforgettable to me. Here and now I could play every shot of a break of over six hundred I saw him make."

Walter gave his father plenty of headaches in the early days at Belfield's Hotel. Being short of stature, Walter's first efforts at billiards were made with some difficulty. Walter had to stretch unduly to play many of his shots and as a consequence he developed the bad habit of throwing the elbow of his cue arm into the air. After vainly trying to counteract this tendency in his son Fred Lindrum went home one night most distraught. He exclaimed to Mrs Lindrum: "I have tried to straighten him up, but there appears to be no hope." After some further reflection he added: "Perhaps it will wear off, sooner or later."

Eventually Walter's cue action did straighten up somewhat. However, it was not completely straight. Although shots that demanded a very correct cue action were played with a straight, orthodox action by Walter he did play many shots with an unorthodox round-arm action. He never completely overcame his early habit which had developed as a response to his lack of reach at the table. That habit did not seem to hinder his billiards in later years.

It was at Belfield's that Walter scored his first hundred break. His opponent was the South African batsman, Dave Nourse, who along with several team-mates frequented Belfield's during the 1910–11 tour. The *Referee* of 14 December 1910 made the following mention of the Lindrums:

> The '3 Lindrums' — father and two sons, are to be seen daily in the upstairs room at Belfield's making long runs and showing how the game is played by experts. The lesser Lindrum — the wee, small ten-year-old [should read twelve-year-old], with the old-fashioned face — surprises visitors, and takes the conceit out of most oldsters who take him on at the 3-ball game, by his great skill for one so young and so diminutive.

Apart from the factual error, referring to Walter as being ten years old, it is interesting that the writer regarded Walter as being so small for that age. What would have been the reporter's thoughts if he had realised the lad was twelve years of age? Though Fred Lindrum senior was pleased with Walter's first century break he certainly did not greet the landmark with nearly as much delight as Walter. Fred senior was paying most of his attention to the billiards of Fred junior who was continuing to shape as a potential champion. Walter continued to live in the shadow of his older brother who with the advantage of age and experience was approaching the zenith of his game.

The year of 1911 was probably the high point of Fred Lindrum junior's career. In May he made breaks of 800 and 821 in a successful title defence against the former Englishman, Albert Williams. An even finer performance was registered a few weeks later against the English professional, Tom Reece. Fred junior scored a comfortable win, in the process making breaks of 830, 840 and 1239. The latter break was to prove the highest of Lindrum's career and it exceeded the previous Australian break record of 1238 by a solitary point. The previous record had been set by Memmott in 1892 under conditions which allowed the free use of the spot stroke. Lindrum's record break was far more meritorious being made under rules which only permitted two successive pots of the red off the spot. It was obvious that Fred junior was ready to enter the true testing ground for any billiards player — England. Passages were booked on the S.S. *Malova* for Fred Lindrum junior and his father for 27 September.

Young Walter Lindrum, who had made a break of 150 on a standard table in August, had visions of practising hard during his father's absence so as to impress him when he returned. These plans were quashed by Fred senior who demanded: "All the time I'm away, you must use only two balls and play only two shots, the spot stroke and the cushion run-through." (The *Sporting Globe,* 16 July 1938.)

Walter was perplexed and disappointed by his father's edict. He thought, with some justification, that he was developing into quite a proficient three-ball player. Fred, however, was a very astute man and he had good reasons for this apparently retrograde step. He never bothered to tell Walter that the cushion run-through was designed to cultivate touch while the spot stroke was to build Walter's top of the table game. Walter was left under the watchful eye of Joe Andreolli who was the attendant at the Billiards Limited Saloon. Despite his feeling of frustration Walter stuck religiously to his father's instructions for the eight months of his absence.

Fred Lindrum junior's tour to England was preceded by George Gray's visit to the Old Dart in 1910–11 season. Gray was under contract to the manufacturers, E. J. Riley Ltd who transported the same table to the venue of each of Gray's matches. Rileys also provided the cloth for the table with a new length being cut from the roll for each match. Gray was thus playing under ideal conditions week in and week out with the only variation due to changes in the weather. Gray used the reliable crystalate balls which were uncommon in England where ivories were still in vogue. Gray's tour was an overwhelming success. He systematically defeated all the leading players and compiled an unprecedented 23 breaks in excess of 1000. The eighteen year old's best break was 2196 unfinished. He made his breaks, as always, with losing hazards off the red ball into the middle pocket. Gray was dubbed the 'red phenomenon' because of his complete mastery of this facet of play. Despite Gray's obvious superiority to the English professionals he never seriously threatened to take the championship from them. He was not nearly as dangerous an opponent when removed from the sanctuary of his Riley environs. However, the over-riding reason why Gray did not win the championship was because he could not handle the ivory balls which were mandatory for all championship matches. It was a tragedy for billiards that Gray did not develop other aspects of play besides the losing hazard game, which had only limited spectator appeal, for he would have been better-equipped to handle the inconsistencies of the ivory balls. An even greater tragedy was that Gray's cue arm gradually 'went' on him. His game disintegrated so markedly that by the time he was forty Gray could not even make a century break.

Although George Gray's first tour of England was an unequivocal success, Fred Lindrum junior's trip could only be described as disastrous. Lindrum might be excused for losing against Melbourne Inman but there was little excuse for his losses to lesser professionals in Harverson and Aiken (the Scottish champion). Lindrum did record some wins, including two victories over Reece, but his general play was described as being 'too bad to be true'. Whether Fred's drinking problem was starting to affect his play by this time is unknown. In an interview after his return to Australia Fred junior claimed that his failure on the tour was due to the winter which was of exceptional severity and the slowness of the tables which did not suit his style of play. Whatever the reasons for Fred Lindrum junior's dismal showing on the tour it was to be the turning point of his career. He continued playing billiards for many more years, and even made another trip to England, but he was never again regarded as a likely world champion.

Fred junior made some interesting comments on the up-and-coming players in England.

> Amongst the young players who are coming to the front, the most proficient appears to be W. Smith, of Darlington, who will probably be invited to take part in Burroughes and Watts next tournament. Tommy Newman, whom Mr John Roberts has in hand, is being boomed as a coming champion, but if he ever reaches that high elevation I will be most surprised for he has about the worst style of any player of experience that I have seen. (The *Referee,* 5 June 1912.)

Smith and Newman both later became world champions, a position that Newman was able to reach despite having a suspect cue action with his cue arm drawn in behind his back. Fred junior was quite correct in his criticism of Newman's playing style but very wide of the mark in his prediction of the effect that this weakness would have on Newman's subsequent development. The example of Newman illustrates that there is far more to billiards success than merely possessing a correct style of play. It can be argued that a good style is more likely to facilitate the development of prowess at billiards (and snooker). Still it was Fred Lindrum junior who, with his superb style, was stagnating as a billiards player much to his consternation and to the disappointment of those who had predicted that he would become a very great player.

Facing page, top left: *Harry Evans (1839–1909), the English-born billiards player who was champion of Australia, 1884–1892. (State Library of Victoria, Australian* Sporting Celebrities, *a pamphlet published in Melbourne in 1887 by A. H. Massina, edited by 'Vigilant)*

Top right: *Walter at 15 years — about the time of his first tours with Miss Ruby Roberts. (Referee, 24 August 1929)*

Below: *A view of Kalgoorlie in the early years of this century. The grand building in the background is the Palace Hotel where Fred Lindrum II ran the billiards room at the time of Walter's birth. (National Library, Canberra)*

Miss Ruby Roberts, who toured with a young Walter Lindrum, 1913–14, and was regarded by Walter as the greatest of all women players. (Alcock's Sporting Review, 14 February 1913)

After returning from England Fred Lindrum senior found that the popularity of billiards was continuing unabated. During his absence the Empire Billiard Theatre had opened in Pitt Street, opposite the City Tattersalls Club. It was the largest billiard saloon in Sydney being equipped with forty Alcock & Co. tables which were spread over two floors of the building. It became the haunt of sharps and cads and those who misspent their youth. The Saloon later became known as the Forty Thieves Saloon, undoubtedly because on each of the forty tables there was sure to be a hustler who would take money from the unsuspecting — by fair means or foul.

4 Apprenticeship

I feel certain that he [Walter Lindrum] will turn out to be the best player
Australia has produced.
Charles Memmott (Australian Billiards Champion, 1892–1908) in 1913

As the chapter of the Lindrum family saga revolving around Fred junior
came to an abrupt anti-climax, so unfolded another. The central character of
this chapter was young Walter. After returning from the disastrous English
tour, Fred Lindrum senior realised that his first son was never going to fulfil
his dreams by becoming a world champion. Fred senior turned his attention
to young Walter who, although not possessing the natural ability that was so
evident in Fred junior, did show a dedication and determination in his
approach to the game that would stand him in good stead for the long hours
of practice. Fred senior's obsession for greatness was thus transferred from
Fred junior to young Walter. It was true that Walter had already been
engulfed by the family obsession. His determination to succeed had
intensified when his father had 'neglected' him and been pre-occupied with
coaching Fred junior. When Fred senior started devoting more time to the
coaching of Walter the lad grasped the opportunity firmly with both hands.

A timetable was drawn up and from seven until half past eight in the
morning Walter was locked in the billiard room. It was then time to head off
to school. As soon as school was over for the day Walter would go straight
home for more practice in the billiard room. The evening session would finish
at ten. The practice sessions were always carefully organised — there was 'no
knocking the balls about' and wasting time with Fred senior as a tutor!
Walter had to keep records of his practice in a notebook. A series of training
routines was listed in the book. Walter would commence with the balls in a
set position and see how many points he could score. The starting point for
the practice routines was often difficult with the balls placed in awkward
positions. Walter had to first work the balls into good position and then
proceed to score as many points as possible. The score from each routine had
to be recorded in the book and over a period of time a series of results was
built up. Walter could compare the results and see how he had progressed
with each of the routines. The result book thus served as an incentive for
Walter to go on and make bigger breaks. It was also a guide to Fred senior
as to which areas of the boy's game were below standard. Extra practice time
would then be allocated to these weaknesses until they became strong links
in Walter's game.

A special routine was devised for the sole purpose of improving Walter's
touch. One ball was placed tight against a cushion with the cue ball placed
about 75 millimetres away and directly out from the other ball. The object
of the exercise was to play onto the object ball to get a double-kiss and
rebound the cue ball to its original position. This was known as the 'tap, tap,

tap routine'. For hour upon tedious hour Walter worked at this most mechanical of strokes. The result of this dogged task was that Walter's touch was refined to a very acute degree. The 'tap, tap, tap routine' was later to become one of Walter's most important practice strokes for it cultivated the touch that is so essential to nursery cannon play.

The benefits of the hours of practice began to accrue and Walter's breaks slowly, but surely, started to increase. When he was up near the 200 mark Walter's father told him that he would not be allowed to leave the billiard room until he had scored a 250 break. It took 6½ hours for Walter to make that break and many times he protested that he had had enough. But Fred senior was a hard taskmaster and refused to listen to Walter's pleas: "If you want to be a champion, you must have pluck and stamina", he explained as Walter struggled off to dinner holding his aching back.

Walter had a love/hate relationship with his father. The intensity of the billiard training that Fred senior organised and the degree of perfection that he demanded often made Walter think of his father as an 'old nark'. It was many years later when Walter reaped the benefit of his countless hours of enduring training that he realised what a marvellous mentor his father had been.

Shortly after his fourteenth birthday Walter made a break in practice of 504. He was highly delighted with his achievement and whistled and sang as he went about the house. Fred senior asked the reason for his son's unusual antics.

"Why Dad, I've just made a five hundred break," boasted Walter. Fred soon brought Walter's castles tumbling down when he growled: "You think you can play billiards? Why, in twelve months time you'll look back and realise what a dunce you are today!"

Walter left school in 1912. He had received most of his education at St Francis' Boy's School, Darlinghurst and the Albion Street School, Paddington. He had been a good sportsman, representing the school at both cricket and football. Cricket was his first love and he made many centuries. Although he was a left-handed batsman Walter bowled with his right arm. When he was not committed to practising billiards Walter would be down at Moore Park playing cricket until dark. He spent many hours at the nets fielding for Charlie Macartney, Warren Bardsley and other great players. His fingertips would often tingle from stopping their shots. Fred senior hastened to bring this pleasure to a halt. He reminded Walter that his hands were required for a game that called for a more sensitive touch than that for merely stopping cricket balls. Walter dearly wanted to continue playing cricket but his father insisted that he make a 'choice' between billiards and cricket. (One of the joys of Walter's cricketing days was to see the legendary Victor Trumper compile an innings of 292 at Hampden Oval).

Immediately after leaving school Walter became a professional billiards player. There was little discussion on the issue and no protest from Mrs Lindrum. It had been understood for some years that young Walter would be following in the footsteps of his father and elder brother. One of Walter's first professional engagements was at Bondi with his father. In the first game of 750 up Walter received a start. Fred senior scored 380 in his first visit, 250 in his second visit and went out on his third. Walter was very disappointed that his father had not allowed him a chance to make a decent break. However, as usual the wily Fred had a good reason for his actions: "The men you meet in later life at billiards are likely to treat you the same way. To take your defeat badly is a sign of weakness," he explained.

It was another valuable lesson for Walter which would stand him in good stead in later life. Towards the end of 1912 the Lindrum family left Sydney and settled in Fred senior's old hunting ground of Melbourne. Eventually Fred senior took over the billiard room at the London Tavern in Elizabeth Street. The room, which contained three tables, had been run since 1907 by Charles Memmott and he continued running it for some time after the arrival of the Lindrums in Melbourne. This becomes apparent from a brief mention in the *Referee* on 5 March, 1913: "Young Walter Lindrum puts in a lot of work in Memmott's room, and has grown at least a couple of inches during his few months residence in the Southern Capital."

The next week the *Referee* carried an interesting report on young Walter:

> The 14 year old left-handed brother of the Australian champion is coming on fast in his billiards. When in Melbourne last week he informed me that in a recent game he made a break of 312, mostly off the red ball. Within the same week, however, the young lad put up a more classical 200 when pitted against Charles Memmott. This run was made by diversified billiards, and points to the youngster as a coming champion, even though he is still handicapped by having to elevate the butt of his cue for most strokes, owing to lack of stature. Later on, as he elongates, that even action, with the cue fired as true and straight as a piston-rod of a locomotive, should come naturally to him, and the wee laddie is sure to make the family name even more prominent in billiards than it is today. (12 March).

This indicates that although he was 14½ years old Walter was still on the smallish side, certainly not anywhere near his adult height of about 170 centimetres. Lindrum's smallness was continuing to make access to the table awkward, necessitating a raised butt and a round arm action for many shots. It is little wonder that, after spending so many of his formative years making compensations for his lack of height, Lindrum's round arm, unorthodox action became so entwined in his game that it remained a characteristic of his style throughout his playing career. A similar verdict on Walter was given in *Alcock's Sporting Review* of 13 March, 1913:

> If one were asked who would be the next champion of Victoria, I think young Walter Lindrum would be a good tip. The boy is much improved. He is growing also, and with increasing height many shots that were very difficult at one time are daily becoming easier. He is of the stuff that champions are made of and if he takes himself seriously, as he seems inclined to do (for he is a very sensible, modest young gentleman), he should go far in billiards. There ought to be no honour indeed to which he might not reasonably aspire.

One of the trademarks of Walter Lindrum's life was his modest nature which, judging by this report, was apparent from his earliest days of public exposure. In May of that year Walter undertook his first major tour when as the 'Boy Wonder' he travelled with Miss Ruby Roberts, the 'Lady Champion'. The duo made a novel combination and drew good crowds on a nine-week tour of South Australia. Walter finished the tour with 26 breaks over the century, the highest being 357 at Semaphore. Ruby Roberts showed her skill in an Adelaide match with breaks of 109, 107 and 102. The trip was of great benefit to Walter for he lost all crowd consciousness with the result that his play improved noticeably.

It was generally accepted, by the end of 1913, that young Walter Lindrum was destined for billiard greatness. The former champion, Charles Memmott gave a professional verdict on Walter's potential: "What I like about Walter is the intelligent interest he puts into his work. He is a truly marvellous player for one so young, and I feel certain that he will turn out to be the best player Australia has produced." (The *Referee*, 5 November 1913.)

It was inevitable that Walter and Fred junior would meet in a match in public. Their first match was in May 1914 at Alcock's Parlour with Walter receiving 4000 start. The fact that Fred junior was conceding such a sizeable start was not necessarily any indication that he was a vastly superior player to Walter. It was the champion's privilege to give start in his matches. It was something of a tradition which had been inherited from England. The champion was the leading player of the game (officially at least) and it would be denigrating to allow an opponent to play off level terms for this inferred that player was of equal status to the champion. By conceding start the champion also had an 'escape clause' if beaten by his opponent. It was Walter Lindrum who with the aid of his 4000 start won his first match against brother Fred by 18 000 to 15 831. Walter also had the highest break of 322. The result was satisfactory to both players for even though Fred had lost he had made up almost half the handicap. The match prompted conjecture as to the relative merits of the Lindrum brothers and that would augur well for the success of their future encounters.

Walter played further matches with Ruby Roberts but the 'Lady Champion' was now in receipt of a hefty start from the rapidly-improving 'boy champion'. Before good crowds in Melbourne and then Sydney young Walter defeated Miss Roberts by 16 000 to 14 530 (received 6000) and 16 000 to 14 778 (received 7000) respectively. In May 1915, Walter challenged Fred junior for his Australian title. The War had drawn heavily on the ranks of the younger men with the consequence that the billiard room proprietors had lost a considerable proportion of their most regular patrons. Although there was somewhat of a recession in the playing of public-room billiards the interest in the professional matches was sustained at a high level. The attendances at the clash of the Lindrum brothers at Alcock's Parlour were very healthy throughout the fortnight's play. The match, of 16 000 up, was a close encounter which kept the spectators enthralled. On the afternoon of the final day Walter hit the front with a break of 111 amidst enthusiastic applause from the packed audience. However, he could not sustain his effort and Fred junior recaptured the lead and went on to win by 16 000 to 15 271. The champion had the highest break of 461 while the challenger made one of 434.

Walter issued a further challenge for the championship in April of 1916 but Fred junior retained his title by a margin of 14 000 to 13 285. Walter thought he had played quite well and expressed his disappointment at being beaten. He had not expected brother Fred to produce such a barrage of big breaks, the highest being 532. This break included a beautiful run of nursery cannons which commenced with the balls above the spot. Fred took the balls to the corner pocket then carried them around it and down to the middle pocket. He steered the balls past the middle pocket and received a round of applause for achieving this most difficult feat. Fred junior continued the run down to the bottom cushion, along it and around to the other middle pocket. He ended the sequence of cannons there and resorted to open play.

Walter had a great admirer at this time in Tom Taylor, a well-known bookmaker who spent many hours watching him at practice. Taylor spurred Walter on by laying him bets to nothing that he could not make certain breaks. Eventually Walter had to make a break of over 600 before he could collect from Taylor but he continued to do so. The bookmaker never had his hand out of his pocket but he was not concerned for he knew that he would recoup his 'investment' in the not too distant future.

The New Zealand champion, Clark McConachy, arrived for a tour in late April. His first match was with Fred Lindrum junior and after receiving 2000 start the visitor won by 18 001 to 17 876. The first match between McConachy and Walter Lindrum followed and the 'House Full' sign was out at Alcock's Parlour to see the clash of the two young players. Comparing their ages, Mac had just turned 21 while Walter was into his seventeenth year. Prior to the match Tom Taylor had offered £10 to Walter if he could make a 700 break. On the second day of the match Walter made a break of 785 and later followed up with an identical score of 785. Two further breaks of 766 and 704 meant that Walter received the veritable fortune of £40 from Taylor. The bookmaker was only too happy to hand over the money for he had made a bundle betting on the match. Walter won the match by 18 002 to 12 469 and had made fifty breaks over 100 as well as averaging 78 per visit to the table. McConachy, whose highest break was 601, was basically a red ball player and was described as being 'raw at the all-round game.'

There were two further matches for McConachy against Walter Lindrum during his visit. Walter confirmed his superiority in both encounters with wins by 18 000 to 16 587 and then by 16 000 to 12 543. Sandwiched between these two latter matches with McConachy was a match between Walter and brother Fred. It was not a title match, fortunately, as Walter easily accounted for the champion by 16 000 to 14 802. The highlight of the match was a fine break of 463 made by Walter at the top of the table. On the last day of the match Walter had outstanding sessional averages of 107.5 and 133.1. One special condition of the match which was agreed to by the brothers was to limit losing hazard sequences to 25. The move, which encouraged more variation in play, was successful and became a standard condition of future matches between the brothers.

The win by Walter over Fred junior was not unexpected. The Lindrum family had known for some considerable time that Walter was capable of beating Fred junior. It was only a question of when. The visit of McConachy probably advanced the day when Walter would decide to defeat Fred junior in public. It would have been highly suspicious if Walter, after his comfortable wins over McConachy, had suddenly lost to his brother, Fred. With the New Zealander as a yardstick by which to compare the brothers it would have been a major form reversal for Walter to lose to Fred junior. Content with having recorded his first win in public over Fred junior Walter never again issued a challenge for the championship of Australia. He was happy simply for the title to remain in the Lindrum family. Over the years the newspapers made several demands for a title match between the brothers, claiming that Fred junior was holding the title on sufferance. This was, of course, true but Walter would not remove the one symbol of status that Fred junior possessed. Although this was a fine gesture by Walter it did have a damaging effect on later matches between the Lindrum brothers. The anomolous position was so transparent that their matches were regarded as nothing more than exhibitions. The public interest in their matches subsequently waned and a number of these were run at a loss.

By the end of 1916 at the age of eighteen years Walter Lindrum was the king, albeit uncrowned, of Australian billiards. It had been a meteoric rise for Walter but it created something of a problem. Apart from Fred Lindrum junior there was no other local professional who could offer Walter any serious opposition. If he was to continue improving his game Walter needed the incentive of regular competition from opponents who were capable of extending him in his matches. Fred Lindrum senior attempted to find that competition by issuing a £200 challenge to any billiardist in the world to play Walter. The one stipulation for any match was that bonzoline balls were to be used. This condition was perhaps the reason why there was no response from England for the English still preferred to cling to the traditional ivory balls. The only alternative left for Walter was to travel to England and meet them under their own conditions. The preliminary arrangements were made for the trip with cabins being booked on the S.S. *Medic*. However, the War continued unabated and a disappointed Walter had no option but to abandon all thoughts of making the trip.

The degree of Walter's superiority over the local talent was typified by the results of some matches that he played with prominent amateurs. He conceded 8000 start to Will Abotomey in a fortnight's match but won easily by 18 000 to 14 562. In a match at Alcock's Parlour, Melbourne, in September 1917, scheduled for a fortnight's duration against the Victorian champion, E. J. Campbell, Lindrum conceded 7000 start. The match was abandoned at the end of the first week because Walter had already made up the 7000 leeway. It was a frustrating time for Walter. He had exhausted the potential of the local billiard scene but was prevented by the War from travelling to England and playing their leading professionals. Lindrum had little alternative but to put his cues away. He gave up his rigid hours of training and played just sufficient billiards to keep 'in touch'. Walter became disenchanted with the game of billiards for it seemed as if all his years of meticulous practice were to be of no avail.

The break from the intense demands of billiards training proved to be a blessing in disguise for Lindrum. He had the chance to explore other fields and develop interests which had not been possible when he had been restricted by the rigid demands of his billiard practice. It was probably during this period that Walter acquired his love for horse-racing which was to remain with him for the rest of his life. On one occasion he accompanied the champion pigeon-shooter, Donald Mackintosh, to a shoot at Tottenham. Walter showed some potential at the sport but would not consider taking it up as a recreation. He was too concerned that he might damage his shoulder or arm muscles and interfere with his billiards.

Walter spent most of his time in the family billiard saloon where he helped in the everyday running of the room. He also gave lessons for a small fee which brought in a modest, but valuable income. One of Walter's regular pupils was the jockey, Hughie Cairns, who was quite a handy snooker player. Cairns was a reticent character who developed a reputation as the 'punter's friend' because the little punter always knew that any Cairns mount would be given every possible chance to win. Cairns was a straight-shooting, unpretentious man who treated all people in the same manner whether they were a millionaire who owned a string of racehorses or a battling punter who was on the lookout for a winner. It is easy to understand why Hughie Cairns and Walter Lindrum had a mutual respect for each other. The highlight of Cairns' career was when he won the 1926 Melbourne Cup on Spearfelt. Probably his most classic ride was in the A.J.C. Derby of 1924 when he nursed the strong-headed, hard-pulling Heroic to victory after the colt had appeared beaten at the top of the straight. Cairns met a tragic ending when he was killed in a hurdle race at Moonee Valley in 1929. His enormous popularity and respect was clearly illustrated when a crowd, estimated at 10 000 attended his funeral service. When Cairns had finished his track work of a morning he would often head for the city centre and the Lindrum's Saloon. He was often waiting on the footpath for the saloon to open. Cairns would play two or three frames of snooker and then rush off to the Victoria Club to play for money against the bookmakers. The 'nob turners' were often surprised at how quickly Cairns found his touch but they never learnt the reason.

The Victoria Club staged an annual billiard tournament, run on a handicap basis, which was renowned for its heavy betting. One of the most infamous moments in the life of the Club revolved around the staging of their tournament in 1899. After the first two rounds of the event it was obvious that one player, 'Prosper', had been treated very leniently on the 160 mark for he had recorded two easy victories. The bookmakers were faced with a payout of about £2000 if 'Prosper' won the tournament. They alleged that 'Prosper' (who was a Mr Charles Graham in private life) had displayed remarkably improved form and he must have deliberately deceived the handicappers. The bookmakers went out on strike and refused to operate on the reading of the card on the Grand National in the afternoon, and again in the evening when the card was called, they held aloof. The Club held a special meeting to resolve the situation and it was ruled that the tournament would go on and if 'Prosper' won the bookmakers must honour all bets. 'Prosper' proceeded to win the event, defeating Sol Green, the biggest bookmaker of his time, in the final by 250 to 220. It was something of a hard luck story for Sol Green who had backed himself heavily in the Tournament only to be defeated by a 'dark horse' who had slipped under the handicappers guard. After winning the event Graham denied the spate of rumours that had circulated about him; he was not a great player and had not tried to deceive anybody. It was the end of an affair that reflected very little credit on the bookmaking section of the Victoria Club.

During his years of semi-retirement Walter Lindrum was not completely out of the public eye. He gave exhibitions at clubs including the Victoria Club and the Commercial Traveller's Club as well as many private residences. He also played matches with brother Fred and usually recorded a win by a very comfortable margin. Occasionally Fred junior scored a narrow (and unexpected) win. In one of these matches in Melbourne Walter made a personal best break of 802 on 27 May, 1920. This was the pattern of Walter's existence from 1917 through 1921. He earnt sufficient from his engagements and matches to cover his living expenses. They were long years with little reward and the prospects for the future were no different.

5 Qualified Success

Lindrum has a long row to hoe before being a danger to any of the leading players at home [England].

H. W. Stevenson (Former World Champion) in 1922

In 1922 the game of billiards enjoyed a level of popularity that rivalled the boom years prior to the war. The late teens/early twenties age-bracket provided the billiard rooms with the bulk of their business. The War had drawn heavily on the young male ranks with a subsequent marked decline in the patronage of the billiard saloons. The return of the troops from the trenches caused something of a revival in the billiard saloon business. However, with some 60 000 not returning from the War the revival was only moderate. By 1922 the adult male population was strengthened by an influx of new graduates to the workforce. With the economy recovering from the setback caused by the War, conditions were ideal for a resurgence of interest in recreational activities such as billiards. There was heavy demand for billiard-playing facilities, so heavy that the saloon operators explored ways of extending their premises to cope with the demand. The rearrangement and remodelling of a billiard room enabled a few more tables to be installed. New rooms were springing up in both city and country areas to capitalise on the boom conditions. A typical example was the seven-table room that opened in the Manchester Unity Building in Melbourne. The room opened with an exhibition between Walter Lindrum and the jockey, Hughie Cairns. Cairns received 400 start but it was to no avail for Lindrum won in a canter by 750 to 567. Fred Lindrum senior had, in 1921, shifted from the three-table room at the London Tavern to much larger premises at 317 Flinders Lane. The room was later remodelled and extended to provide twenty tables for the public. The renovated room opened for business in July of 1923.

For Walter Lindrum 1922 offered a chance to escape from oblivion. The former world champion, H. W. Stevenson, was to visit Australia under contract to the Sydney-based manufacturers, Heiron & Smith. When Lindrum was offered the first match with Stevenson he jumped at the chance, advising Heiron & Smith of his availability for matches in any part of Australia. The final match arrangements were left in abeyance until Stevenson's arrival. In the meantime Walter returned to the rigours of training with renewed enthusiasm and dedication. He was determined to make the most of his chance to gain recognition against one of the English players.

Walter Lindrum's lay-off from billiards produced some problems that needed to be remedied before the arrival of Stevenson. He lacked the confidence and tough mental approach that can only be acquired from regular competition. Fred Lindrum senior decided that the best remedy was a tour of Western Australia and South Australia with an intensive schedule of matches. In a Perth match with leading amateur, Ted Thompson, Lindrum compiled a break of 1237 on a non-standard table. The break was a milestone in Lindrum's career, being his first four-figure break in public. More importantly the break showed that Lindrum had regained the mental attitude essential for his forthcoming match with Stevenson. He was ready to take on the Englishman! Stevenson, world champion in the 1909–11 period and runner-up in the 1919 Championship, had since been displaced from his pre-eminent position by the younger brigade of professionals led by Willie Smith and Tom Newman. Harry Stevenson, though, was still regarded as being more than capable of repelling any threat from the colonials.

In late April Stevenson's boat docked in Sydney. Walter Lindrum was waiting with a car to escort Stevenson into the city. Stevenson, though, immediately showed that he was not interested in socialising with Walter. In a lofty tone he said:

"Lindrum, I'll see you at Heiron and Smith's at eleven o'clock".

Walter was very annoyed by Stevenson's aloof attitude and disregard of his efforts at hospitality. Matters did not improve when the pair met at Heiron and Smith's. Stevenson's first words were:

"Lindrum, the only conditions on which I will meet you are that you receive 6,000 start and get a fifth of the gate receipts".

Walter dismissed these ridiculous terms and looked for a way to destroy Stevenson's superiority complex.

"Mr Stevenson", he politely began, "if you want to play me, you can meet me for £100 aside, winner take all, off level terms". (*Sporting Globe,* 23 July, 1938.)

It was a rude shock for the former world champion to receive such a preposterous offer from a completely unknown quantity such as Lindrum. The negotiations became very heated. Finally it was Eugene A. Boyle who suggested that the match should be a fair encounter off level terms with the visitor to receive 60 per cent of the gate. The two players agreed to a three-match series under these conditions. Boyle, who was known as 'Hughie' — a natural misconception which stemmed from the abbreviation of Eugene to Euie, was a leading figure in the billiard fraternity. He was the foundation secretary of the Amateur Billiards Association of New South Wales, a post he held from 1910–1925, and became a life member of the Association. Boyle was a leading referee in the days when they enjoyed no official status but had to rely solely on their public displays for promotion. He refereed many important matches and contributed articles on billiards to newspapers. In later years Boyle was referred to as 'The Grand Old Man of Australian Billiards', a title which was thoroughly deserved because of his devoted service to the game.

The first match between Lindrum and Stevenson opened at Hogan's Billiard Parlour in Bathurst Street, Sydney. Lindrum was on edge and very anxious to perform well as the match was regarded both as a comeback and his first real test. The guiding presence of his father helped to steady Walter and he strung together a series of breaks to reach the required 750 sessional points. As the match progressed Lindrum's confidence soared as he dominated the play. On the other hand Stevenson was completely rattled.

On the fourth day one enthusiastic spectator was anxious to get Stevenson's opinion of Lindrum's game. "What do you think of the boy?" he asked Stevenson who is alleged to have replied, "He can't even dress properly."

Stevenson was making a reference to a slight tear on Lindrum's trouser pocket, the result of his frequent delving after his cue chalk. Stevenson's comment was made in a voice which carried to the table where Lindrum was about to commence play. Walter's response was to play a cannon, then pot the white ball. He then proceeded to score 1413 points off the red ball, making his total break 1417. It was a personal best for Walter and earnt him a cheque for 20 guineas from Mr F. A. Alcock. Stevenson was made to regret his ill-chosen remark and realised how absurd were his original terms for the match. Lindrum continued to be his nemesis throughout the first week of play. Stevenson repeatedly left his ball in the jaws of the pocket. Lindrum did not hesitate to pot the white ball and make further red-ball breaks. Stevenson was not strong on the losing hazard game, relying heavily on the more refined top of the table game for the bulk of his points. Lindrum, of course, was very adept at the top-of-the-table game but he chose to concentrate on red-ball play with the intention of unsettling Stevenson. The tactic was successful. As Lindrum continued to score heavily off the red ball Stevenson became more and more dishevelled. Inevitably Stevenson's play deteriorated and he fell further and further behind. During the second week of play Lindrum relented with his tactics but still scored the easiest of wins by 16 000 to 6540.

The second match of the series was scheduled for Melbourne but in the wake of his first drubbing Stevenson refused to play under the agreed terms. There were fresh negotiations with Lindrum offering 10 000 start in 20 000 up, with the winner to take all the gate takings. Stevenson countered by offering 2000 start in 16 000 up with hazard sequences limited to ten. The players failed to agree on terms and Stevenson decided to return to England.

In the company of Hughie Boyle he went to book his passage with Thomas Cook & Son. The booking clerk quite innocently asked: "Would you care to travel by the All Red Route, sir?" The staff at Cooks were certainly not expecting Stevenson's reply, delivered with a burst of invective: "I've seen all I want to see of the blasted all red route if I live to be a hundred!" (*Sporting Globe*, 23 July 1938.)

Hughie Boyle could not contain himself and burst into laughter. Stevenson eventually saw the lighter side of the situation and joined in the laughter. Subsequently Boyle was able to persuade Stevenson to remain in Australia and undertake a tour with Fred Lindrum junior. This duo played a series of matches under terms which permitted only ten hazards in succession. After a highly successful tour Stevenson left Australia with a bulging wallet. He also carried home the memory of his severe thrashing at the hands of Walter Lindrum. Stevenson bemoaned to the English reporters that during his match with Walter one journalist from the *Referee* actually offered Lindrum £5 for a thousand break and urged him to beat Stevenson by as many points as possible. Stevenson had not impressed the Australian public with some of his actions. He had earned the ire of many with his habit of leaving the room when his opponent was in play and for his failure to honour his agreement to play three matches with Walter Lindrum. As his final comment on the tour Stevenson declared that "Walter Lindrum had a long row to hoe before being a danger to any of the leading players". Such a declaration was his own indictment for the former champion had been systematically annihilated by Walter Lindrum. It is difficult to reconcile the H. W. Stevenson of 1922 with the player who had proved a popular personality on his previous visits to Australia. On those visits Stevenson, who was approaching the top flights of the game, had displayed no signs of arrogance or bad sportsmanship. By the time of his 1922 visit Stevenson's status was on the decline and to be beaten by Walter Lindrum, whose reputation in England was non-existent, must have been a severe blow to Stevenson's ego. This may account for Stevenson's strange behaviour following his defeat.

One incident that occurred during the Lindrum–Stevenson match had a more agreeable ending. It stemmed from Walter's school days when he used to play truant in order to watch the good players who patronised Billiards Limited in Sydney. Unfortunately Walter's teacher found out about these little escapades. Apart from getting six whacks with the cane Walter had to write out the word 'billiards' 500 times each night for a week. Shortly after this experience Walter happily left the school and that teacher. It was during an evening session of the Stevenson match that Walter renewed his acquaintance with his old foe. As he was potting the red ball into the middle pocket Walter spotted his former teacher seated in the front row of spectators. He bided his time, waiting for an opportunity to settle an old debt. Finally, when he had the balls along the side cushion, Walter forced the cue ball off the table and caught his old foe flush on the knee. The spectators all laughed, thinking it was simply a bad shot. After the session the teacher went to the dressing room and asked if Walter remembered him. "Remember you," said Walter, "What do you think I whacked you on the knee for?" (*Sporting Globe,* 23 July 1938.)

The pair had a hearty laugh, agreed the score was even as far as hitting was concerned, and became great friends. Lindrum returned to his regular round of club engagements and private exhibitions with renewed enthusiasm. He knew that he had 'arrived' as a billiard player, that it was only a matter of time before he would reach greater heights. Walter continued to play matches with brother Fred but there was little public interest in these matches. Walter's superiority was beyond question and the informed billiard follower knew that matches between the Lindrum brothers were virtual exhibitions. It was a difficult period for the professional game in Australia with the scene being so completely dominated by Walter. Alcock & Co. continued to promote matches and keep billiards before the public despite the financial losses that occurred frequently during this period.

One of a small number of professionals who was active in the early twenties was the Englishman, A. E. (Albert) Williams who had migrated to Australia some years previously. Williams, who was originally from Staffordshire, had unsuccessfully challenged Melbourne Inman in 1909 for the Championship. In the latter part of 1923 Williams played two matches with Walter Lindrum who proved vastly superior in winning both the 8000-up games by over half the distance. Despite the ease of the wins Lindrum always had a high regard for Williams as a player. Williams cued a beautiful ball and his touch was unsurpassed on some parts of the table. He possessed a very powerful cue action which allowed him to execute strokes that other professionals seldom attempted. He played a forceful drag shot and was also a dainty nursery cannon player. One of the reasons, according to Lindrum, why Williams never reached greater heights was because he tried to play every shot too perfectly. Said Walter: "Big breaks seem to elude the player who does not take an occasional risk." (*Sporting Globe*, 27 August 1938.)

In one match with Fred Lindrum junior, Williams made a break of 328 at the top of the table. What made the break so noteworthy was that the object white was on the 'wrong' side of the spot. Williams would play a cannon and only just brush the white, barely moving it. He would then pot the red twice before scoring another cannon. The white ball moved less than fifteen centimetres during the entire break. Walter regarded it as the finest break that he ever saw at the top of the table. Lack of opportunities was another reason Williams never devoted more time to billiards. He found it was easier to make a living by training racehorses. In an era when even top players such as the Lindrum brothers were earning only modest incomes from billiards there was little prospect for the lesser professional.

With the professional scene being dominated by firstly George Gray and Fred Lindrum junior, and later by Walter Lindrum, the amateur ranks held a number of players who, in another time, would have been of professional standard. There were scores of amateur players who regularly made their hundred breaks while the better amateurs were those capable of making breaks of at least 200 or 300. These amateurs knew that it would be futile trying to compete against Lindrum & Co. so in the amateur ranks they stayed. The end result of these strong amateur ranks was the emergence of two very fine players who went on to win the World Amateur Championship. Bob Marshall, from Western Australia, won the title on four occasions, the first being in 1936. He won the Australian title on nineteen occasions and had a best break under match conditions of 702. Tom Cleary, from Victoria, usually had to play second fiddle to Marshall but in 1954 he won the world title, defeating Marshall in an early match and setting a championship record break of 682 in a later match against the South African, Taffy Rees. Marshall and Cleary kept Australia at the top of the amateur scene for over twenty years.

The early months of 1924 saw Lindrum on a tour of country New South Wales, playing such centres as Albury, Holbrook, Wagga Wagga, Yass and Goulburn. In late May he commenced a match in Sydney with brother Fred. It was described as a top class encounter until the final session when a number of easy shots were curiously missed. Fred junior won another of those Lindrum exhibitions by 18 000 to 17 841 and also had best break with an 834.

The month of July was marked by the arrival of a dapper, little Englishman, Claude Falkiner, who had heard that there was good money to be made in the Antipodes. Falkiner had a delightful touch at billiards. Walter Lindrum, later in life, acknowledged: "The best nursery cannon player of all the Englishmen, Falkiner could make more nurseries in a given space and time than anyone, including myself." (*Sporting Globe*, 27 August 1938.)

Falkiner, who had been runner-up in the 1920 and 1922 championship also possessed one of the best masse strokes in the game. He was a great collector of things, including stamps, antiques and assorted treasures from the many places that he visited during his numerous overseas trips. It was partly his vast range of interests that prevented Falkiner from devoting his singular attention to billiards and thus developing his game to its potential. Falkiner was a jovial personality and upon his arrival he greeted Lindrum with: "Now Walter, I want you to promise me that you will not travel by the all red route when playing with me." (*Sporting Globe*, 23 July 1938.)

It was an obvious reference to the tactics which Lindrum employed against Harry Stevenson. Lindrum was, by this time, far more than just a red-ball player. He possessed a strong top-of-the-table game as well as having some knowledge of close cannons. Falkiner described Lindrum's nursery cannon game as 'rudimentary' but by the end of his tour that description had altered to 'strong'. Claude opened Lindrum's eyes to the potential of these close cannons as the ultimate scoring force. Lindrum began devoting much of his practice to the development of his nursery cannon play. It was to prove the turning point of his career as he reassessed his game and remoulded it around these close cannons. Little did Lindrum realise that the nursery cannon would later be a source of controversy and at the heart of a dramatic climax in the game of billiards.

The first match of the tour went to Lindrum by 16 000 to 15 403 and Falkiner won the second by 16 000 to 15 574. The third match, played at Home Recreations, Sydney, was one of the highlights of the tour. Good crowds witnessed a fine match which Lindrum won by 16 000 to 15 147 with a best break of 1219. Lindrum also had a run of 253 consecutive nursery cannons which illustrates that he had been working feverishly on his cannon game since Falkiner's arrival only two months earlier. Falkiner topped the thousand mark also with a break of 1001. There was an incident at the end of this break when Falkiner protested to the referee, Hughie Boyle, that the break was not 1001 but in fact 1101. He claimed that there had been a mistake in the counting but Boyle rejected the appeal and refused to award the extra 100 points. When he was refereeing, Boyle would never call the score while the break was in progress. He would keep tally in his head and when the break was completed announce its magnitude. This led to Falkiner's claim that Boyle had forgotten to credit him with the last 100 points.

The fourth match of the series was played in Melbourne. Falkiner won by over 800 points to level the score at two matches each. The deciding match of the tour was set down for Perth. The duo travelled to Adelaide to play a week-long exhibition. Falkiner's health was causing some concern and he took part in the exhibition against doctor's orders. Lindrum predictably won the game under these circumstances but he was in top form, making breaks of 1272 and 1005. The final match commenced in Perth on October 21 but was soon abandoned as Falkiner's health problems intensified. The Englishman decided to return home but agreed to return for another visit in the following year.

Lindrum was in Sydney in May of 1925, preparing for a challenge match with Frank Smith junior. Having completed arrangements for the match and satisfied himself with the playing conditions, Walter went for a stroll around the city. In one particular street he came across a recently-opened billiard saloon. Lindrum walked into the room which contained four tables set in well-appointed surroundings. On one of the tables were two young men playing a game of billiards. Walter stood intently watching the game, engrossed by one of the players who happened to be cross-eyed, and who proceeded to compile a stylish break of more than 100. The proprietor of the room was justly proud of his prodigy. He walked over to Lindrum and, not recognising him, asked:

"Would you like to play him?"

"No fear", Walter declared hurriedly, "I've just seen him make a hundred break looking out the window."

Frank Smith junior had trained solidly for his match with Lindrum and declared himself to have a strong chance of winning. Frank Smith senior was the old-time professional who had played many matches against Fred Lindrum senior in the 1890's. Smith senior had eventually established his superiority over Lindrum senior. When Frank junior and Walter renewed the family rivalry the result served to even up the score for it was the Lindrum representative who won easily by 18 000 to 14 803. Smith junior was more highly regarded as a snooker player and was considered Australia's leading exponent of the game until young Horace Lindrum defeated him in the early thirties. Frank Smith senior maintained for many years that it was he and Henry Alcock who invented the game of snooker. They had done so at the request of the Indian Army officers who had visited the Victoria Club, Melbourne in 1887.

It is more widely accepted that snooker was first conceived at Jubbulpore, India in 1875. A game called 'Black Pool' was played there by members of the English regiment. The black ball was placed on the centre spot and acted as a 'rover' ball. It was suggested that a pink ball be added and gradually other balls were stained various colours and allocated specific spots on the table. At that time Neville Chamberlain was a subaltern with the Devonshire Regiment. One day he was visited by a young subaltern who had trained at the Royal Military Academy, Woolwich. The youngster mentioned that as one of the first cadets at Woolwich he had been referred to as a 'snooker', meaning a person of low and devious habits. Shortly afterwards Chamberlain was playing a game when his opponent unexpectedly played a shot which left the object ball obstructed by another ball. Chamberlain was surprised by the stroke and without thinking declared: "Why, you're a regular snooker!"

After necessary explanations and apologies the players agreed that it would be appropriate to call the game 'Snooker'. Eventually in 1885 John Roberts junior, who was on one of his many visits to India, sought out Chamberlain. He learnt the rules of the game and took them back to England where official rules were issued by the Billiards Association in 1903. It seems likely that Frank Smith senior had seen the visiting army officers playing an improvised form of snooker at the Victoria Club. He reasoned that the game had come from the wilds of India and decided to rescue it from obscurity and introduce civilisation to the game of snooker. Unbeknown to Smith, John Roberts junior had already done this service to the game. Although Frank Smith senior may not have invented snooker he was certainly one of the early stalwarts of the game in Australia. Along with Frank Smith junior he did much to popularise and help establish snooker during those infant days.

While waiting for Falkiner to arrive for his second visit Walter played a match with his brother, Fred, at the Elystan Billiard Parlour, 147A King Street, Sydney. Walter won, in the predictably close finish, by 18 000 to 17 641. Falkiner arrived via New Zealand in late June to play another series of matches with Walter. The tour was somewhat of a failure with poor attendances at several matches. It was suggested that professional billiards had been on the wane for several years — a situation partly due to Walter Lindrum's domination of the local scene and also to the continuing charade of

Walter, at about five years of age, pictured with his sister, Florence, at Donnybrook.
(Dolly Lindrum)

Walter at 11 years — a small boy with a very long cue. (Dolly Lindrum)

close matches between the Lindrum brothers. One of the low points of the tour was a match in Melbourne where excessive nursery cannon play was given as the reason that there were so few spectators after the first few days of play. Falkiner made one run of 210 close cannons and Lindrum made a number of lengthy cannon runs as well. Falkiner won the match in the usual close finish. After another close result in Adelaide the duo set off by train for the long haul to Perth.

There were lengthy stops at desert outposts to take on supplies of coal and water. The American band of Bert Ralston was also on the train. Ralston's band was on the final leg of its visit to Australia which was part of an extensive world tour. The band travelled on to South Africa where Ralston met with an untimely death as the result of a shooting accident. During one of the outpost stoppages Walter Lindrum exuberantly showed the band members how to throw a boomerang. Falkiner was also a competent boomerang thrower having been taught the art by 'Black Charlie', an Aboriginal who operated a thriving business only a few kilometres out of Sydney. 'Black Charlie' charged one shilling for a boomerang and also gave lessons for a similar fee. It was during one of these stoppages that Lindrum met a 21-year-old cycling fanatic by the name of Hubert Opperman. Little did the duo realise that when they next met they would both be household names in their respective fields.

Lindrum and Falkiner disembarked at Kalgoorlie for an exhibition at the Tattersall's Club. Walter had intentions of producing some dazzling billiards on the occasion of this visit to his birthplace. Falkiner, though, had different ideas and during the first session of play he blotted Lindrum out of the game to win by 750 to 153. Walter was not at all impressed by Falkiner's domination of the table and he was more than a little annoyed. Lindrum was never content to take second place to anyone in a billiards match, whether it be a championship match or an obscure country exhibition. During the second session Lindrum managed to record a win by 750 to 563 but he was still not satisfied that he had evened the score.

The pair travelled on to Perth for the final match of the tour at the Town Hall. Lindrum still carried the memory of his resounding defeat at Kalgoorlie and he was looking for some way to square the ledger. Walter broke the balls and left a difficult position from which Falkiner failed to score. On his second visit to the table Lindrum quickly worked the balls into good position for a run of open play. With 291 on the board Lindrum attempted to pot the red in the middle pocket and screw back and cannon on the white. He did just that but in endeavouring to set the object white up for an easy in-off he accidentally potted the white. Unperturbed, Lindrum went to work on the red ball and proceeded to score 1581 points off it. The vast majority of the points came from red losers into the middle pockets, with an occasional long loser to restore position. On only two occasions did Lindrum find it necessary to pot the red ball. The break ended when Lindrum missed a fine in-off into the left-hand middle pocket. The cue ball rattled in the jaws and threw out. One spectator, carried away by the excitement of the moment, jumped to his feet and called for three cheers for the Western Australian-born champion. Falkiner hastened to congratulate his opponent who seemed a little downcast at having broken down. Lindrum was in fact very disappointed because his ball had been thrown off its path by a piece of chalk grit on the table. Lindrum had set himself to make a 2000 break and he could be excused for showing some dismay. It is one thing for a break to end through bad play but quite another for a break to end through circumstances beyond a player's control. Nonetheless Lindrum was delighted with the break which was a personal best. The break remains a record for the first scoring visit to the table and it seems safe to predict that it will never be beaten.

As Falkiner went to the table the referee called the scores: "0 plays 1879."

The amicable Falkiner burst out laughing and could not play his shot for some minutes. Falkiner realised that it was pointless to upstage Walter for any such attempt was sure to be repaid with a generous rate of interest. Lindrum went on to win the match by a wide margin. It was the end of a disappointing tour for Falkiner and its financial failure effectively discouraged visits to Australia by the English professionals.

When Falkiner returned to England he was loud in his praise of the exploits of Walter Lindrum. The billiard fraternity was generally sceptical of these glowing reports of a potential star. There were some who showed faith in the judgement of Falkiner, including the current champion, Tom Newman, and two former champions, Willie Smith and Melbourne Inman. All three made separate offers in their endeavours to secure Lindrum for a season in England. All the offers were rejected by Lindrum who claimed that he was "too busy and there was more money to be made in Australia". These were not the first attempts to secure Lindrum's services for an English visit. In 1924 Henry Hutton, an English promoter, had offered Lindrum £2000 to play a season of billiards in England. The offer was firmly rejected. Lindrum was obviously reluctant to go to England but the reason for his repeated refusal of attractive terms remained obscure. The English press seized on this point and suggested that the Australian was afraid of the tougher competition and was thus an over-rated player. As each year went by and Lindrum continued to decline offers, the English press believed that its suspicions were confirmed.

Lindrum thus spent the year of 1926 busying himself on the local scene but not making as much money as he suggested was available. He had simply used that as an excuse to reject the lucrative offers that flowed in from England. Lindrum's strange reluctance to visit the Old Dart was virtually a self-imposed sentence to the obscurity of an isolated billiards outpost. One match result of interest in 1926 was Walter's win over brother Fred, by 16 000 to 11 241 at Alcock's Parlour, Melbourne. Maybe Walter was growing tired of playing these matches at half-pace. The big news of the year came from England where the controlling body brought in a rule change that restricted the number of consecutive hazards (winning or losing) to 25. There seems little doubt that it was Walter Lindrum who had prompted the rule change. He was the only player in recent years to make thousand-plus breaks by hazard play — 1879 against Falkiner in 1925 (the last 1581 off the red), and 1417 against Stevenson in 1922 (the last 1413 off the red). No English player had made a red-ball break that even remotely approached these Lindrum breaks. Of course George Gray had in the 1910–1911 English season made a staggering 23 breaks over the thousand by playing the losing hazard game. On that occasion the Control Council stood impassively by and watched the breaks being made right under its nose. However, when Lindrum made his break of 1879 they acted with relative haste to prevent any repetition of the red-ball methods that Gray had employed so effectively. Walter Lindrum thus made his first mark on the course of billiards history but it was not to be the last mark he made and, comparatively speaking, it was merely a drop in the ocean.

Indeed the controlling authorities in England were undergoing a period of some activity. In May of 1927 the Control Council's attention was drawn to a break of 3964 made by Tom Reece against Arthur Peall. The break was made by use of the pendulum cannon, a stroke that had been secretly developed by Reece to use as a shock weapon against Melbourne Inman who was the scourge of his life. Just a week later and in the same match Reece made another pendulum cannon break, 6417. The pendulum cannon was played with the object balls locked in the jaws of a corner pocket. Once the balls had been worked into that position it was a simple matter to tap the cue ball across them. The one stroke that called for skill and judgement was when the player was required to play an indirect cannon — when the cue ball, in making a cannon, struck one or more cushions. To play an indirect cannon, which was required at least once every 35 cannons, Reece would play his ball onto the cushion before it made contact with the object balls. The indirect cannon rule had been introduced in 1907 to put an end to the anchor cannon, another type of close cannon which was played with the two balls resting dead on the angle of the corner pocket jaws. It was Reece who, by making a break of 499 135 unfinished with the anchor cannon, had prompted the indirect cannon rule. As Reece compiled that break the object balls became embedded in the cloth and a track was formed along which the cue ball travelled. The break was never officially recognised as a record because no single spectator was in attendance for the entire 85 hours that it took Reece to compile the mammoth score. Only the hapless referee, W. H. Jordon, was present for every stroke of that enduring performance. The reason that Reece did not continue his break to the half million mark was because when the break commenced he had already scored 865 points in the match which was 500 000 up.

Reece's latest endeavours with the pendulum cannon failed to over-awe Joe Davis who exploited the stroke in a desperate attempt to wrest the Championship from Tom Newman. When news reached Walter Lindrum of Reece's new stroke he had a simple answer. In an exhibition at the Footscray Men's Club in Paisley Street, Footscray, he made a pendulum cannon break of 8000 unfinished before walking away from the table through boredom. The English legislators soon amended the rules to eliminate the pendulum cannon from the game. They redefined an indirect cannon, so closing the loophole that Reece had discovered. The rule now read:

> 4i) An indirect cannon is made when the striker's ball, after making contact with the first ball, strikes a cushion or cushions before making contact with the second ball. All other cannons are direct.

None of the professionals wept as the game swung away from the pendulum and back to its former balance. Even Tom Reece readily accepted that the removal of such repetitive strokes was in the best interests of billiards. Reece was one of many personalities who belonged to what has been dubbed 'The Golden Era of Billiards'. When this era began remains open for conjecture. It was probably around 1919, when the championship resumed after the diapause caused by the War. There is no question that the era ended after the staging of the 1934 championship. The Golden Era was an unprecedented period when the standard of play improved at a relentless rate. The professionals refined and developed billiards towards its potential and their breaks and averages inflated accordingly. Walter Lindrum was to prove the greatest refiner and inflationist that the game had ever seen. It was not merely the player's prowess that denoted the golden era. It was the players themselves with their myriad of idiosyncrasies and eccentricities that gave the era its 24-carat touch.

The most famous duo of the period were the mutual antagonists, Tom Reece and Melbourne Inman. Their style of play and personalities were diametrically opposed but they agreed on one thing: each hated the other's intestines. Inman was a man of great determination, self-reliance, willpower and obstinancy. Reece was a sensitive and temperamental artist who was easily upset. Inman played the all-round game and especially enjoyed playing the forcing loser (losing hazards requiring a powerful stroke). Reece disdained the 'agricultural', sometimes crude strokes that Inman played, preferring instead the delicacy and refinement of nursery cannons and other close play. The pair conducted a running duel, which began during their very first match in 1903, and continued throughout their playing careers. It became a custom for them to bicker before each match over the financial and playing conditions. They argued about which set of balls would be used, the type of cloth that the table should have and so on. During the sessions of play, no opportunity was ever lost to make derisive comments about each other. Inman and Reece played to the gallery with their caustic contempt for each other but there was never any doubt about the sentiments that lay behind the remarks. Inman was the antagonist and formulated tactics for his matches with Reece. He would set out to upset Reece, for once this was accomplished he was virtually assured of victory. Inman usually succeeded in this ploy, much to his own delight but to Reece's disgust. During one of their encounters two urchins were watching through a half-open doorway: "Put it across him, Tommy!" yelled one. In a twinkling, Inman asked: "Would you mind keeping your friends quiet, Mr Reece?"

In the 1910 Championship Inman duly won his semi-final against Reece only to go down to Harry Stevenson in the final. Lord Alverston, president of the Billiards Association, had earlier in the week sentenced Crippen to death for the gruesome murder of his wife. As Inman went up to receive the runner-up trophy from Lord Alverston, Reece arose from the ranks of the spectators and said: "Excuse me, my Lord. But if you knew as much as I do about Inman, you would have given Crippen the cup and sentenced Inman to death."

Inman owned a car in the days when they were considered a real status symbol. There were no formal driving tests in those times and Inman was one of many who had a less than basic knowledge of the art of car-driving. One night after an exhibition at a club Inman was motoring home in the early hours when he came across a line of red lamps warning that the road was under repair. At the end of the line of lamps sat a night-watchman, outside a workman's hut, warming his hands over a brazier. Inman ploughed into the first red lamp and, despite taking evasive action, proceeded to demolish the entire row of lamps before grinding to a halt. The irate watchman rose to have words with Inman but as he approached the car Inman quickly found first gear and as he moved off into the night he shouted: "I've taken all the reds. Now where are the colours?"

Clark McConachy was, like Inman, a very determined fellow. He was probably even more strong-willed and once he had made up his mind on a subject he would not budge. He had a fetish for physical fitness and exercising was part of his preparation for his billiard matches. He would do anything for a dare and often walked around a billiard table on his hands. On one occasion, before a session, he walked into a dressing room to find his opponent, Walter Lindrum, slumped in a big chair.

"How are you, Mac?" asked Walter from his reclined, half-asleep position.

"As fit as a buck rat", replied Mac. To prove his point McConachy picked up the chair, Lindrum and all, and held it up in the air. Both players were shaking for some time after the incident: Mac from the physical exertion and Walter from the nasty fright.

Willie Smith was a colourful character who always seemed to be in disagreement with someone. He was not afraid to take a stand on an issue and was always prepared to support his principles with appropriate action. Apart from this admirable strength of character, Smith also possessed a sharp sense of humour. After he had won the 1920 Championship and received the trophy Smith began his victory speech with 'Gentlemen, and members of the press'. The spectators burst into laughter at Smith's concise venting of his attitude towards the press. It was no laughing matter when Smith's later use of his own newspaper column to conduct a verbal battle with Joe Davis led to a threat of legal action. The paper persuaded Smith to associate himself with their official withdrawal of the statement and apology to Davis for making false claims.

Tom Newman was cast in a different mould from his more boisterous contemporaries. All who knew Tom immediately recognised his genuine sincerity and the considerable generosity under his quiet demeanour. He was a most amiable gentleman who thought nothing of remaining behind after a session of play to explain shots and talk with the fans for an hour or more. Newman was a true sportsman who took both victory and defeat in the same gracious manner. This was perhaps the major factor that prevented Newman from attaining greater glory as a billiardist. He simply lacked the 'killer' instinct. It seemed very unjust for this most popular of players to suffer an early death, in 1943, at the age of 49, after a prolonged illness caused by cancer of the throat.

In Melbourne on 10 April 1928 Lindrum caused a sensation in the Flinders Lane saloon. The room was fairly busy at the time with sixteen of the twenty tables occupied by customers. Lindrum decided that he needed a little practice and so began playing on one of the vacant tables. The players on the adjoining table interrupted their game to watch Walter in practice. As the minutes ticked by, and Walter continued his break without missing a shot, other players abandoned their game and joined the crowd of onlookers. It was not long before every table in the room was idle. Lindrum's break went on and on but not a single spectator moved off to resume playing at his own table. They stood silent and spellbound as Lindrum just kept scoring. Finally, after being at the table for two-and-a-half hours, Lindrum stopped playing. It was not because he had missed his last shot. He had received a message from his father that he must cease playing immediately. Fred senior was very concerned that every table in the room was lying idle. He could not afford to have Walter keeping the patrons away from the tables. Walter had no idea of the number of points that he had scored for he hadn't bothered to keep count. Using a conservative estimate of 1500 points per hour the break would have totalled at least 3750!

After almost twelve years' absence, Clark McConachy made a visit to Australia. The New Zealander had in the intervening years made a number of trips to England and had developed into a far more polished player than he was back in 1916. In a match at Sydney McConachy scored a narrow win that was described as "unexpected and revealing the New Zealander's skill and determination". It was Lindrum who provided most of the highlights of the tour. He scored a break of 815 in 23 minutes, breaks of 1006 and 1273 in Sydney and 1380 and 1415 in Melbourne. The nursery cannon had played an integral part in each of these breaks. At one stage of the 1415 break Lindrum had the balls running sweetly at nurseries but then broke away from the position and played some top-of-the-table and open play. He then reverted to cannonading. Lindrum's play brought praise from McConachy, who said: "Walter, there is not another player in the world who could have done that." (The *Argus*, 29 June 1928.)

One of the most remarkable aspects of Lindrum's play was his capacity to switch between the various scoring methods. He could, seemingly at will, change from top of the table play to nursery cannons to open play to top of the table to nurseries and so on. It was one facet of his billiards that no other professional could even remotely approach. It is apparent that, by 1928, this amazing facility was becoming well established.

Lindrum spent the latter part of 1928 on a tour of New Zealand with McConachy. It was his first journey out of Australia and by its conclusion he had made a further six breaks over the thousand, making a lifetime total of 16. At Christchurch against McConachy he set a New Zealand record with a break of 1461. Four weeks later at Dunedin he broke this record with a 1475 against a leading amateur, Mr Stewart. Clark McConachy developed a penchant in early life for new cues. Regardless of the deeds that he had performed with his old cue he would readily discard it for another that had taken his fancy. This habit seemed to continue throughout his life for when he was into his seventies McConachy discarded one of his old faithfuls and replaced it with one of the new two-piece models. In one match with Lindrum, Mac decided to try out his latest acquisition. Lindrum was in play as the session commenced and he remained at the table until he had scored the required sessional points. After the session, one wag in the crowd asked McConachy: "How is that new cue playing, Mac?".

6 Triumph and Tragedy

> My tip is that there will be a scream from certain quarters to lower
> the cannon limit after Walter has opened their eyes at home next season.
>
> Willie Smith, in the *Referee*, 28 August 1929

Throughout 1928 and the early months of 1929 a spate of cablegrams had been exhanged between Australia and England in an effort to arrange billiard matches between Walter Lindrum and Willie Smith. Lindrum was anxious to play Smith who, although not holder of the Championship, was commonly regarded as the leading English professional. He was therefore also regarded as the best player in the world — at least by his fellow-countrymen. The English could be excused for this biased attitude because in the history of the game of English billiards it had always been one of their fold who was the best in the world. Besides, Willie Smith was a great player, probably the best up to that time, with a personal best break of 2743. It was inconceivable that Smith could be beaten by anyone, especially an Australian or, more precisely, a non-Englishman. With his own reluctance to visit England, Lindrum hoped that Smith could be persuaded to visit Australia for matches. It would be necessary to offer Smith some travelling expenses and financial guarantees if he was to be lured to Australia. Walter Lindrum was not in a position to offer Smith either of these things. He needed someone to provide financial backing and so decided to contact the well known Melbourne sportsman and entrepreneur, John Wren.

Wren was a self-made millionaire who had been involved with a wide variety of sporting projects and astutely-planned betting plunges. Wren started on the road to wealth when, as a youth of nineteen, he risked all his savings on a horse called Carbine in the 1890 Melbourne Cup. Wren won the princely sum of £180 when Carbine humped ten stone five (65.8 kg) to win the Cup by two-and-a-half lengths. By 1900 Wren had accumulated wealth from many projects which included his controversial Collingwood tote. In 1901 he pulled off the biggest coup in the history of Australian cycling in the Austral-1 mile at the Melbourne Cricket Ground. 'Plugger' Bill Martin won the race and Wren netted about £8000 on the result. It was in 1904 that Wren landed his biggest plunge when his own horse, Murmur, won the Caulfield Cup. Wren started backing Murmur as soon as weights were declared. Bets were placed with bookmakers in Sydney, Perth, Adelaide and Melbourne. Lucrative odds were secured in the early stages as Murmur had little form on the board to suggest that he could win such a testing race as the Caulfield Cup. In the months leading up to the big race Murmur won a few middle-distance races and on Cup day his price had shortened to 10–1. The favourite for the race was the mare, Gladsome, owned by Sol Green, the biggest bookmaker of his time. Both Wren and Green owned clubs which provided a betting service for their members. Wren ran the City Tattersall's

Club in Bourke Street while Green ran the Melbourne Tattersall's Club in nearby Royal Lane. Wren and Green competed fiercely for the punter's money by offering better odds than each other. To win the Caulfield Cup thus carried more than the usual reward for these arch-rivals. Murmur carried the luxury weight of six stone twelve (41.5 kg) to victory while Green's mare, Gladsome, carrying around nine stone (57.2 kg) finished fourth. Wren collected £51 000 from his wagers on Murmur. In 1915 Wren netted £27 000 when another of his horses, Garlin, won the Doncaster

Walter Lindrum contacted Wren who, upon the recommendation of a friend, agreed to support Lindrum. Wren, despite having never seen Lindrum play, cabled Smith and challenged him to play Lindrum for £1000 aside, the match to be played with composition balls. Wren offered Smith half the gate takings as well as £200 for travelling expenses. In reply Smith said that he required a 60% share of the gate, an additional £70 for expenses and for there to be a return match in England. Further cables were sent to Smith, offering a compromise on the terms and conditions. After some progress had been made, and the negotiations appeared to be nearing fruition, Smith suddenly stopped replying to the cablegrams. Following some months of silence news was received from England that Smith was to visit Australia in the winter of 1929. He had arranged to play two matches with Fred Lindrum junior but there was no mention of any matches with Walter. Fred junior had made a trip to England during the 1928–29 season. It was a disastrous tour with Fred suffering a series of heavy losses, the most staggering being a 19 178 points defeat at the hands of Willie Smith. Despite the imbalance in this result Smith made a verbal agreement to visit Australia and play two matches with Fred junior.

Walter Lindrum was very disappointed that Smith had given no indication that he would play him. He became desperate and decided that he would have to do something which would make Smith realise that he was a classy player and a worthy opponent. Walter arranged to play a match in Melbourne with his seventeen-year-old nephew, Horace, the son of Violet. Young Horace had been reared by Fred Lindrum senior and his wife from about six years of age, following the separation of Violet and her husband, Horace Morell. Horace Lindrum (he changed his name by deedpoll at an early stage of his career) always maintained in later years that he was a self-taught player. With his childhood background it seems inevitable that Horace received some coaching from his grandfather and uncles. The match with Walter, to be of a week's duration, was Horace's debut into the big league of billiards. It was certainly not a very enjoyable experience for the youngster. Prior to the match Walter had told Horace that it was his intention to put together a string of large breaks for the perusal of Willie Smith. Horace agreed to be a figurative punching bag and thus gave Walter plenty of access to the table. Walter piled on the breaks, making four thousands: 1953, 1381, 1052 and 1002, and scoring a very comfortable win by 18 001 to 7729. Surely that would impress Smith!

There was no indication from England that Smith was suitably impressed by Lindrum's efforts or even if he heard of them. He did not send a cablegram in an attempt to re-open negotiations. Instead Smith set off on a leisurely journey to Australia, part of which was made overland. Lindrum was left in a quandary. He was desperate for a match with Smith but he would have to wait until the Englishman's arrival before he could hope to make further approaches. In the meantime newspaper reports from England left no doubt as to their opinion of Smith's ability. A number of these reports were reprinted in the local papers and undoubtedly some of them reached Lindrum. Typical of these reports was one that appeared in the *Referee* of 10 April:

> One other wish is that Lindrum is as good as the Australian judges him out to be. He will have to be all that and then some, for if Smith reproduces in Australia anything like the form he has recently shown here, it is difficult to imagine how any player could beat him.

The report also said that Smith was warlike and after Lindrum's scalp. Walter Lindrum was beginning to wonder just how good this Smith fellow really was. With a total of fifteen four-figure breaks in the last English season alone, Smith must rank as a fine player. Lindrum was puzzled by the reports that Smith was after his scalp. As far as Walter could discern, Smith had no intention of playing him on the forthcoming visit. Yet, according to the reports, Smith was suggesting that he would be playing Walter. If this was so, why had Smith not given Walter some indication of his intentions?

It certainly was a perplexed Walter Lindrum who awaited the arrival of Willie Smith. Meanwhile Clark McConachy arrived from New Zealand and played a match with Lindrum in Sydney. It was a marathon three-week encounter that went Walter's way by 34 845 to 33 951. Lindrum's score included four breaks over the thousand with a top of 1492. Lindrum and McConachy then set off on an extensive tour of country New South Wales. They gave exhibitions at places such as Walcha, Scone, Tamworth, Muswellbrook, Armidale, Lismore, Ballina, Canberra, Goulburn and Temora. The duo travelled to Melbourne where they played a match with each session of two hours' duration. This innovation was Lindrum's idea. He thought that the old system, when each session was played up to a set number of points (usually 750), allowed for an element of luck that could decide the result of a match. He explained. "It may not be the size of a break that beats one's opponent so much as the time at which it comes." (The *Argus*, 10 April 1928).

Despite scoring three breaks over the thousand Lindrum lost this match to McConachy by 19 239 to 19 932. Willie Smith and his wife had arrived in Sydney in late May after an eventful journey which saw him robbed of £300 on a train in India. Smith was met in Sydney by Fred Lindrum junior and this duo played a fortnight's match at the YMCA Hall in Pitt Street. Smith conceded 10 000 start but still beat Fred junior easily by 26 061 to 23 839. Willie and Fred junior travelled to Melbourne for the return match. Finally Walter Lindrum had the opportunity to meet Smith and find out why the Englishman had failed to answer some of the cablegrams. Smith explained that he had finished with betting on his matches, so he could see no reason for continuing the negotiations. He told Lindrum that he was interested in playing him provided that no side wager was involved. Smith and Walter agreed to play two matches after the conclusion of Smith's second match with Fred Lindrum junior. Walter informed Smith that, due to other commitments, he would be unable to see him in action against Fred junior at Alcock's Parlour. Walter had every intention of watching the match — but not from the comfort of the spectator's seats. He viewed the match through a ventilator while perched up on a stack of timber. The reason for Walter's clandestine behaviour was to ensure that Smith had no reason to disguise his real form. With Walter being absent Smith would be free to play his natural game against Fred junior. From his vantage point Walter saw Smith make a beautiful break of 460. It was the break of a champion and Walter realised that Smith would be his most formidable opponent to date. Smith defeated Fred junior by 26 374 to 24 681 after conceding 10 000 start.

The first match between Walter and Willie commenced on 1 July. It was a gala occasion with Prime Minister Mr Bruce, Lieutenant-Governor Sir William Irvine and their wives in attendance. Lindrum scored a comfortable win by 24 234 to 22 147. His best break was 991 and Smith made one of 1058. Although the end result was well in Lindrum's favour, such might not have been the case if Clark McConachy had not been present at the match. In the first sessions of play Smith struck form and established a handy lead. As Walter sat watching from the player's seat, Smith was scoring freely from the 'postman's knock' position at the top of the table. With the red on the spot and the object white resting on the top cushion above the spot Smith was building a sizeable break from the pot red and cannon sequence. Lindrum was becoming quite agitated and turning to McConachy said: "I've got no chance of beating this bloke. The only shot that he is likely to break down on is when he has lost position at the top and has to play a long loser. My ball will be hard up on the top cushion and what chance have I got to score from there?"

It was McConachy who had to reassure Lindrum and prevent him from becoming completely downcast: "Look Walter", said Mac, "Smith can't keep scoring forever. You'll get a chance to get your nurseries going and once you do he won't be in it."

It was sound advice from McConachy. It helped to steady Walter and he was able to watch Smith's play with greater equanimity. When it was Lindrum's turn to play he was in a sufficiently confident mood to take advantage of the position left by Smith. Just as Mac predicted, Walter was able to get his nursery cannons into action and go on to an easy win. By the end of the match Walter was no longer afraid of Smith's scoring power. He realised that in comparison to his own play Smith's methods were slow. He knew that he could score a thousand break in almost half the time that it would take Smith. Lindrum expounded: "Time, of course, is the main factor in modern billiards. The moral effect in such matters plays a part, to say nothing of the extra strain there must naturally be on the slower player." (The *Sporting Globe,* 2 July 1938.)

Lindrum also deduced that because he was strong at the top of the table, mixed billiards and close cannons he could spell one game against another. When he was starting to feel the strain of concentrating on one particular scoring method Lindrum could switch to another scoring mode and so rest himself. Stated simply, Lindrum believed that 'a change was as good as a rest'. Smith, because he did not play nursery cannons, was not able to vary his game for the purpose of resting himself. It was another advantage Lindrum knew he had over Smith.

Having analysed his scoring ability against that of Smith, Walter began to conceive a plan for a mammoth betting coup. When the first match with

Smith was completed Lindrum signed a contract with Smith to visit England in the 1929–30 season. He was to play the season under the aegis of the manufacturers, Burroughes and Watts. The firm had sent Smith to Australia for the express purpose of persuading Lindrum to visit England. Walter contacted John Wren and made an appointment to see him at his Studley Park mansion. He explained to Wren that he was confident that he could beat Smith whenever he so wished. Wren had a golden opportunity to make a killing by backing Lindrum to beat Smith. The place for such a betting coup was unquestionably England with its betting shops scattered all around the country. Wren agreed that the plan had good possibilities but before he committed himself he would like to see Walter in action. Wren possessed a fine billiard table and Walter began playing with the intention of dazzling the millionaire. It was not long before Wren was flushed with excitement as he timed Walter making a thousand break. Lindrum offered to go on and make a second thousand but Wren was satisfied. Wren asked Lindrum to show him how he missed a shot. Walter replied that his game did not allow for misses. Wren laughed heartily and said: "There is no limit to the amount I will back you for in any match in which you tell me you think you can win." (*Sporting Globe*, 2 July 1938.)

Wren's plan was to send a manager to England with Lindrum to organise the elaborate betting plunge. As Walter was departing from Wren's home he was given a piece of advice by the discerning sporting man: "You will find lack of concentration your greatest enemy in compiling big breaks. Move quickly between your shots. A second gained is a point added."

Walter saw the logic of the suggestion and, although he had always been a fast player, he resolved to lift the tempo of his game to an even higher level. Lindrum returned home that night inspired by the confidence of John Wren. Despite the lateness of the hour he adjourned to the billiard room for a practice session. He played for six hours without a miss in amassing a break of 8000. He had three ten-minute spells while making the break. With plans at foot for the English betting coup Lindrum decided that in future matches with Smith he would coast along and not show his best form. It was important that the match results be close enough to suggest that Smith was capable of beating Lindrum on English soil.

The second match between Lindrum and Smith was played in Sydney at the YMCA Hall. It was an epic struggle which attracted capacity crowds during the fortnight's play. Lindrum took the initiative with a break of 1434 but Smith replied with a 1383. Lindrum scored a later break of 1090 but going into the last day it was anyone's match. A timely break of 1028 saw Smith put the issue beyond doubt, with the final scores being 23 446 to 22 317 in the Englishman's favour. The match proved a huge financial success. The players shared net proceeds of £1265/13/0 which came down to £13/3/8 per hour of play or 6/6d per point scored. It was the first big gate for Walter and he did not know what to do with so much money. He had thoughts of giving it to his mother. Willie Smith took Walter to a bank and helped him open a savings account. It was a new experience for Walter for he had never had any previous need for a bank account.

Willie Smith's relationship with reporters on his Australian tour was never very rosy. Smith felt as if the journalists were deliberately 'hounding' him and he complained publicly about it. There were definite grounds for Smith to feel persecuted for there certainly was some adverse commentary on some of his matches. Most of the newspaper reports carried a common theme: that some of Smith's matches were not genuine encounters — one (or both) players were running 'dead'. Though none of the reports was quite so blunt there was no doubt as to the inference. Before expanding on a delicate topic such as match fixing it must be placed on record that both Willie Smith and Clark McConachy have denied any knowledge of any such 'arrangements'.

The first report that hinted at the question of a match not being a genuine encounter was printed after the second match between Smith and Lindrum. The *Referee* (31 July 1929) said:

> Smith is certainly the most formidable English opponent Walter Lindrum has faced and his play is full of variety. But in the second week he was not so consistently brilliant as he has been in his previous play in Australia. This was the opportunity for Lindrum to walk right away. But he failed to do his remarkable ability full justice. On many occasions close followers of Lindrum's play went away with the impression he was not all out.
>
> It was hoped that these contests would provide a real test of strength and enable us to gauge the limit of Lindrum's ability. It seems that we have not yet realised the extent of his powers. He cannot be severely criticised for making a close fight of it. The game must be kept interesting to attract the public. The attendances would soon dwindle if one or the other established too big a lead and got into an impregnable position.
>
> But the fact remains that so much widespread publicity has been given to the matches and such Empire-wide interest has been developed that Lindrum should win on every occasion if he is capable of doing so. In fact, the interest of Australia and England has been so greatly kindled that each has the honour of his country in his hands. In addition, Lindrum's defeats will go down in the records, and future generations will sum up his ability by figures which are ineffaceable.
>
> There are countless thousands outside the ranks of billiardists following the Smith-Lindrum duels who accept only figures as their guide.

Of course Lindrum was playing within himself in this match but his motives were not quite as were suggested. He was in fact laying the foundations for the English betting coup. Although this second Lindrum-Smith match opened the subject of 'arrangements', it was a following match between Smith and McConachy that brought the question to a head. This match was meant to be an interlude before the next match between Smith and Lindrum. After their first two matches Smith and Lindrum had each recorded one win, thus the third match would be the decider. It was expected that Smith would not have any difficulty in beating McConachy and so set the stage for the third and final match with Lindrum. The doughty McConachy, though, had other ideas on the situation. He had never beaten Smith and to do so against the player who was commonly regarded as England's best would be an enormous boost. McConachy set about the task with great determination and midway through the second week of the match he had built up a considerable lead. This was despite a brilliant break of 2030 by Smith. There is an incident which supposedly occurred at about this stage of the match. It must be stressed that this account is only hearsay which is often a very unreliable source of information. While Clarke McConachy would, if he was still alive, vehemently deny that any such conversation took place, the following is an account of that alleged incident.

'McConachy was approached by Walter Lindrum. It was during the second week of Mac's match with Smith and the big New Zealander had established a sizeable lead. Lindrum told Mac that he wanted him to lose the match, the reason being that if Mac beat Smith the forthcoming "decider" between Lindrum and Smith would lose all appeal and be a financial flop. Mac at first refused to "run dead" for Smith, arguing that he had been trying to beat the Englishman for years. Walter persisted with his request and Mac finally agreed after he was promised a win in a return match with Smith at Melbourne. McConachy declared, however, that he would make it so obvious that he was not trying that the spectators would see through it.'

That is, according to hearsay, how the alleged conversation ran. An article in the *Referee* (14 August 1929) details the conclusion of the Smith-McConachy match:

> The final session was one of the poorest on record, under present rules, between first class professionals. Nearly 40 visits were made to the table by the players in 2 hours. At one period McConachy scored 6 points in 5 innings, four being fruitless.
>
> It was hardly the merit of Smith's play that was responsible for McConachy's eclipse. The Englishman, apart from his break of 2,030, has not shown to such disadvantage in Australia. The New Zealander, in consequence, seemed to have the game well won when he was over 1,500 ahead on Wednesday. The poorness of his showing in subsequent sessions, therefore, was disappointing to his admirers. He had won a reputation as a fighter, but if his display on this occasion is a guide, he is probably not endowed with the temperament with which he has been credited, or something else was awry.

The final words of the report, "or something else was awry", hinted at the possibility of pre-arranged matches. The report was another in the continuing saga of the Press versus Willie Smith. Such reporting only served to strengthen Smith's contempt for the Australian Press. During the period from August 11–20, 1929, a number of reports and comments appeared in the *Sportsman* and *Truth,* which carried very definite suggestions concerning the pre-arranged results of billiard matches. These reports were the work of one Richard Thomas Harrison who was a freelance journalist in the employ of The *Sunday Times* Company. Harrison had been a regular bowls reporter for the *Referee* for seven years, writing under the nom-de-plume of 'Boomerang'. His reporting had caused some ill-feeling amongst members of the Waverly Bowling Club in 1927. He had been expelled from the Club's premises and subsequently took action against the president, Mr Howe. Harrison did not enjoy the best of reputations in racing circles either, having been formally warned off the course by the Australian Jockey Club for defaulting on a debt of £400 to a bookmaker, Walter Kelly. The interest created by the Lindrum-Smith matches had prompted the sporting editor of the *Truth & Sportsman*

Ltd, Alec Boyd, to engage Harrison to cover the matches. Following the scrappy ending to the McConachy-Smith encounter Harrison reported in the *Sportsman*:

> . . . Then "all of a sudden" Mac got a fit of the stops. We knew that half the community hasn't been feeling well these weeks, and perhaps the New Zealander went off his oats, as they say in horseland. Any person who had the dire misfortune to be present at the last session on Saturday night won't soon forget the display.
>
> McConachy looked as if he didn't care whether "Joeys" or the "All Blacks" won the next boat race, he could do nothing right; and Willie Smith, when not otherwise engaged, carried on a tete-a-tete with veteran J. R. Hooper. But what concerns us is the match between Smith and Lindrum. Will Smith beat the young Australian?
>
> "Sportsman" doesn't know, but one thing it does know: Exhibition billiards lies on a special slab at the morgue. It wants to see both these top-hole professionals all out.
>
> "He could beat Mr Smith with his jaws tied in a knot with neuralgia", said an ex-Melburnite.
>
> But it didn't work out that way the second time, did it?

These reports by Harrison, bordering as they did on being libellous, must have made Willie Smith most uncomfortable. It seems reasonable to suggest that the relationship between Smith and Harrison was not amicable. On the evening of 22 August, 1929 Harrison went to the YMCA building to attend a session of the third match between Smith and Lindrum. Upon seeing Harrison arrive at the building, Smith left the building and returned with a Constable Whittle. Under instruction from Smith the constable escorted Harrison to a quieter part of the building. After some discussion of the reasons for Smith's. action, the constable advised Harrison to leave the building.

The following day a writ was issued out of the Supreme Court by Mr E. R. Abigail, acting on behalf of Richard Thomas Harrison, against William Robert Smith, claiming £5000 damages in connection with an occurrence at a billiard match. The next day (Saturday) a writ of *caveat,* or *ca re,* was served on Smith. This writ, for £5050, was to prevent Smith from leaving Sydney, and later Australia, and so avoiding a proper defence of the action. Smith had given no indication of such an intention but Harrison was taking no chances. Acting on the writ of *ca re* the Sheriff "arrested" Smith who was held at his solicitor's office for about half an hour. After entering into a bond for £5100 to remain in the jurisdiction Smith was released from custody. A few days later the writ of *ca re* was set aside after an application by Mr Dovey who was acting on Smith's behalf. It was not permissible for the defendant to be held to bail for an amount which exceeded the original claim for damages. It was only through this legal technicality that Smith was free to leave Australia. One interesting upshot of the ill-conceived writ of *ca re* was that Harrison dispensed with the services of Abigail who had advised him to take out the writ of *ca re.* Harrison later took Abigail to court, alleging professional negligence in the handling of the writ of *ca re.* Harrison won the case and was awarded £300 damages plus costs of £39/8/6. It was something of a blemish on the record of Abigail, a criminal lawyer who had a reputation as one of the most skilled advocates of the day.

The original action by Harrison, claiming £5000 damages from Smith, was not settled until 2 April, 1931. In his testimony during the Supreme Court proceedings Harrison said that after an article had appeared in the *Truth* on August 11, 1929 he had a somewhat heated conversation with Willie Smith at the YMCA about his reporting of the matches. Smith is said to have denied any suggestion of McConachy running dead. Harrison said that Mac was tied up and it was the opinion of everybody that he was tied up. On the last days he became a new man; he was sulky and, in his opinion, tied up. Harrison said that he knew McConachy and Smith were not friends and that is why McConachy wanted to go on. He said that a conversation with Walter Lindrum at Home Recreations on August 12 had brought about his belief that Lindrum had told McConachy to pull up. Harrison alleged that in reply to his question, "What is the matter with McConachy?" Lindrum said, "They sometimes play bad." Harrison continued: "I went over the position with him and I said, 'He was playing so brilliantly, and suddenly he ceased to be, and appeared to be a different man. Everybody in the town has got him crook,' and all he replied to that was, he just sniggered."

Evidence which had been taken on commission in London from Smith stated that there was no arrangement with Lindrum or McConachy about what was to be the result of any of the matches. Smith claimed that while the play was in progress Harrison waved his copy paper about and conversed with a man who was sitting with him. Evidence from Lindrum, also taken on commission in London, claimed that Harrison carried on a conversation with another man and moved about in the line of fire. It was because Harrison's conduct in the Match Room had disturbed their play that Smith and Lindrum had decided to exclude him from the YMCA Match Hall.

In summing up the case for the jury, Judge Ferguson said that as Smith and Lindrum had hired the hall in order to give their exhibition of billiards they had a perfect right to say who should come in and who should not. To turn someone out of the lounge, or any other part of the building, apart from the match hall, was not their prerogative. The Judge continued:

> The plaintiff's case was that "I had been writing criticisms which annoyed them. I was there as a reporter and I was writing what rightly or wrongly I considered to be a fair account of the match. It annoyed Smith, it annoyed Lindrum, they did not like it. They did not like the criticism, and what they did was not really because of anything I had done in the room but because they wanted to punish me, to have their revenge on me for having exposed them in the public press to criticism they did not like."
> If that was so, what they really wanted to do was to damage him in the eyes of his employers and to have their revenge upon him because he had written criticisms about them which they did not like. (Supreme Court, Harrison vs Smith, March-April 1931).

The jury (of four) returned a verdict in favour of Harrison of £200. In a cross-action, heard at the same time, Smith had sought £1000 damages for wrongful arrest. The jury found in Smith's favour and awarded him the sum of one farthing. Judgement was thus entered for Harrison for £199/19/11¾.

The third match between Lindrum and Smith during the Englishman's 1929 tour should have been a promoter's dream. With the scores standing at one match each the stage was set for a gripping 'decider'. That ideal situation was spoilt by the adverse publicity which had erupted following the dismal ending to the Smith-McConachy match. That seems to be the reason the attendances for the third Lindrum-Smith match declined noticeably from the frenzied level of their second match. This was despite the fact that the *Sun* newspaper donated a silver tea service, valued at 100 guineas, for the winner of the third match. When Walter's girlfriend, 'Rosie' Coates, saw the tea service, she said: "Wally, you've got to win that tea service for me."

Rosie had been Walter's 'girl' for over two years and she often accompanied him to his matches and exhibitions. The match opened at the YMCA Hall on 12 August. After Lindrum had won the string for break and left the balls in a safe position Smith played his first shot. Smith miscued and the top of the cue, measuring about a centimetre, snapped off and flew among the spectators. Although Smith was upset at the irreparable damage to his cue, which he had used for 28 years, he was still able to quip: "It is the biggest break I have made in my career."

An inspection showed that the cue had been tampered with. Smith always maintained that it must have been the work of a professional punter who was trying to ensure a Lindrum victory. That does seem the only logical explanation for this lowly act.

For the first five days of the match Walter played strongly and established a lead of 2254. During the Friday night Walter's girlfriend, Rosie, was suddenly taken ill. Some two months previously Rosie had been injured in a traffic accident in Melbourne and had not fully recovered. Rosie's condition was critical but she rallied sufficiently on the Saturday morning to ask Walter how the match was going. When she heard that Walter was doing well she urged him to go on. Walter had been on the point of calling off the match so that he could be with Rosie. The two Saturday sessions were dominated by Smith who slashed Lindrum's lead to only 441. During the evening session Lindrum spent about eight minutes at the table and scored only 189 points. A paper reported that "never had Lindrum been so completely overshadowed" but little did they realise that Walter's heart was not in his billiards. Two leading specialists attended Rosie over the weekend and her condition improved sufficiently to put Walter's mind at rest. Upon the resumption of play in the second week Lindrum was back to his best and at the close of play on Tuesday night he had built his lead up to 2226. Rosie's condition declined overnight and was again causing Walter great concern. His play on Wednesday was very indifferent and at the end of the day the scores stood at, Lindrum 16 865 to Smith's 16 222. After the evening session Walter went to the hospital to find Rosie had improved slightly but she was still not out of danger. Walter still wanted to call off the match so that he could be with Rosie but she urged him to go on. In the Thursday afternoon session Walter's concentration was broken by his concern for Rosie. Willie Smith began to dominate play and Walter saw his lead dwindling away. Walter rallied slightly, ending the session with a break of 155 unfinished. Prior to the evening session Walter visited Rosie and when she learnt of the lapse in Walter's play she urged: "Wally, you've got to make a 2000 break for me". "I'll try", promised Walter as he left Rosie to return to the YMCA Hall.

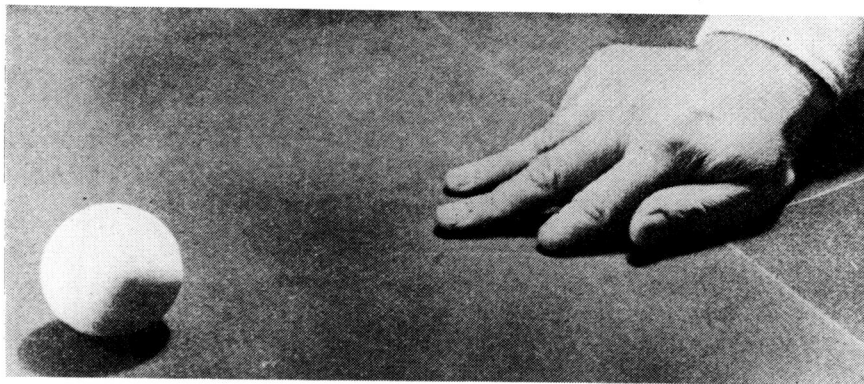

Above: *Walter's bridge hand, clearly showing his damaged index finger — the result of an accident with a mangle at the age of three. (Dolly Lindrum)*

Below: *Walter's playing card in 1920. (Dolly Lindrum)*

Fred Lindrum III (left) and Melbourne Inman at the Inman Club, London, 1928. (John Fairfax & Sons Ltd)

Above: *Walter with the New Zealand champion, Clark McConachy, during June, 1929 when they played the first match under a time limit of two hours per session.* (Herald & Weekly Times)

Preceding page, above: *A youthful Claude Falkiner, the English professional who, on his first visit to Australia in 1924, opened Walter Lindrum's eyes to the scoring potential of the nursery cannon. (Norman Clare)*

Preceding page, below: *England, 1929. Lindrum's tour under the management of the manufacturer, Burroughes and Watts. Taken from a Burroughes and Watts advertisement, this photo shows Walter Lindrum and Willie Smith examining a set of balls while Clark McConachy looks on from the left. (Norman Clare)*

> Lindrum dazzled in the evening, and performed the most prodigious feat of his career. Continuing his unfinished break, he scored at an amazing rate. The rapidity and accuracy of the young Australian and the wondrous nature of his billiards held the big crowd enthralled. Hundred after hundred flowed from his cue, greeted with intense applause as each was called by the marker. He passed the thousand mark, and it appeared that he would never break down. (The *Referee*, 28 August 1929.)

When the break reached 1500 Walter was showing some signs of strain. Willie Smith, in a fine sporting gresture, brought a glass of water to the table and assured Walter that all was well at home.

> Excitement grew as the 2000 mark approached, and he received a tumultuous reception when the goal was reached. He had a hard fight for the last few points. Then he missed a cannon off the cushion with the second object ball well up the table, in endeavouring to bring the red into play again, the break terminating at 2002. (The *Referee*, 28 August 1929).

Walter had made it! He always regarded the break as one of the greatest of his life. In the evening session he had scored the final 1847 points in 102 minutes. The break had left Lindrum completely flat and for the remainder of the session he added only 31 points in five innings. Walter left the YMCA Hall to visit his girl in hospital. Rosie's first words to him were:

"Wally, did you make it?"

"Yes", he replied in a thick voice.

"Good", said Rosie as she drifted off to sleep.

Willie Smith made up some leeway during the two sessions of play on Friday. As Walter returned to the dressing room after the evening session he was informed that Rosie had suffered a relapse. Her condition was critical. Walter rushed to the hospital to find Rosie barely conscious. After exchanging a few words with her he hastened out of the room. Some time later he returned with an Anglican minister, Arthur E. Morris. In the obscurity of a room at the Omrah Private Hospital Walter and his sweetheart, Rosie, were quietly married. The marriage was witnessed by Austin Frauenfelder and Amy Breakell. The critical nature of Rosie's condition can be gauged from the fact that she was incapable of signing the marriage register with her usual signature. Instead she placed an X in the register. In the early hours of the next morning — Saturday — Walter's bride of a few hours, his precious Rosie, died. It was the toughest break of Walter Lindrum's life.

The match with Willie Smith was abandoned. With the scores favouring Lindrum by 21 431 to 19 308, Smith conceded that he had no chance of winning. He agreed that the silver tea service should be presented to Walter. The body of Mrs Lindrum was taken to Melbourne for burial. Walter was very upset over Rosie's death. He was scheduled to depart for England in a few weeks' time but he wanted to abandon the trip. Members of the Lindrum family urged Walter to make the trip for they realised it would help take his mind off his painful loss.

Smith and McConachy played a return match in Melbourne in which the New Zealander scored a well-deserved win by 21 459 to 20 073. Following the conclusion of this match Smith and McConachy made arrangements for their departure for England. McConachy had also been signed up for the forthcoming English season. Walter Lindrum had demanded that before he signed up for a season under Burroughes and Watts, Mac had also to be offered a similar contract. Smith was so anxious to secure Lindrum for an English season that he agreed to this condition. Smith was besieged by Walter's sister, Violet, who pleaded for her son, Horace, to be taken to England. Smith refused for he had already signed up one more player than he originally intended.

7 There's More to Billiards

There is no doubt that Lindrum is the finest player the world has ever
seen. We used to think that Willie Smith was unbeatable, but in
comparison with the Australian artist he is but an imperfect artisan.

Morning Post, December 1929

On 10 September, amidst an air of uncertainty and depression, Walter
Lindrum left Melbourne on the S.S. *Cathay* bound for England. He was
accompanied by Willie Smith, Clark McConachy and their wives and
Horace Morell who was to act as his manager. As the *Cathay* was preparing
to dock in Perth, Smith took the incredible step of locking Lindrum in his
cabin. Smith had been told that, some years previously, Lindrum had
jumped ship at Perth when he was suppose to accompany Claude Falkiner to
England. Smith was taking every precaution to ensure that he did not lose his
prize possession whom he had travelled half way around the world to secure.
The reason that Lindrum had previously jumped ship (and why he had
refused the attractive offers to visit the Old Dart) was because he had a
chronic fear of the damp English climate. Lindrum suffered from a
bronchial condition and he was convinced that the cold and wet of the
English winter would play havoc with him. Lindrum's fear had reached such
immense proportions that only for the efforts of Willie Smith he probably
would never have visited England. It so happened that Lindrum suffered less
bronchial congestion in England than he did in the relatively dry climate of
hometown Melbourne.

Upon their arrival in London on 13 October Lindrum and McConachy
were given a luncheon of welcome by Messrs Rainbow and Billington-Greig,
the managing directors of Burroughes and Watts. Willie Smith, in an
introductory speech, at Frascati's Restaurant said of Lindrum: "I did more
than any professional has ever done in Australia, yet I went under to this
modest young man. The hottest stuff I have met." (The *Argus,* 14 October
1929.)

Walter was embarrassed by Smith's praise but he was nonetheless pleased
to receive such a warm welcome. He was not at all pleased, though, to learn
that the first match of his tour was scheduled for Glasgow. Lindrum's
contract with Burroughes and Watts meant that he had to comply with any
arrangements that they made whether he agreed with them or not. Smith,
who had been associated with Burroughes and Watts for several years by
means of a lucrative contract, acted in an advisory capacity to the firm
throughout Lindrum's tour. Smith's advice was usually accepted and thus it
was he who virtually controlled Lindrum's tour programme. It was an
arrangement that placed Smith in a powerful position and led to a conflict of
interests from the very outset of the tour. Lindrum could not understand why
he was being sent to the provinces to open his tour. He claimed that he
should have given star-billing and opened his tour in London at the heart of

the billiard world. Burroughes and Watts did not seem to regard him as a drawcard but merely as another player.

Lindrum won his first match at Glasgow, defeating Clark McConachy by 22 694 to 21 962. He made two breaks over the thousand: 1083 and 1330. Tom Newman had made a special trip to Glasgow to have a close look at Lindrum's game and he was so impressed by the sheer speed and ease of scoring that he wrote in his column in the *News of the World* that Lindrum was "a superb player, the greatest billiard player that has ever been".

Lindrum travelled to Newcastle for his first encounter with Smith. To his dismay he found that the match was to be played in a 'cellar' which was little better than the 'smokey basement' in which he had played at Glasgow. Lindrum realised that there was no money to be made in small halls in the provinces. He complained to Smith about the low admission charges and Smith responded by increasing the rates to a higher level. Attendances at the match dropped off and it was necessary to revert to the lower charges to secure moderate crowds. These working class people could not afford to pay what Lindrum considered was a reasonable charge. Smith always adopted a working man's approach to the game of billiards. He insisted that the average man in the smaller cities had just as much right to see professional billiards as the aristocrats who patronised Thurston's Hall in London. Smith could afford to adopt this stand for his contract with Burroughes and Watts guaranteed him an income of at least £60 per week. Lindrum had no such guarantees, relying solely on his share of the gate proceeds for his income. He felt that having travelled to the other side of the world he should not be used to provide cheap entertainment for one section of the public while there were others who were prepared to pay considerably more to see him perform. Lindrum had two breaks over the thousand, with a best of 1721, in beating Smith by 23 400 to 22 039. Although the win caused some surprise it was not regarded as any real indication that Lindrum was a better player than Smith. In a match that followed at Leeds a few of the sceptics were converted when Lindrum scored a decisive victory by 28 333 to 20 350. He had made an unprecedented 8 thousand-plus breaks with a top of 1925 which was followed later on the same day by one of 1228.

The London public learnt of the remarkable deeds of Lindrum and waited in excited anticipation for his arrival in their city. Fortunately Burroughes and Watts took notice of Lindrum's complaints regarding the playing conditions and especially the size of the match halls. They scoured London and secured a lease on the spacious Memorial Hall in Farringdon Street which had seating for over 800 spectators. Lindrum was pleased with this improvement and decided that if his tour was going to be successful he would have to try and fill those seats. Lindrum's first match at the Memorial Hall, against Willie Smith, commenced on 25 November. The London fans had an immediate taste of the Lindrum magic when he served up a break of 1057 on the first day of play. This was followed by a break of 1725 on the second day and later by three more breaks over the thousand. Going into the last of the match, 7 December, Lindrum had a sixth thousand on the board, 1350 unfinished. The 1350 points had been scored in only 43 minutes which, calculated at an average scoring rate, meant that Lindrum had scored a thousand of the points in less than 32 minutes.

Upon resuming play in the afternoon session at three o'clock Lindrum played with perfect coolness and reached the 2000 mark by the aid of a delightful screw back loser off the white. Smith rose from his seat and shook hands with Lindrum who resumed play and immediately passed his previous best break of 2002. There was an expectant atmosphere around the room for every spectator felt that the real test was yet to come — it was not so much a question of whether Lindrum would lower his own record, but whether he would lower Smith's world record set at Manchester just twelve months previously. Lindrum was perhaps the last person to realise that he had a chance of breaking the record. He had been so intent on the task at hand, that of keeping his break going, that he was oblivious to any thoughts of Smith's record. The enthusiastic applause of the spectators and the intensifying atmosphere of the room made Lindrum aware that the record was within his grasp. A certain tenseness came into his play. When the applause had died down Lindrum continued scoring with spells of open play varied with long strings of nursery cannons.

At 2,650, when playing winners and cannons at the spot end of the table, he got into temporary trouble, but by going into baulk and playing a few losers and two drop cannons he soon regained position.

Presently the scores were called:— "2,735", "2,737", "2,740". A cannon followed and he potted the red.

Smith's record had been lowered at last. Smith was the first to offer his congratulations, and for the first time in the afternoon Lindrum was beaming with satisfaction. Insistent cries arose of "Speech! Speech!" but Smith, stepping forward, appealed for silence. "Yes, I know it is a world's record", he said, "but I hope you will keep quiet for a little longer because I want to see Lindrum pass the 3,000 mark. (The *Argus*, 9 December 1929.)

Lindrum continued with top of the table play and then switched to nursery cannons and ran his score up to 3000. The time was ten minutes past four, which meant that Lindrum had taken a total of 113 minutes to make the 3000 points. Once this landmark was passed the strain was lifted from Lindrum's shoulders. His play was free from all care and he went on scoring without any apparent effort. The break ended unexpectedly, at 3262, just when Lindrum was playing so well that he thought he could have gone on scoring till the end of the session. A small hair had caused the object white ball to 'kick', ending in an unplayable position. Lindrum used the rest and attempted a desperate cannon off two cushions but missed by a whisker. There was plenty of discussion about that hair. Willie Smith said it must have been one of the hairs off his head as Lindrum was sending him bald. One writer ridiculed Lindrum's claim, arguing that as he had already made a couple of thousand upon exactly the same part of the table he would have had trouble much earlier if the hair was on the table. In fact the hair had not been on the table for more than a few strokes. The hair was from the brush that had been used to sweep the table prior to the commencement of the session. The sweepings, as was common practice, had been swept into the pockets. When the red ball had been potted a hair had adhered to it and thus found its way onto the table. The hair had caused only a slight deviation of the object white but it was sufficient to result in the unplayable position. It had taken two hours and three minutes for Lindrum to make the record break.

For the second time in the session there were insistent demands for a speech. With his characteristic brevity Lindrum thanked the London public for the wonderful reception that it had given him. His one regret was that his record had been made against such a good sportsman as Smith, but he added that he was proud to have made a world record for Australia.

Lindrum's feat made the stop-press column of almost every one of the afternoon newspapers. Claude Falkiner interrupted his match with Joe Davis to send his congratulations to Lindrum:

> I had predicted a 3,000 for Lindrum, but now I predict a 5,000 break
> for him. Anything is possible for that boy! He could make a 500 break
> on the floor. (The *Argus,* December 9, 1929.)

In a comment in its leading columns the *Morning Post* said that the comparative merits of Lindrum and Smith are summed up as follow: "There is no doubt that Lindrum is the finest player the world has ever seen. We used to think that Willie Smith was unbeatable, but in comparison with the Australian artist he is but an imperfect artisan".

Writing to the *Evening Standard* Melbourne Inman said that "Walter Lindrum has no rival, and that if perfection is possible Lindrum is perfect. Inman thinks that the Australian could give one-fourth of the game in 18 000 up to the leading professional and one-third to the rest: and even if a man backed himself to win on his own terms he would be an optimist."

With Lindrum's performances eliciting such high praise from players of the calibre of Inman and Falkiner it is hard to believe that only two months earlier the *Daily Express* carried the following opinion:

> If the handicapping of the five principal players for fortnight time-limit
> matches would be brought about I would place Willie Smith on the
> scratch mark as he is undoubtedly the greatest player of the day. I would
> give Joe Davis and Tom Newman a start of 2,500, Walter Lindrum 3,500
> and Clark McConachy 4,500 (October 1929.)

It is difficult to understand how the *Daily Express* reporter could have arrived at these handicaps. If he had examined Lindrum's record at the time of his arrival in England he would have found that the Australian had thirty four-figure breaks to his credit, the highest being 2002. It was more than any player had ever made, exceeding George Gray's tally by just one. At the same time Willie Smith had made 26 breaks over the thousand including two scores in excess of 2000. The records of Davis, Newman and McConachy did not even approach these figures. It seems as if the *Daily Express* reporter, come handicapper, was somewhat biased towards his fellow-countrymen. He found it difficult to imagine that any overseas billiards player could be superior to the local champions. The reporter was not alone in holding this view. He was one of many who believed that at billiards the English were invincible. During his first English tour Lindrum destroyed this myth. By the conclusion of Lindrum's tour even the most patriotic Englishman had to acknowledge Lindrum's claims to the number one position.

Lindrum's record break of 3262 had thus brought him the recognition which he had worked so hard to obtain. It also had forced the English bookmakers to revise the odds of Lindrum beating Smith. When Lindrum had first arrived in England the bookies were offering as much as 10-1 about his prospects of beating Smith. In only two months these odds had been dramatically slashed. Lindrum's price was now closer to 10–1 on! What had happened to the betting coup that Lindrum and John Wren had envisaged? It had not eventuated. It was not because Wren had lost any confidence in Lindrum's chances of success. Wren was, on the contrary, keener than ever to back the greatest certainty that he had seen in his illustrious career. It was the death of Walter's wife that had indirectly caused the planned coup to be abandoned. Rosie's death had thrown Walter's life into confusion. He had been so distraught that he had forgotten all about Wren and the betting plunge. Wren had learnt of Lindrum's sad loss and decided not to press the matter. Thus a golden opportunity to make a 'killing' had been missed. It was only through chance circumstances that the English bookmakers were saved from an enormous payout. They had realised that their assessment of the relative merits of Smith and Lindrum had been totally inaccurate. Lindrum's price was slashed. The lucrative odds that had been on offer were gone forever. Charlie Hannon was a noted punter of the racing world who also gambled on billiard matches. He was a keen amateur snooker player who over-estimated his own ability and as a result lost large sums on a few matches. On one occasion he played Stanley Newman, brother of Tom and a professional of some standing. When the game concluded in the early hours one morning Hannon owed Stanley and a backer the sum of £4,000 each which he paid without a grumble. Hannon caught his first glimpse of Lindrum during the first match at the Memorial Hall. Hannon was introduced to Lindrum after the session and said: "Sonny, until seeing you tonight I would have laid £20,000 to £2,000 on Smith trouncing you. I'm lucky. It's money saved." (*Sporting Globe*, 2 July, 1938.)

Following the completion of the match Lindrum sent a cable to his parents. He said that he was feeling the strain of the tour. He had played since the middle of October with hardly a spell of rest, for even on Sundays he sometimes had to travel. In the few hours that he had been away from the table he had to accept invitations to luncheons, suppers and fill other social engagements that took up what little spare time he would otherwise have had. He would be glad when the tour was over so that he could return home.

Apart from his demanding schedule of engagements Lindrum was faced with other pressures. He continued to be unhappy with Willie Smith's handling of the tour arrangements. With both players contracted to Burroughes and Watts they were destined to be playing each other for most of the tour. This caused an outcry from some English professionals who claimed that Smith was monopolising Lindrum. Burroughes and Watts replied that as they had taken the time and expense to bring Lindrum to England they were entitled to first preference to his services. They had a contract that gave them the legal right to decide who would be Lindrum's opponents. It was this contract that led to the greatest disappointment of Lindrum's tour.

The Billiard Association and Control Council (B.A. & C.C.) was preparing to stage the 1930 Championship. The championship had for many years been played at the famous Thurston's Hall in Leicester Square. Thurston's was a leading billiard firm and its match hall naturally contained one of its own tables fitted with Thurston cushions and cloth, etc. There was intense rivalry between the major billiard firms with each doing its utmost to gain recognition as the leading firm. The management of Burroughes and Watts was not in favour of its contracted players (Smith, Lindrum and McConachy) competing on the table of a rival firm. If any of these players had set a world record on the Thurston table then that firm would have a decided advantage gained at the expense of Burroughes and Watts.

Therefore Burroughes and Watts wanted to negate any advantage that Thurstons might gain through the participation of Lindrum, Smith and McConachy in the Championship. Burroughes and Watts suggested that the table for the championship be a combination of cushions and cloth from one firm and slates and table frame from the other. As an alternative it was suggested that the table be supplied by a neutral firm other than Thurston's or Burroughes and Watts. The only stipulation made by Burroughes and Watts was that the match should be staged in the spacious Memorial Hall. The firm guaranteed not to use the event for any form of advertising. Despite a declaration by the B.A. & C.C. that it naturally wanted all the leading players to compete for the Championship it refused to make any form of compromise to facilitate the entry of Smith, Lindrum and McConachy. The B.A. & C.C. issued the following statement:

> The Council would draw attention to No. 3 of the conditions of the Professional Championship which states that 'Play will take place at Messrs. Thurston's and Co.'s Hall, Leicester Square, London W.C. on one of their Standard Tables, covered with West of England woollen cloth and fitted with 'Stanfast' cushions, and at such other venues and on such other tables as the entries may render necessary.' Deeply as the absence of these three players from the Professional Championship is deplored, their participation in it would have been purchased too dearly upon terms involving the forfeiture of all authority or right to govern, on the part of the governing body, and no other decision was possible. (The *Billiard Player*, January 1930.)

The B.A. & C.C. argued that they could not accept any of the conditions suggested by Burroughes and Watts because by so doing it would lose its independence and authority. The Control Council ignored the fact that Thurston's had been given an implicit privilege in the written conditions of the Championship. This had already cast doubt on the supposed independence of the B.A. & C.C. The refusal of the offers by Burroughes and Watts left the Control Council open to accusations of favouring one particular trade interest (Thurston's). If the firm of Burroughes and Watts was to release the three contracted players and allow them to compete in the Championship it would have to be done under the terms and conditions that removed all the advantages that had been acquired at some expense. Although Burroughes and Watts were prepared to forgo these advantages it was not prepared to hand them on a platter to one of its fiercest rivals. The situation was thus deadlocked and Walter Lindrum was prevented from competing in the 1930 Championship for which he would have started a prohibitive favourite.

The next two matches between Lindrum and Smith were won by the Englishman. At Birmingham the result favoured Smith by 1101 points after Lindrum had been in front with the aid of breaks of 1231 and 1812. The match which followed at Glasgow was the one classic encounter of the tour. Lindrum established a large lead in the first week of play. On the third day of the match, Christmas Day, he made breaks of 1086 and 1213. Smith replied in the evening session with a break of 1038. Smith produced some outstanding play in the second week to record a well-earnt win by 24 713 to 24 147. This was despite a fine break of 2140 by Lindrum which established a Scottish record. The match had a slightly curious ending when, with the scores very close, Lindrum gave what was described as a 'virtual exhibition of masse shots'. After he had congratulated Smith on his win Lindrum said that his own play had been affected by a summons that had been served on him. He thought it a shame that a visitor to Great Britain should be the victim of such treatment. The summons was issued by Mr J.G. Williamson in whose rooms Lindrum had opened his tour in October. It claimed that Mr Horace Morell was guilty of defamation of character. The incident was due to an item in a balance sheet in which a certain sum was charged against refreshments to representatives of the press. The summons was withdrawn a few weeks later.

Around this time Joe Davis was reported to be devoting much practice to the nursery cannons. This was an ominous sign not so much for Walter Lindrum but for billiards in general. The history of billiards showed that whenever one player perfected a shot, others followed suit and tried to emulate his deeds. The result was that the shot was overdone and became either restricted or eliminated from the game altogether. The 'spot' stroke was a case in point. It was the oldest specialised shot, dating from 1825. It received its death warrant in 1890 when W. J. Peall made a break of 3304 of which 3174 points were made off the spot. The history of the losing hazard is very similar. In 1850 John Roberts senior recommended it as the backbone of the game. Sixty years later George Gray went far beyond this— he made it the entire game. At first the public flocked eagerly to see the marvellous young Australian play two-ball billiards. Fred Lindrum junior followed suit to some extent and Clark McConachy first won the New Zealand Championship solely by the use of the red loser. Walter Lindrum, with some large breaks made mainly off the red ball, emphasised the need for some restriction of hazard play. Hazards (whether winning or losing) had been limited to 25 in succession since 1926.

Thus the news of Davis's practice of nurseries was a sign of things to come. Already cannons were restricted to 35 ball to ball cannons but this proved no obstacle to Lindrum and Co. An inundation of close cannon play into the game would probably bore the public and necessitate another rule change. Certainly Davis could not be criticised for practising nursery cannons. If it was possible to beat Lindrum it had to be done by playing him at his own game. That at least was how Davis saw the situation at this stage.

Although Burroughes and Watts could have restricted Lindrum to playing only Smith and McConachy for the duration of his tour, it is to the firm's credit that the other leading professionals, Davis and Newman, were given matches with him. The first non-Burroughes and Watts player to be opposed to Lindrum was a Derby professional, Willie Leigh, who was not regarded as a first-flight cueist. The match was played at Sheffield from 6–11 January and for the first time in England Lindrum conceded a start to an opponent. Leigh received 7000 points but proved little more than a sparring partner for Lindrum who, with four breaks over the thousand, won by 19 781 to 10 080.

An amusing incident occurred before this match. Willie Leigh visited the hall and was approached by someone who asked if he had come to examine the table. "No" replied Leigh, "I've come to select a comfortable chair!"

Joe Davis, the champion, had his first taste of the Lindrum wizardry in a match in London from 13–25 January. Davis scored 26 172 points for the match. It was the most points he had ever scored during a fortnight's play but it still left him almost 3000 points behind Lindrum who made five thousands and 23 breaks over 500. The match aggregate was 55 228 — a world record.

Lindrum travelled to Manchester for his next match with Willie Smith and set another record when he made ten breaks over the thousand (with a top of 2419) in thrashing Smith by 30 817 to 19 344. One of those ten breaks over the thousand was 1011 and it had been made by Lindrum in just thirty minutes. Lindrum returned to the Memorial Hall in London for a match with Clark McConachy who had been enjoying a very successful tour with wins over Davis, Smith and Newman. The match went to McConachy who recorded a most unexpected win by 24 224 to 23 387.

In a following match at the Memorial Hall the genial Tom Newman had his first dose of the Lindrum success formula. On the second day of play, 25 February, Lindrum made a break of 2053 which was his fiftieth break over the thousand for his tour. During the session in which he made the 2053 break Lindrum scored a total of 2664 points, a record aggregate for one session of play. For that session Lindrum had only one completed visit to the table which gave him a further record — a sessional average of 2664. It seemed as if Lindrum had an insatiable appetite for devouring records. He was certainly keeping the B.A. & C.C. busy with the issuing of a certificate for each record that he set. Lindrum went on to defeat Newman by 28 722 to 24 090. He had therefore beaten the three players who were commonly regarded as the best in England — Davis, Smith and Newman.

The rest day (Sunday) during this match was a cold, wet, uninviting day. It was a good day to be indoors. Lindrum was sitting in the lounge at the Strand Palace Hotel, thumbing through a magazine, when another guest struck up conversation with him. Lindrum learnt that the gentleman had been ordered by his doctor to have regular light exercise. He had decided that billiards was very suitable. Lindrum readily accepted an invitation to adjourn to the billiard room. It was agreed to play a match of 500–up with the loser paying for the table. Lindrum ran up his 500 points before his opponent had even scored. Lindrum suggested that they play another game. Came the reply: "No thank you. I only played that game for a bit of exercise."

Lindrum's visit to the United Kingdom was drawing to a close. The one major match he had yet to play was a seventh encounter with Willie Smith at the Memorial Hall, London. The tour had seen many remarkable performances by Lindrum with a spate of records flowing from his cue. The tour had also been marked by the controversy that had prevented Lindrum's participation in the Championship. Lindrum believed that this was the direct result of the dominating influence of trade interests which impinged on the running of the event. Some years later, after four visits to the United Kingdom, this first tour was described by Lindrum as the "most harassing season I have ever experienced". By the time Lindrum was due to play his last match with Smith he was inwardly at boiling point over the niggling problems that had confronted him throughout the tour. Of course the relationship between Smith and Lindrum had been strained since the outset and it had gradually worsened as the tour progressed. This state of affairs prompted Lindrum to recall the ruthless thrashing that Smith had handed out to his brother, Fred, on his trip to England in 1928. Smith had annihilated Fred by 19 178 points and virtually destroyed Fred's prospects of a successful tour. Walter Lindrum had arrived in England with some thoughts of settling the family debt but had decided it was wiser to forget the idea. With the decline in his relationship with Smith, Walter resolved to repay that family debt. Lindrum later recalled: "I opened the match in what I can only describe, with some feeling of shame, as an antagonistic and almost unsporting spirit." (Melbourne *Herald,* 28 December, 1934).

Lindrum played devastating billiards throughout the fortnight of the match. He released his frustration on Smith with a relentless barrage of breaks in the most unmerciful performance of his career. Lindrum had set out to defeat Smith by a greater margin than the 19 178 points by which Smith had beaten Fred Lindrum. This he achieved comfortably, being 21 285 points in front when time was called. He had avenged family honour in full. Lindrum scored 11 breaks over the thousand during the match and average 262 per visit to the table. These were both record performances. Lindrum's aggregate of 36 256 for the fortnight's play was a further record which he added to his already substantial collection. On one day, 19 March, Lindrum, with the aid of breaks of 1978 and 1824, totalled 4815 points for the two sessions of play — yet another record. During the evening session of the last day of the match, Lindrum was chasing one further record. His appetite for records was insatiable. And he was relentless in his determination to avenge both family honour and his 'mistreatment' by Willie Smith. One journalist tried to corner Lindrum after his dominating play on 19 March, by stating: "You are wasting no compassion on Smith." Lindrum effectively defused the issue with a reply worthy of the most expedient politician when he said, quietly, "Well, what can I do when they say I am slacking?" (The *Argus,* 19 March, 1930).

The record which Lindrum pursued during the last session of the match was to make two thousand breaks in that one session. Lindrum made a break of 1462 in the first part of the session. During his next visit to the table, which commenced at 9.30 with 30 minutes of the session remaining, he set out after the second thousand. To compile a thousand break in 30 minutes was certainly within the capabilities of Walter Lindrum (his fastest thousand break probably took 27 or 28 minutes) but to do so in the latter part of a session, when he could be expected to be slightly drained, both physically and mentally, was surely a daunting task. Certainly it was a task which no other billiards player in the world could perform, under even the most favourable conditions. To claim, though, that such a feat was beyond the capabilities of Walter Lindrum was another matter for he was different — oh so very different — from any other billiards player that the world had ever seen.

Lindrum set off after the second thousand in his deceptively effortless style. He scurried around the table, combining his top of the table game and his nursery cannons in his inimitable way. At one minute to ten Lindrum's break stood at 996. After glancing anxiously at the clock he attempted to carry the break to the 1000 mark. The balls were in line along the top cushion with the red near the pocket. With a most remarkable shot he achieved a seemingly impossible cannon, amid loud aplause. He was now on 998, but unfortunately the balls ran in line and once again Lindrum was faced with a shot which called for every atom of his skill. While Lindrum was considering the situation the referee turned to look at the clock, but Willie Smith whispered to him, "Let him get his 1000". It was a fine gesture by Smith, considering the severe hammering which he had taken from Lindrum from the very outset of the match. Or was it that Smith had resigned himself to the inevitability of it all? With the hands of the clock resting exactly on ten o'clock Lindrum played for a cannon off the white ball. The cue ball headed for the red ball only to pull up within a quarter of an inch of its objective. There were cries of "Bad Luck", followed by a sustained round of applause for Lindrum's dazzling display, both in the session and throughout the match.

Walter had timed his onslaught to perfection. Smith would have no opportunity for a return match in which he could redeem himself. Although Smith had suffered a humiliating defeat he had won the respect of Lindrum. Despite being faced with a hopeless task Smith had, with his characteristic Yorkshire determination, battled on until the last day of the match. He had averaged a respectable 109 per visit to the table — a figure which would have virtually guaranteed success in any match in the pre-Lindrum era. The match was the only occasion in Lindrum's career during which he was 'flat-out' for the entire journey. Lindrum made the following comments which gave an insight to how he approached his matches:

> Championship or exhibition billiard matches, unlike many outdoor sports, cannot be played on the 'flat-out' plan. The concentration necessary for big break making requires conservation of mental and nervous energy in a higher ratio than many outdoor games demand conservation of physical energy.
>
> Opportunity is another vital factor in the decision of a fortnight's match. It may happen that, for the first two or three days, he will be kept right out of the game by an unlucky run of the balls. If he has set himself to a plan of getting hundreds ahead of his opponent from the start, such a run would so affect his temperament as to ruin his chance when things did break his way. (Melbourne *Herald,* 28 December, 1934).

One young Australian, Jim Morgan, was especially pleased with Lindrum's devastating win over Smith. Morgan was stationed at Wolverhampton where he had been sent by his father's engineering firm to improve his knowledge of steam power-houses. The local inhabitants were extremely patriotic English citizens and they did not have a very high opinion of Australians. Morgan, who was the only Aussie living in the area at the time, was made patently aware of their attitude. He was frequently reminded of the whereabouts of the last Australian to visit the area — at the bottom of a mine shaft with his throat cut.

Morgan's hometown was Melbourne and it was there that he had seen Lindrum display his wonderful ability. When he learnt that Lindrum was coming to England to play Willie Smith, Morgan openly declared that his fellow-countryman would beat the Englishman. He went further and claimed that Lindrum would win one match by at least 20 000 points. Whether it was the impetuosity of youth or Morgan's own brand of loyalty that prompted him to make this claim is unknown. It certainly was a startling statement for Smith was regarded locally as the patron saint of billiards. The Wolverhampton people found it difficult enough to conceive of Smith being beaten. To suggest that he could be beaten by 20 000 points was a ludicrous idea which was only possible in the outer reaches of a fertile imagination. The Wolverhampton inhabitants rushed to defend their idol from the reckless claims of the young invader from Australia. Morgan was besieged with bets and although these were mostly for only sixpence or a shilling the total amount was quite a considerable figure.

It was thus a great relief to Morgan when Lindrum scored that final win by over 21 000 points. Morgan was able to live like a king on the proceeds of his wagers — at least for a few weeks. Lindrum's win did more than earn Jim Morgan a few extra pounds. Lindrum had earnt the respect of the Wolverhampton people for all Australians. Although these people were poorly educated, living hard with little money or pleasure they considered themselves to be civilised in comparison to the wild colonials. Lindrum's extraordinary deeds did much towards altering this opinion. Some months later a young Australian cricketer by the name of Don Bradman, who was also on his first tour of England, gave confirmation that Australians were people of some substance after all.

It seems incredible, in retrospect, just how blindly the English supported their own players against Walter Lindrum. The Wolverhampton people were not alone in believing that Smith was invincible. It was a popular view across the whole spectrum of English society. A major reason that Smith was regarded as a superior player to Lindrum was because the Australian was looked upon as another red-ball fiend, in the George Gray mould. The English knew that despite Gray's extraordinary scoring under certain conditions, he was not really a serious threat to the local players under championship conditions. Thus, once Lindrum had been labelled as another red-ball fiend, it was concluded that he would suffer a similar fate to George Gray. There was one person who never seriously entertained this notion, and that was Willie Smith himself. Smith was better-informed than most and knew that Lindrum was much more than merely a red-ball player. Smith had concluded that he could not beat Lindrum even before he had seen him in action. Smith's highest break of 2743 was made in November, 1928. During the progress of this break he met Jimmy Wilde and Jim Driscoll, two great boxers of the day, and Leo Oppenheimer, a professional backer, for tea. Wilde asked Smith how he was getting on.

"Not bad, I'm 2250 unfinished," replied Smith. Oppenheimer immediately made out a cheque for £500 and gave it to Smith to back himself against Lindrum.

"I put a match to it," said Smith. "They couldn't understand it. What was I doing? 'I'm saving your money,' I said. 'I've no chance.' I couldn't make them fast enough. I could make a hundred in four or five minutes but if he got nurseries on he could do it in less than half the time." (*The Story of Billiards and Snooker*, Clive Everton.)

During the progress of the final Smith match, Lindrum received an invitation to visit the Prime Minister, Ramsey MacDonald, at No. 10 Downing Street. On or about 20 March, Lindrum met the Prime Minister and was introduced to members of the world naval conference which was meeting in London at the time. When Lindrum told the Prime Minister that he often practised for eight or ten hours a day Mr MacDonald replied: "You would be an ideal person to sit on a naval conference with such patience."

It seems as if it was not only Walter Lindrum who was having a difference of opinion with Willie Smith. Following his last match with Lindrum at the Memorial Hall Smith travelled to Manchester to play Clark McConachy. During the Monday of the second week an incident occurred that resulted in Smith being granted a summons against McConachy for alleged assault and threats. In the ensuing court case Mr Butlin, appearing for Smith, declared that McConachy had complained that the balls had not been washed and that the cloth was not properly stretched. After tests of the cloth by the referee and manager it was ordered that play would continue. The next night McConachy declared that a ball was flawed and that he was playing under a disadvantage. The referee and manager examined the balls and decided the complaint was not justified. Smith agreed to go out and weigh the balls, and the players and the referee took a taxi-cab to the office of Burroughes and Watts for the purpose of weighing the balls. Mr Butlin claimed that McConachy was in a vile temper, and heated remarks were exchanged, after which McConachy assaulted Smith.

Mr Rycroft, McConachy's counsel, declared that McConachy simply leaned forward in the taxi and pushed Smith back on the seat. The words suggested as threats, if uttered, were only terms of abuse. Cross-examined, Smith said it was ridiculous to suggest that he was jealous of McConachy. He did not regard him as one of the coming players in a brilliant world. He was too old. McConachy tried to goad him into a quarrel at the outset of the match. The summons for assault was dismissed and McConachy was bound over until 10 April (when he was leaving England) on the assault charge. He was also ordered to pay costs. After the court case the magistrate's clerk, in a private conference with the billiardists, vainly appealed to them to shake hands.

Meanwhile Walter Lindrum was spending the final weeks of his tour in Ireland. At Belfast, against Tom Newman, he set an Irish record of 1364 only to set a new figure with a break of 1531 just three days later. Lindrum scored a very comfortable win over Newman in the one week match by 15 157 to 9783. The duo travelled to Dublin where Newman turned the tables with a 14 145 to 13 955 victory. At Dublin Lindrum met President Cosgrave who was a keen billiard enthusiast and visited many of the sessions.

Walter returned to London to prepare for his return to Australia. The tour could only be described as an outstanding success. Lindrum had broken virtually every imaginable record on the way to compiling an unprecedented 67 breaks in excess of the thousand — a figure that no one (probably not even Lindrum) had envisaged when Lindrum had arrived in England just six months before. Walter had won an enormous following among the English public and was touched by their generous appreciation of his play. Lindrum was very disappointed with the financial result of the tour. He had grossed £2843 for the tour — £2443 from Burroughes and Watts, £100 from the Composition Ball Co. for his record break of 3262, £300 for the Ireland matches and the earlier match at Sheffield. That figure did not include any payments for newspaper articles or any fee that Lindrum might have been paid for appearing in a short, newsreel film. These two sources would have added a very modest amount to the tour's income.

Lindrum believed that mismanagement had been the major reason he had not earnt considerably more on the tour. He could not understand why Smith had persisted with playing matches in small halls in the provinces. Lindrum claimed that when Smith had visited Australia he had misled him about the amount of money that he was likely to earn in England. On his arrival in Australia Smith had said:

> There is a £2000 guarantee if he does (go to England). But I would advise him not to worry about the guarantee. He could make more taking a percentage of the gate receipts. His matches would draw big crowds.
>
> (The *Referee*, 29 April, 1929)

At that time Smith had not met Lindrum, let alone seen him play billiards. He had no real concept of just how good Lindrum really was. Lindrum, of course, did earn more than £2000 but only by performing a seemingly endless sequence of incredible feats. The sum of £2843 might sound like a veritable fortune for the times. However, there were many expenses to meet on such a long and intensive tour. It is difficult from this distance in time to judge the relative merits of Lindrum's complaints. It does seem reasonable to suggest that Lindrum's earnings on his first English tour were not commensurate with the reputation he now enjoyed of being the hottest piece of billiard property that had ever walked the earth.

At the end of his first English tour Lindrum was guest of honour at a dinner to commemorate his marvellous performances on the tour. Amongst the identities who attended the dinner were the Earl of Lonsdale (who acted as chairman), Jack Hobbs (still regarded by many as the greatest of all English batsmen) and Steve Donoghue (who rode to victory in 6 English Derbies). During his tour Lindrum had been nicknamed "Pokerface" and "Mille" — French for thousand.

Lindrum bade farewell to England on April 10, 1930, carrying a total of 17 official certificates from the B.A. & C.C. for record performances. Lindrum was accompanied by Mr and Mrs Clark McConachy and Horace Morell, his manager. Those who farewelled the group included Joe Davis, Newman, Falkiner, Inman, Willie Leigh and John Bissett (chairman of the B.A. & C.C.). Despite his swag of world record certificates Lindrum had been denied the title of World Champion following the stalemate between the trade and the Control Council. Joe Davis retained the world title by defeating Tom Newman by 20 918 to 20 117. Davis, though, was regarded by many as only caretaker of the championship trophy which would surely go to Lindrum when he was able to enter for the title.

8 Commanding Performance

Lindrum has been called the 'Bradman of Billiards'. He was far more
than that, the Bradman-Trumper-Grace-Hobbs combined.
Great Moments in Australian Sport, by R. S. Whitington

After returning to Australia, and enjoying a respite from the intense activity
of his first English tour, Walter Lindrum again set sail for the Old Dart in
early August 1930. He was now free from the shackles of the Burroughes
and Watts contract which had been the source of so much disappointment on
his first tour. Instead Lindrum would play on his second tour under contract
to the firm of Reddaway & Co. of Pendleton, Lancashire. Lindrum, along
with Davis, Newman and McConachy, had accepted the lucrative terms
offered by Reddaways to play for the season on the firm's "Janus" cloth.
Reddaways was making every effort to establish the Janus cloth, made
entirely of cotton, as a suitable alternative to the traditional woollen cloth.
There could be no better advertisement than to have the leading
professionals playing on tables fitted with the Janus cloth. A special event
was organised and, known as the International Tourney, it was to be
managed and promoted by Bill Camkin, a livewire billiard trader from
Birmingham.

Lindrum commenced the English season with a match in London against
Claude Falkiner. The game was intended to serve as a warm-up for Lindrum,
allowing him to find his touch after the sea trip and to adjust his game to the
napless cloth. Lindrum opened the match at Thurston's in some discomfort.
He had arrived in London with three teeth missing as the result of a painful
injury suffered on a night train. Walter's gramophone (which was a regular
part of his luggage) had slipped from an overhead luggage rack. It was
immediately followed by a suitcase, which struck him in the face and
dislodged three of his teeth. Walter managed to locate a London dentist who
carried out the necessary repairs over the weekend in order that he could
commence the match on schedule. The injury did not prevent Lindrum
scoring a very comfortable win by 28 799 to 19 523 after conceding Falkiner
8000 start.

During this match, on 19 September, Walter Lindrum was visited at
Thurston's by Don Bradman. The young batsman, himself a keen billiards
player, was in the last days of his first tour of the United Kingdom. It had
been an overwhelmingly successful tour for Bradman and he had established
strong claims to the title of the most prolific batsman of all time. There are
some interesting parallels and comparisons which can be made between
Lindrum and Bradman. First, both emerged as superstars on the sporting
horizon during their first visits to England. Lindrum reached that status with
his record break of 3262, made during 6–7 December, 1929. Bradman had
been establishing records from virtually his first match in England. Arguably

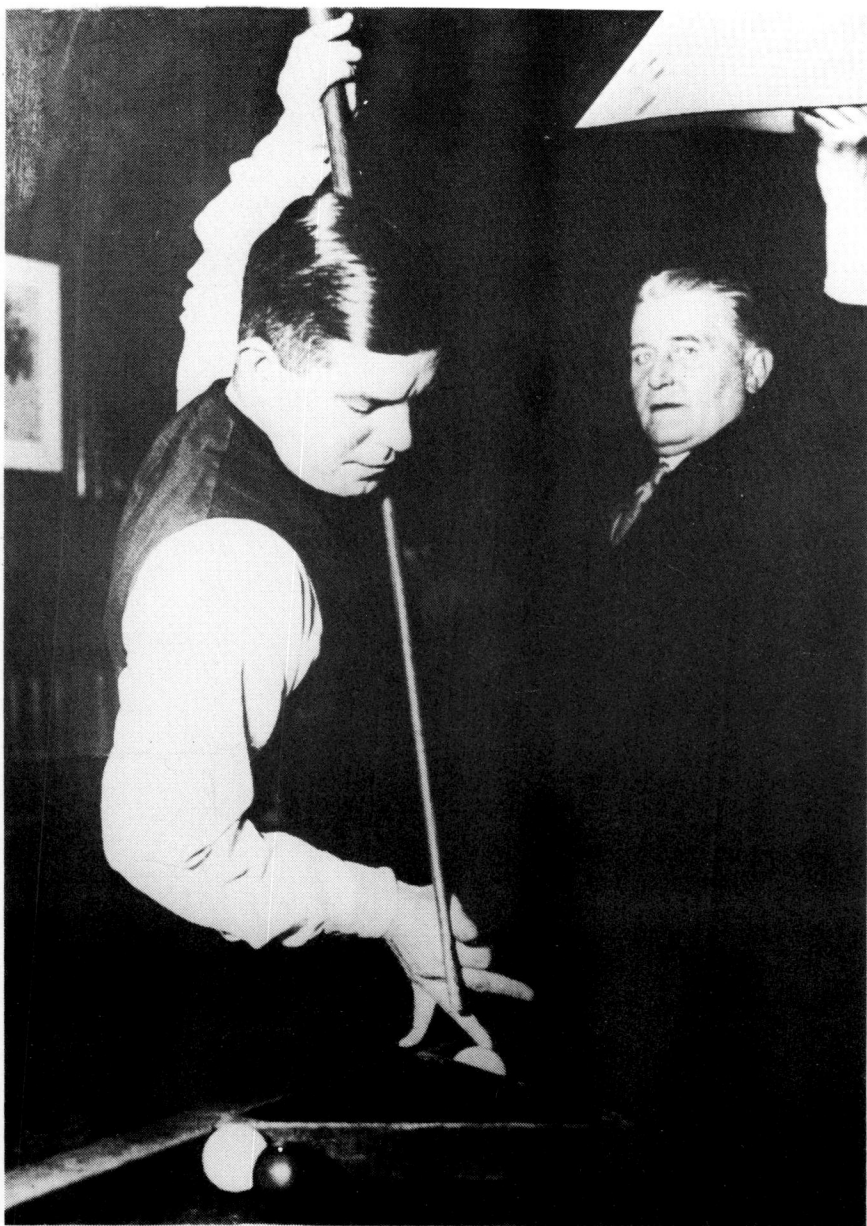

Playing a masse stroke around the triangle to score a cannon. (Dolly Lindrum)

The cherished photo of Walter's first wife, Rosie, who died at an early age. Walter took the photo everywhere he went during the first few years after her death. (Dolly Lindrum)

Walter Lindrum in action during his first visit to England, 1929–30.
(Norman Clare)

Walter Lindrum with England's Prime Minister, Ramsey MacDonald, in 1930. (John Fairfax & Sons Ltd)

he set the seal on his greatness with his record innings of 334, made on 11–12 July, 1930, in the Third Test at Headingley, Leeds. It is remarkable that these two Australian champions, regarded by many as the most outstanding of all time in their respective fields, should establish themselves within such a brief interval. It is interesting to note that this dual rise to fame occurred within the scenario of the Depression, a fact which may be more than just coincidence. It will never be known what the exact motivations were that led to the rise to fame of Bradman and Lindrum. Of course, both were heavily endowed with the will to win, the determination to succeed — what champions have not been? But that does not explain why Lindrum and Bradman emerged when they did, during the Depression. In such times sporting success can take on an extra dimension. It can become a means by which a sporting champion can gain immunity from the awful uncertainty and hardship of the times. Maybe it was a lurking knowledge of the bleak economic conditions which, consciously or unconsciously, spurred Bradman and Lindrum on to greater and greater heights. One of the greats of Australian cycling, Hubert Opperman, also reached the pinnacle of his career in the Depression when he won the 1931 Paris–Brest–Paris race.

Boxing was one sport that provided a means of survival for some of the less-gifted victims of the Depression. Amateurs, who in times of plenty would never have contemplated turning pro, stepped into the ring for the price of a feed. The Depression had found Australia rich in boxing talent, especially the little men. There were gifted glovemen such as Syd Godfrey, Bert Spargo, Bert McCarthy, Billy Grime, Harry Stone, Jamito and Bert Restuccia. Shortage of work and money kept many coming back when they were no longer good boxers but merely battlers. Inevitably it led to tragedy. A typical case was poor Bert McCarthy, who came out of retirement, overweight and in poor condition, to meet a young, hard-hitting Aboriginal named Alby Roberts. The bout would never have been permitted if there had been proper medical supervision. But times were tough and for a meagre purse McCarthy climbed into the ring because he wanted food for his family. McCarthy died for his family — killed by the Depression.

How fortunate were those sporting champions who could avoid the ravages and desperation of the Depression as typified by Bert McCarthy. Contrary to what might be expected, attendances at sporting fixtures during the period increased rather than decreased. Despite the acute shortages of money the public flocked in vast numbers to see their sporting champions. These heroes offered a means of escape, at least for a few hours, from the overwhelming problems that faced so many at the start of each and every day. Bradman, Lindrum and Opperman represented success stories in times when success in other fields of human endeavour was far from being the norm. It must have been reassuring to know that each time Bradman went in to bat he was almost certain to score at least fifty runs. Or that Lindrum would beat his opponent out of sight. These idols were the symbol of hope, the thread of positiveness which helped many to battle on through the Depression and eventually rebuild the tattered fragments of their lives. It is little wonder that the sporting heroes of the Depression were so lionised that they became legends in their own lifetimes. Who could forget the immortal Phar Lap, the 'Red Terror' who won 37 of his 51 starts including the 1930

Melbourne Cup, and who galloped his way into the hearts of hundreds of thousands of Australians. It is remarkable indeed that several of our greatest sporting heroes should emerge during those years.

A further interesting comparison can be made between Lindrum and Bradman in regards to style. Neither could be described as perfect stylists. Lindrum had certain idiosyncrasies of style, which had developed in his childhood and which were frowned on by some purists. Likewise Bradman was subject to criticism of his technique which, among other things, suggested that a cross-bat action was apparent in the execution of some strokes. In his biography of Bradman in 1949, the celebrated cricket writer, R. C. Robertson-Glasgow said of Bradman: "About his batting there was no style for style's sake . . . His aim was the making of runs, and he made them in staggering and ceaseless profusion."

Bradman himself said to the *London Star* in 1930: "Style, as style, I have never studied; my batting is dictated by the needs of the moment." The deeds of Lindrum and Bradman demonstrated that genius is not subject to any laws. Their achievements are explicit reprimands for those experts who find it necessary to define success in terms of mechanical correctness.

It was inevitable that sporting scribes would draw comparisons between Lindrum and Bradman. R. C. Robertson-Glasgow said, of Bradman: "Like his fellow-countryman Walter Lindrum in billiards, he sought and achieved a numerical standard not previously contemplated". Neville Cardus, in his classic essay on Bradman in 1930 wrote: "And now that a Bradman has come to us, capable of 300 runs in a single day of a Test match, some of us are calling him a Lindrum of cricket!" The reference was not meant to be a complimentary one. Cardus was suggesting that Bradman might put an end to the glorious uncertainty of cricket in the same way as Lindrum had done in billiards. Cardus continued: "It is a hard world to please! Perhaps Bradman, by making a 'duck' in the Manchester Test match, will oblige those of his critics who believe that there should always be some strangeness, something unexpected, mingled with art and beauty."

Both Bradman and Lindrum were the cause of later moves to restore balance to their respective games. The rules of billiards were to be changed with the introduction of the baulk-line rule which was designed to restrict long runs of nursery cannons. It was very difficult for the rules of cricket to be altered to restrict Bradman. However, it was the success of Bradman in England in 1930 that prompted the development by English players of a new cricket strategy which became known as 'bodyline' bowling. It was during the English tour of Australia in 1932–33, under the captaincy of D. R. Jardine, that bodyline became an effective but highly controversial weapon. There was also controversy with the baulk-line rule in billiards although certainly not in such an acrimonious and divisive way as was the case with bodyline. It suffices to say, at present, that it was the respective genius of Lindrum and Bradman which pre-empted baulk-line and bodyline and so changed the history of the two games.

Those who have an interest in astrology may find some link between the birth dates of Lindrum (29 August 1898) and Bradman (27 August, 1908). It is sufficient to record these dates and leave it to the astrologers to decide if this is more than mere coincidence. A comparison between the full names of each:

Walter Albert Lindrum and Donald George Bradman; reveals that there are six letters in the first name of each, six letters in the second names and seven letters in the surnames. Totally superfluous but intriguing nonetheless. When Don Bradman visited Walter Lindrum at Thurston's an enterprising photographer took the only photos of the two that are in existence. That occasion was one of only a few times that Lindrum and Bradman met each other. This is contrary to what some newspaper reports have suggested, with one paper going so far as to invent an anecdote which is based on a visit by Lindrum to the home of Sir Donald. Lindrum, in fact, never visited Bradman's home and that anecdote is entirely without foundation.

The first matches in the International Tourney commenced on 29 September. It was to prove the greatest billiard tournament ever staged. The *News of the World* added to the prestige of the event by donating a magnificent gold cup valued at £500. Bill Camkin, in his role as promoter and manager, made a bold decision that contributed to the success of the Tourney. He was confident that the public wanted to support the game if "big break" players were matched in spacious halls. In a daring move, typical of his flair and foresight, Camkin organised for matches to be played in the provincial cities of Liverpool, Cardiff, Leicester, Bradford, Southampton and Plymouth. By hiring large halls and installing as many seats as possible the admission prices were kept at a relatively low level. The public responded by flocking to the matches and filling the halls to overflowing.

One of the problems that confronted Camkin was the handicaps for the event. After Lindrum's performances on his first tour the critics had called for him to concede start to his opponents. All sorts of handicaps had been suggested, freakish and otherwise. The situation was unique in that although Joe Davis was champion of the world it was obvious that he could not beat Lindrum off the stick. It was a ticklish situation and one which Camkin had to handle with great care. After much deliberation Camkin called the 'Big Four' together and announced his decision. Davis, Newman and McConachy were each to receive 7000 start from Lindrum. Davis, being a realist and a sportsman agreed to the start. Clark McConachy, though, was an unexpected stumbling block. At first he refused to accept any start, claiming with his usual unbounded confidence that he was too good a player to receive start from anyone. Finally Camkin convinced the New Zealander that if one player accepted the handicap then all the players would have to. McConachy agreed but declared that he was a certainty to take out first prize.

The heats of the Tourney were scheduled to last twelve weeks, with each player meeting the other three players on two occasions — once at Thurston's Hall and once at a provincial centre. The matches at the provincial centres were refereed by Arthur Goundrill, the one-armed player who had been dubbed 'Goundrill the Scoundrel' because of his devilish sense of humour. The matches at Thurston's were in the charge of Charlie Chambers who, despite an impediment in his speech, had established himself as the doyen of referees. Chambers was a quiet, solitary character who led a lonely life but as a referee he handled the big matches with absolute authority and impartiality that earnt him the respect of all players. The way in which he counted the nursery cannons, kept a mental note of losing and winning hazards and the total break — sometimes running into four figures — all done with care and precision, aroused the admiration of the spectators. His movement round the hallowed precincts of the Leicester Square Hall were so beautifully timed to the rhythm of the players that they hardly knew he was there.

When the first two rounds of heats were completed Davis was holding down first position, following two wins over McConachy. Second place was shared by Lindrum and Newman with each player having recorded one win. The more interesting clash of the third round appeared to be the Davis-Lindrum encounter. If Davis could record a win (his third in succession) he would be in a very strong position to take out the event. A loss for Lindrum would virtually put him out of contention. The backmarker realised the importance of the match and played throughout at a consistently high standard to win comfortably by 29 276 to 24 775. Lindrum had made eight thousands for the match, including a break of 2063 — his first double thousand for the season. When Davis' handicap of 7000 points had been deducted from the score the world champion had in fact been beaten by 11 501.

In the fifth round of heats Davis staged a major reversal of form to beat Lindrum by 24 613 to 23 867. The win was the fourth for Davis and he was again a clear leader in the tournament. Lindrum and Newman had each recorded three wins while McConachy had yet to win a match. Thus if Davis could win his sixth and final match (against Newman at Plymouth) he would take out first place. In their first encounter Davis had disposed of Newman easily by 4 590 points. He was therefore a short-priced favourite to repeat that win and carry off the beautiful gold cup. Newman was not deterred by the odds and, in a real cliff-hanger, which saw the lead change several times in the last day, he scraped home by 26 859 to 26 402. This left Lindrum the chance to level up with Newman and Davis who were tied on four wins each. Lindrum's last match, at Thurston's with McConachy, was played concurrently with the Newman-Davis encounter. The first Lindrum-McConachy match, played in Southampton saw the Australian score an enormous win by 29 554 to 16 867. In the process Lindrum made thousand breaks in five consecutive sessions. It was another world record inasmuch as no player had ever done it before. Therefore it was expected that Lindrum would have little difficulty in accounting for McConachy who had recorded five straight losses. McConachy, though, looked likely to prove the experts wrong, for at the halfway point of the match he was in front by 6892 points. The use of intensive safety play had effectively shut Lindrum out of the match. The form of McConachy during the tournament had been very disappointing and it was puzzling why he should now play such a tough game against Lindrum when he himself had no chance of winning the event. It was a matter of regaining lost prestige for the big New Zealander. Lindrum's form in the first week had not been up to his usual standard although there was some suggestion that his health was partly to blame. (Perhaps it was one of the bouts of lumbago which troubled him from time to time.) As the second week opened Lindrum knew that if he did not quickly make inroads into McConachy's lead he would be faced with a hopeless task. On the Monday he shaved 1732 off the lead but that still left him 5160 in arrears. When the afternoon session on Tuesday opened Lindrum resumed play with an infant run of three on the board. Calling on every atom of determination he forced himself to concentrate in an effort to play himself into form. The points began to build up and at the end of the 105-minute session, Lindrum had 2378 unfinished to his name. In the interval before the evening session Lindrum was placed under pressure by Bill Camkin who was anxious for the world record to be broken. Camkin had been appointed distributor for the Janus cloth in England and there could be no better advertisement than a record break on the napless cloth. Camkin wired Lindrum to let him know that he was following the match on the Thurston's match-room phone. For this reason and others Lindrum had lost his concentration when he resumed play. He was soon in trouble and had to play with great deliberation to keep the break going. His scoring rate dropped appreciably to a level which was palpably slow — for Lindrum at least. He plugged on and finally passed his previous record break of 3262. The strain of the effort eased and some of Lindrum's fluency began to return. The break eventually ended at 3905 after he had potted the white and left a double baulk. He had been at the table for three hours and five minutes — the longest break that he was to make in his career. It was not a champagne Lindrum break for there had been several dogged patches of play which were uncharacteristically shaky. It was, though, to be regarded by Lindrum as the best break of his career, considering the vital stage at which it was made. For the rest of the match Walter played like a true master and went on to win by 27 907 to 21 431. His average for the second week was an incredible 313.

The next morning when being interviewed about the break Lindrum said: "I seemed to have a voice ringing in my ears all night, saying, 'The break is 3905'. I now understand the sentiments of the soldier in Kipling's poem who complained of 'boots, boots, boots'." (The *Argus,* 16 December 1930.)

The win by Lindrum had thus resulted in a three-way tie for first place. No one could have hoped for a more exciting ending. A play-off would be necessary. Davis and Newman were to meet, with the winner to play Lindrum in the final. Apparently Davis must have folded under the pressure for Newman had a comfortable win by 30 663 to 25 515. There was no shortage of pressure on the players, with considerable sums being wagered around the clubs.

The Final, to be played at Thurston's, started on February 1. Tom Newman was very confident about his prospects. He declared: "Every circumstance favours the greatest battle in the history of the game. I am firmly convinced that I am too close on Lindrum's heels for him to give me 7,000 in a fortnight in the 'pit'." *(News of the World,* 1 February 1931.)

Newman was justified in making such a claim. He was in the best form of his career. He had beaten Joe Davis, the world champion, twice in three encounters during this tourney. In a heat against McConachy he had made seven breaks over the thousand. Lindrum was in for a tough match. No one was more aware of this fact than Lindrum himself. He was very apprehensive on his chances. He had conceded 42 000 points start in the heats and the strain of catching up the handicap had taken a toll of his energy. What concerned Walter more was that he had been away from London for a month playing matches with McConachy (at Hull) and Davis (at Edinburgh). He was worried that it would take him a few days to adjust to the different playing conditions at Thurston's. Contrarily, Newman had played for a month solid at the Hall and would thus know the table backwards. Lindrum was aware that

Newman would strike form immediately. He hoped that he could at least hold Newman for the first few days until he found his own form.

Thurston's was bulging at the seams for the opening of the match and its Tom Thumb dimensions were stretched throughout the fortnight of the match. Admission charges had been greatly increased but scores of spectators were still turned away from each session. Newman commenced play in even better form than Lindrum had expected and began to increase his lead beyond the 7000 points handicap. Lindrum was struggling to find form and had to watch, almost helplessly, as Newman stretched his lead beyond 8000 points and then past the 9000 mark. After the seventh session Newman's lead was 9177. He was making a mockery of the handicaps. Lindrum's form in the first few days brought the following comment from the *News of the World*, per Tom Newman:

> About the only weak spot in his armour is that he is curiously responsive to his environment. No matter how often he may have played in a hall, he always 'feels strange' there for the first few days. I suppose we all do to an extent, but Lindrum seems to feel this sort of influence rather more than others. (8 February 1931.)

Lindrum walked his bedroom floor on the Thursday night and wondered if it was somehow possible to get back into the match. A photo of his beloved wife, Rosie, served as a source of inspiration for Walter. He resolved to lift his game. As he entered Thurston's for the fifth day of play, Lindrum overheard a patron placing a hefty wager on a Newman win. Lindrum ground his teeth and became more determined. He declared to Bill Camkin:

"I will show the patrons billiards they have never seen before!"

"They must break for you soon", sympathised Camkin.

"I'll make them break or bust!" added Lindrum, recklessly.

The scope of wagering on the Gold Cup Tourney can be gauged from the fact that Lindrum was approached prior to the final and offered a substantial sum not to try. Those responsible for the offer were not in any way associated with any of the players. Lindrum bluntly refused the offer.

> Although I refused to have anything to do with that offer, there were times before and during the final when I wondered whether I had been a little hasty in telling the people who had made the offer to go somewhere. It seemed, at times, that as I appeared to be right out of the running I could have accepted the offer without the least thought of deception of the public or the interests offering the bribe. (Melbourne *Herald*, 18 December 1934.)

Lindrum went to the table intent on whittling away Newman's enormous lead. He was not quite sure how he was going to do it. He just knew that he had to peg Newman back and somehow he was going to do it! After the tenth session Newman's advantage was back to 7429. His average for the first five days was 204 — far greater than what was expected from a player in receipt of 7000 start. The sixth day saw the Lindrum fightback gain momentum. He produced a break of 2835. His next visit added a further 451 to his score. He finished the day, still in play, with 1794 on the board. At the halfway point Newman was leading by 3780. Lindrum resumed on the second Monday but added only two points to his break, which thus ended at 1796. At his next visit

Lindrum continued the onslaught with a break of 2583. In four successive visits he had amassed 7665 points at an average of 1916 per visit. What was more remarkable about Lindrum's play was that he had made two breaks over 2000 within four visits to the table. If there ever was an achievement that underlined the degree of Lindrum's superiority over his nearest rivals, then this was surely it. Under the existing rules Joe Davis made two breaks in his lifetime over the two thousand mark: 2052 in 1930 and 2002 in 1935. Similarly, Willie Smith passed the double-thousand mark twice with 2743 in 1928 and 2030 in Australia in 1929. Both Newman and McConachy failed to record a two-thousand break. Walter Lindrum had done, in the space of four visits to the table, what two of his nearest rivals took a lifetime to achieve. What is just as important, Lindrum made those two breaks when he was under extreme pressure and facing defeat.

Lindrum's incredible scoring brought him back into the betting with a vengeance. At the end of fifteen sessions it looked as if Lindrum had the measure of Newman, whose lead was only 1590. Lindrum still had his reservations. His heavy scoring had drained him of his reserves of energy and he went as 'flat as a pancake'. Newman went to the table and soon dashed Lindrum's hopes with some strong play. After sixteen sessions the Englishman's lead was back up to 2439. The Thursday afternoon session, the nineteenth of the match, saw Lindrum reduce the leeway. Newman, in attempting to get out of a double-baulk, had put his ball in a baulk pocket. Lindrum was left with the red ball and after playing 25 hazards he demanded his rights under a newly-framed rule which stated:

> Should the non-striker's ball be off the table, as a result of the non-striker's last stroke, such ball shall be spotted after the 25th hazard, on the middle spot of the 'D'; or if that is occupied on the right-hand spot of the 'D'.

Lindrum scored a cannon with his next stroke and went on to make a break of 1201. The break kept his hopes alive and at the end of the nineteenth session he trailed by 1647 points. The twentieth session, though, saw Newman in complete command again as he scored 1613 points to Lindrum's 286 points. With only four sessions remaining Newman's lead was 2974 — surely an unassailable margin. The situation was desperate, for if Lindrum did not quickly make heavy inroads on Newman's lead he would be beaten by time. The grimly determined Lindrum staged a last-ditch effort in the twenty-first session. He scored a 500 break in seventeen minutes and a 1484 break to dominate play and tally 2110 to 107 for the session. He now trailed Newman by only 971. In the twenty-second session Lindrum finally caught Newman with the scores at 23 355, amid the greatest ovation that he ever received. At the end of the session Lindrum was 248 points in front but the match was still wide open.

The final drama of the match took place that night. Several months earlier Lindrum and Newman had agreed to give the journalists of London an exhibition in their club on a certain night in February. That night just happened to be the Friday night on the eve of the conclusion of the International Tourney. Newman and Lindrum were locked in the most momentous battle of their careers and had completely forgotten their long-standing engagement. However, when they were reminded of it they duly obliged the pressmen and finally retired to bed at 5.30 a.m. The two players stayed in bed until it was almost time to leave for Thurston's. As they journeyed to Thurston's on that momentous day both players knew that a good break in the session would virtually seal the match. That break came the way of Lindrum who scored 1163. As the players went to the table for the final session Newman said:

"The Cup looks like yours, Wally."

"You never know", answered Lindrum.

As a form of insurance Lindrum agreed to Newman's offer of a bet of £200 to £10 against him losing. The final session produced an anticlimactic ending to the greatest billiard event ever staged. The two players were mentally exhausted from the tremendous strain of the match and both played like drunken sailors. The final scores were: Lindrum 25 807, Newman (received 7000) 24 436. After his astonishing victory Lindrum gave a speech of acknowledgement:

> Ladies and gentlemen, the great reception and the general kindnesses I have received have helped me to play in my very best form. Without the genial atmosphere and friendly conditions I should not have been able to play as I have done this week. I feel delighted that I have won the game, but believe me, I should have been just as delighted had Tom Newman won. At one time during the match I would not have taken a thousand to one about winning. Tom Newman is a fine sportsman, and his wonderfully sporting spirit throughout the game helped me immensely. I am afraid we played faultily tonight, but perhaps you can understand that this was due to the strain we have been passing through during the past fortnight. All Australia will be thrilled when they see the Gold Cup, and I, personally look forward to coming back to play before such marvellous people as I have found in this country. (The *Billiard Player,* 31 March 1931.)

The outstanding success of the International Tourney had been of great benefit to the overall image of billiards, according to one report:

> The personality and the prowess of the contestants for the Gold Cup . . . has put billiards in England on entirely new plane. Queues begin to form early in the evening and although the prices have been almost doubled, hundreds of people failed to obtain admittance. In the evening sessions the majority of the men attend in evening dress and there is always a large sprinkling of fashionably-attired women. Lindrum might be a popular matinee idol judging by the crowds that wait at the exit doors just to catch a glimpse of him. (The *Argus,* 12 February 1931.)

The game of billiards was to get the ultimate seal of the approval a few days later when Walter Lindrum was summoned to give a special performance for King George V and Queen Mary at Buckingham Palace. Bill Camkin received a message from Sir Derek Keppel, the Private Secretary of the King and went to Buckingham Palace where he was told that the King would like Lindrum to appear at the Palace. The Secretary requested that the command performance be kept secret for several reasons, one of which was the indifferent state of the King's health.

Camkin kept the news from Lindrum for a few days and it was over a cup of coffee at 2 a.m. that Walter learnt that he was to appear at the Palace on 19 February 1931. Lindrum was so elated that he did not sleep that night.

Lindrum was at Wolverhampton where he was playing a match with Clark McConachy. He rang his tailor in London and ordered a new suit for his big occasion. A billiard room some thirty kilometres out of Wolverhampton was secured for Lindrum to practise his trick shots in complete privacy. He wanted to have each trick shot perfect for the Palace was no place to bungle shots.

On the morning of 19 February, Lindrum and Camkin discreetly left for London. In order to avoid arousing any suspicion, the match with McConachy was scheduled to continue as usual in the afternoon. No one was let in on the secret, not even McConachy or the referee, Arthur Goundrill. When Lindrum arrived in London he taxied to his tailors for a final fitting of his new suit. At 2.50 p.m. he caught a taxi to the Palace. When the driver pulled up near the gates Lindrum told him to drive on in.

"Not on your bloomin' life!" declared the driver.

Lindrum and Camkin tried to convince the driver that they had an appointment with the King but the driver simply gave them an incredulous look and demanded his fare. Eventually a detective came forward and assured the driver that it was all right to enter the grounds. The driver straightened visibly and entered proudly through the gates. When the taxi stopped in front of the Palace steps Lindrum moved to open the door. As quick as a flash the driver was out of the cab, saying:

"I'll get it, m'lord."

"And that", Lindrum later mused, "was how I was elevated to the peerage in two seconds flat."

Meanwhile, back at Wolverhampton a capacity house had gathered for the afternoon session of the Lindrum–McConachy match. The referee, Arthur Goundrill, phoned Lindrum's hotel but could not locate him. Goundrill was a one-armed player who had the honour of being the only other billiardist to perform for royalty. Walter Lindrum was giving little thought to the predicament he had left behind at Wolverhampton. He was more concerned with the tense feeling that had descended on him since his arrival in London. He was simply overwhelmed by the situation. He was worried that if he did not overcome the tension he would perform poorly for Their Majesties.

Sir Derek Keppel ushered Lindrum and Camkin into the Billiard Room which was, appropriately, palatial. The panelled walls matched the mahogany table. The cloth was olive green with matching pocket nets. It was a craftsmen's masterpiece. The chandelier was of ornate bronze.

"That'll do me", said Lindrum, in good Australian.

"Is it not a beautiful table!" commented Camkin in very good English.

At precisely 3.00 p.m. the King and Queen came down the stairway, arm in arm. Lindrum stood nervously as they approached. After shaking hands the King immediately put Lindrum at ease by discussing the progress of the International Tourney.

"I was really excited towards the close of the last game in London. It was the first thing I looked for in the newspapers. I really thought you were going to be beaten."

The King greatly surprised Lindrum by referring to his averages and aggregate scores throughout the tournament, which were letter-perfect. The

King then invited Walter to commence his exhibition. Lindrum took out his cue. The King observed:

"So you have an Alcock cue? How interesting! I still have an Alcock cue presented to me by the Melbourne firm years ago. Here it is."

The King handed the cue to Lindrum. Lindrum then showed Their Majesties the various aspects of play. While demonstrating his close cannons Lindrum played the balls along the top cushion and down the left-hand side until he reached the centre pocket. This pocket had often proved a stumbling block in his runs of close cannons but on this occasion Lindrum negotiated the balls past it without losing position. He was interrupted by the hearty laughter of the King, who said:

"Well done sir, I've heard that you were often unable to pass the centre pocket."

Lindrum went on to his range of trick shots which appealed greatly to the Queen who asked for one shot to be repeated three times. When Lindrum had exhausted his repertoire of shots, the King said to him:

"I must congratulate you. That's really wonderful." (The *Argus*, 21 February, 1931.)

The King put his hand in his pocket, took out a small parcel and presented it to Lindrum. In his excitement Walter immediately opened the parcel to uncover a beautiful pair of gold and enamel cuff links, bearing the G.R. monogram. The King and Queen then left the room. The performance had also been witnessed by two ladies-in-waiting and Lords Abermarle and Fitzmaurice.

The King made a brief and apparently hurried entry in his diary:

> Thursday Feb 19th Buckingham Palace. Fine. Have a slight cold so didn't go out. In afternoon Lindrum an Australian aged 39, the finest billiard player in the world gave us an exhibition here in the billiard room, he is a wonderful player. Usual work.

(Reproduced by Gracious Permission of Her Majesty Queen Elizabeth II)

Lindrum made a hurried journey in a taxi to Paddington station to catch a train to Birmingham in order to resume his match at Wolverhampton with McConachy. When the spectators at the match learnt of the command performance they gave Lindrum a rousing reception. He was excused for his absence from the afternoon session for it was understood by all that when the King commands, the subject must obey. Lindrum played very poor billiards in the session. He was still excited and had lost touch completely. Lindrum always regarded the day as the highlight of his life and he proudly wore the gold cuff-links on numerous occasions. Lindrum was inundated with offers from the newspapers for the exclusive rights to the story on his Buckingham Palace visit. He refused to commercialise his honour and all the papers were given equal access to the story.

Following the outstanding success of the International Tourney it was perhaps appropriate that the B.A. & C.C. announced that it would not be staging the Championship in 1931. If the Championship had been held it would have been an anticlimax in the wake of the fervour and enthusiasm that had been aroused by the International Tourney. Lindrum's incredible deeds in that event would have made him a prohibitive favourite for the Championship. The reason for the cancellation of the Championship was, once again, due to trade involvement. Lindrum, Davis, Newman and McConachy were all under contract to Reddaway & Co. and the firm wanted some say in the running of the Championship. Tom Newman, on one of the rare occasions that he opposed the controlling body, made the following observations on the situation:

> There is a principle involved which is at the root of all difference; that the control of billiards shall be absolutely in the hands of amateurs of the standing of those now on the council of the controlling body. But while this is true beyond argument, it must not be forgotten that the Council is in a delicate position as regards its relation to trade interests and the incomes of professional players. Through no fault of its own it has no venue for match play — it is an M.C.C. without Lord's. Consequently, it is compelled to arrange with the trade for a hall, table and everything else connected with the business side of its championships. This is far from an ideal position, but there is less chance of change today than ever on account of prohibitive site values alone. This places the Control Council in the market for trade support, and with all due deference, I venture to suggest that the importance of this factor has not been fully realised by the governing body.
>
> It is useless to pretend that the first of these requests is free from trade interests, but the cardinal point is that the nature of things compels the governing body to join forces with trade interests in the promotion of its championships, and it therefore follows that, provided playing conditions allow professionals to display their skill to advantage, it is injudicious to interfere with any trade interest which is willing to face the serious financial risk of Championship promotion.
>
> Allowance was made for this when the B.A. & C.C. was first formed. The original constitution provided for a trade advisory committee as part of its permanent organisation, and it is a pity that this powerful and useful auxiliary has been allowed to die out. One thing is certain, the present machinery will have to be overhauled to allow for the fact that the trade cannot be treated as it has been during the long period of continual squabbling over the Championships.
>
> (*News of the World*, 11 January, 1931)

In contrast to its implacable stand when faced with an almost identical situation in the previous season, the B.A. & C.C. was now prepared to make some concessions. The controlling body offered to allow half the championship matches to be played on the Janus cloth. This was not a satisfactory compromise for there were considerable differences between playing on cotton cloths and woollen cloths. The negotiations reached a stalemate and the Control Council was left with only one entry for the Championship, none other than Willie Smith. Clark McConachy, despite his apparent obligations to Reddaways, had not joined with Lindrum, Davis and Newman in announcing that he would not compete for the Championship.

Mac kept his options open until the the last minute before deciding against entering the event. Smith was taking no chances, and forgetting his long-standing feud with the Control Council, he entered for the Championship to prevent the title going to the Antipodes by default. Nominations were extended for three weeks in a last-ditch attempt by the controlling body to get the Championship off the ground. This move hardly endeared the Control Council to Willie Smith who saw it as a typical example of pandering to the 'Big Four'. There were no further nominations forthcoming in the three-week extension period and the B.A. & C.C. cancelled the Championship for 1931 and refused to award the title to the sole entrant, Willie Smith. This was in contrast to earlier years when both Harry Stevenson and Melbourne Inman, as the sole entrant in certain years, had been awarded the title. Smith viewed with disdain this change of policy and irately returned to oblivion, more convinced than ever that the Control Council was little more than a self-elected social club.

Lindrum's first match after the final of the International Tourney was against McConachy at Hull. It was a match of little consequence, as were all matches that followed the highly-successful International Tournament. There was one interesting occurrence during the progress of the Hull match when Walter Lindrum and Clark McConachy, through the courtesy of Captain N. Blackburn, were given the opportunity of viewing the city of Hull and its surroundings from the air. While this short flight would not even rate a second thought nowadays it was regarded as newsworthy in the relatively infant aviation days of 1931. The mention of the flight is of special interest because it conflicts with the commonly-held belief that Lindrum never flew in a plane during his lifetime. Certainly in later years Walter was strongly averse to the mere thought of flying. During the Second World War he steadfastly refused the offers of the RAAF to fly him to the more distant and isolated venues for his exhibitions, preferring instead to travel by either train or car. Possibly the flight at Hull was a sufficiently unnerving experience for Walter never to fly again.

During the next six weeks Lindrum played matches at Birmingham (against McConachy), Dundee (Newman), Burnley (Newman), Sheffield (Davis) and Birmingham (Newman). Most of the matches were of one week's duration and both Newman and Davis recorded wins over Lindrum, albeit with the aid of sizeable starts. In the last match of the tour, with Newman, Lindrum made a run of 273 nursery cannons, taking the balls past five pockets. The nursery cannon had, by this time, become the backbone of the professional game. Lindrum, Davis, Newman and McConachy were all playing nurseries, both proficiently and profusely. In some matches these close cannons were responsible for in excess of 40 per cent of the points scored. Despite the enormous public following for billiards in the 1930–31 season, the warning signs were there for anyone who cared to look beyond the current boom. It was apparent to the more astute judges that the public must eventually tire of such a preponderence of close cannons and lose interest in the game.

The popularity of billiards at the time can be gauged from the fact that in March of 1931 a billiard saloon for women only was opened in Liverpool. Men were not allowed into the room unless they were tutoring a woman player.

There were many women professionals in the early thirties and several were, under contract to the billiard manufacturers. The first-flight women players included Joyce Gardner, Thelma Carpenter, Margaret Lennan, Ruth Harrison and Eva Collins. Margaret Lennan was a determined Scottish lass who played a fine all-round game and possessed a strong masse shot. On one occasion when Walter Lindrum asked her how she played a certain shot she replied:

"You know my terms for lessons, Mr Lindrum."

During the 1930–31 season, the book, *Billiards* by Walter Lindrum, was published by Methuen & Co Ltd. Methuen had secured the rights to the manuscript from the *Billiard Player* magazine, which had purchased it from Walter to publish in serialised form. *Billiards* must have been a very sound investment for Methuen because by 1949, the book was into a fifth impression. Walter Lindrum, having relinquished all rights to the manuscript, was not entitled to any share of the profits of the successful book. Lindrum's original decision to sell the manuscript to the *Billiard Player* had proved short-sighted, and illustrated that he needed the services of an experienced agent to handle all his business negotiations.

The presentation of trophies for the International Tourney took place on 13 April. Lord Riddell, in presenting Lindrum with the Gold Cup, said, inter alia: "Lindrum is the greatest inflationist in the world. He has inflated billiard breaks beyond recall".

Lindrum was farewelled from London on 20 April by a large crowd. "I will never forget the scene. It completely knocked me off my feet", said Lindrum. He was accompanied by Tom Newman and the amateur players, Sydney Lee and Laurie Steeples who were to compete in the World Championship which was to be staged in Sydney. Lindrum had won several billiard tables as trophies in England and he deplored the fact than an exorbitant tariff of £250 per table prevented him from taking them to Australia.

The tour had seen Lindrum make 65 breaks over the thousand, including the new record of 3905. Although there are no figures available the tour was probably the most lucrative that Lindrum ever undertook. For the second year running Lindrum had proven that he was unquestionably the greatest player in the world but he was still not the world champion. That honour had once again been denied him by conflict between the B.A. & C.C. and a trade interest. Walter Lindrum would have to wait until the next season to try to satisfy his most burning ambition.

9 Cannon Controversy

He played with such perfect judgement that he made the game look
absurdly easy.   *The Times*, 21 January 1932

Walter Lindrum, along with Newman, Lee and Steeples, left England on the
P&O liner *Mongolia* on 21 April. The journey to Australia was not all plain
sailing for the youthful Sydney Lee. The problem for Lee stemmed from the
fact that he shared a cabin with Lindrum. It was not that Sydney and Walter
did not get along. The duo had developed a friendship during Lindrum's
latest visit to England. There were moments on the *Mongolia* when that
friendship was strained by Walter's fondness for gramophone music.
Lindrum took a gramophone on all his early trips and owned dozens of
records. Lee did not mind Walter playing his gramophone but he did object
to the almost endless playing of one particular tune with the title of
'Goodnight Sweetheart'. "Walter, I'll throw it overboard!" an exasperated
Sydney threatened on several occasions.

'Goodnight Sweetheart' had a very special attachment for Walter. Prior
to the death of his wife, Rosie, they had been to the pictures. As the
programme ended, the pianist played the tune. It was a popular number at
the time and was often played at the conclusion of picture shows. It was
almost two years since the sad death of his wife but Walter still clung
desperately to the memory of her. A photo of Rosie on which she had written
'To Wally, with all my love' was a treasured possession which Walter took
everywhere. On one occasion when Lindrum had been photographed in his
hotel room he quickly jumped to his feet and placed a sheet of paper over the
portrait of Rosie that stood on the mantelpiece. Walter wanted to protect the
photo from the dust of the flash powder that filled the room.

The *Mongolia* berthed in Melbourne on 25 May 1931 with the quartet of
players being given a civic reception by the Lord Mayor, Councillor Luxton
MLA. The amateurs, Lee and Steeples, travelled on to Sydney to contest the
World Billiard Championship which was being held in Australia for the first
time. It was a standard procedure for the amateur championship to be held
in the defending champion's home country. Les Hayes, the Australian
champion, had won the 1929 world title and the right for the next
championship to be staged in Australia. Hayes, though, was no match for the
English players who dominated the event. Steeples scored a convincing win
over Lee in the final.

Lindrum and Newman opened their tour in Sydney with the Englishman
in receipt of the usual sizeable start. The tour was to carry the duo to every
mainland State of Australia. It was to prove a disappointing tour with a
sudden decline in spectator interest, partly due to the effect of the
Depression. One of the few occasions on which Lindrum and Newman did

make good money was during an exhibition at Farmers' Emporium in Sydney. Farmers spared no effort and cost to present the match. They installed elevated seating in a setting which Lindrum described as the best playing conditions that he had ever experienced. At the end of the fortnight exhibition, which had been viewed by large crowds, Farmers was prepared to sign up the players for a return match. Disaster struck when Newman went down with appendicitis. While Newman was recovering from his operation Lindrum undertook a tour on his own. He returned after a two-week absence with the tour proceeds and insisted on splitting them fifty-fifty with Newman. The tour resumed in Melbourne where Lindrum produced some fine play. During one break he passed the thousand mark and when he reached 1200, the soothing 'click' of the balls had put Newman to sleep — audibly. Lindrum turned to where Newman was dozing and laughed heartily. He resumed his break and almost missed a cannon following his laughter and the lapse in concentration. The spectators burst into laughter and awoke Newman from his slumber. Newman apologised profusely and when the break finally ended at 1464 he rose from the player's chair and asked, in mock surprise, "May I have a shot now?"

The tour concluded in Perth in early November. The monetary returns had been poor. The standard of play had been high with Lindrum establishing an Australian break record of 2609, made in one hour and 47 minutes. Lindrum and Newman departed for England on the *Moldavia*, arriving there on 11 December. They found that the popularity of billiards had slumped since the previous season. The reason for the slump was probably due, partly, to the Depression which was now gripping that country. None of the billiard firms or newspapers seemed at all interested in promoting an event similar to the highly successful International Tourney of the previous season. The proliferation of nursery cannons in the game, which proved boring to the average spectator, was probably also affecting the popularity of billiards.

With the professional scene being devoid of any real potential Lindrum and Newman began looking for alternatives to spending a fruitless season on the English circuit. Meanwhile they played a match at Thurston's with Newman receiving 5000 start. The effects of the sea travel and the lack of practice was apparent in both players. Newman won the low-scoring match by 19 930 to 19 008. The pair then travelled on to Taunton where they had been engaged for an exhibition. Upon arrival at Taunton by train Lindrum showed Newman to a hotel where he had stayed on his first visit to England. Walter explained to Tom that the hotel had a billiard room which he had used for practice during his previous visit. Lindrum added that although the room did not appear to be used much it had a fine table on which they could have a little practice before their evening engagement. Entering the hotel, Lindrum recognised the proprietor who immediately made his way towards them.

"Are you Lindrum, the billiards player?" asked the proprietor.

"Yes, I am", Lindrum replied, "And this is Tom Newman", he added.

The proprietor seemed unimpressed that he would have two famous billiard players staying at his hotel. He continued querying Lindrum: "How long is it since you were last here, Mr Lindrum?"

"About two years", suggested Walter and on reflection he added, "Yes two years this very month".

"That's right", said the landlord, "And I went down to the billiard room the other day and found that you had left the light on!"

Lindrum and Newman completed arrangements to undertake a tour of Canada and the U.S.A. It was a fairly ambitious tour and the players had hopes of establishing a universal game of billiards by welding together the English game with the carom (all-cannon) game of the Americans. The two players were to leave for Canada in mid-February. On the eighteenth of January a special challenge match commenced at Thurston's between Lindrum and Joe Davis. The match opened in a very tense atmosphere. Lindrum explained why:

> My match at Thurston's, London, against Joe Davis could be described as a real 'Needle' match. The press created the impression that Davis was a much improved player, and that I would not be able to concede him 7,000. By the bookings, atmosphere and the serious look on Joe's face, I realised that I was in for a tough time.
>
> As a good deal of betting at even money was transacted at some of London's leading clubs, it had the effect of letting me know that some people did not share my views on the ultimate result of the match.
>
> The fact that it was my last game of the season in England, also that I was taking Newman with me on a tour of America, caused a little undercurrent of jealousy between certain players. The atmosphere was charged with electricity. In no game in which I have played, do I remember being so grim about wanting to hit an opponent with a break.
>
> (*Sporting Globe,* 1 October 1938.)

At the end of the first day of play Lindrum had made some impression on Davis' handicap to be 6130 points behind. When play resumed the following afternoon Lindrum showed that he was intent on making rapid inroads into Davis' lead. Resuming with 24 unfinished he made an attractive break of 808, including runs of 116 and 101 nurseries. In the latter sequence he made many of the strokes right-handed until he was able to reverse the position. Later in the session Lindrum adopted more-open methods of play to be on 701 unfinished at the interval. The scores now stood at Davis, 8644, Lindrum 3726. The marker next to Joe's name on the scoreboard had already been stationary for thirty minutes. It was to remain unmoved for the duration of the evening session of play, for 105 minutes, as Lindrum lifted his break to 3151 unfinished. *The Times* reported:

> Lindrum's play was remarkable. His control was so good that he added hundred after hundred without appearing to be in the slightest difficulty.

Facing page: *The menu card for the dinner given in honour of Walter Lindrum at the end of his sensational first tour of England, 1929–30. (Dolly Lindrum)*

Overleaf: *Two great Australian sportsmen. Walter Lindrum and Don Bradman snapped by an enterprising photographer at Thurston's, London, on 19 September 1930. Bradman had just completed his first English tour during which he scored a record 974 runs in the Test Matches at an astounding average of 139.14. 'The Don' was a keen billiard player — his best break was slightly over 100. (Pacific & Atlantic Photos)*

THE GUEST OF THE EVENING OR THE 'DADDY' OF THE LOT.

THE EARL OF LONSDALE.
K.G., G.C.V.O.

Mr. WALTER LINDRUM.

SQUADRON LEADER ORLEBAR.

Mr. DAVID MACMYN.

Mr. TOM NEWMAN.

Mr. BILLY WELLS

Mr. O. PULVERMACHER.

Mr. HAROLD ABRAHAMS.

Mr. CHARLES B. COCHRAN.

Mr. DAVID JACK.

Mr. E. HUSKINSON.

Mr. DICK PRESTON.

Mr. FRED MAY

Mr. W. C. SNOWDEN.

Mr. W. O. McGEEHAN.

Mr. TOM WEBSTER.

Mr. JACK HOBBS.

Mr. HARRY VARDON.

Mr. STEVE DONOGHUE.

SIR HENRY SEGRAVE.

Mr. TOM REECE.

Mr. MELBOURNE INMAN.

Mr. CHARLES GRAVES.

Mr. R. H. GILLESPIE.

Mr. J. BERESFORD.

Mr. GUY INNES.

Mr. MATT McKEIGUE.

Mr. GODFREY DAVIS.

Mr. PETER MAZZINA.

Mr. HARRY PRESTON.

DINNER TO WALTER LINDRUM

Given to Commemorate

His Marvellous Playing Record in Great Britain 1929–30.

IN THE CHAIR :

THE RT. HON. THE EARL OF LONSDALE.
K.G., G.C.V.O.

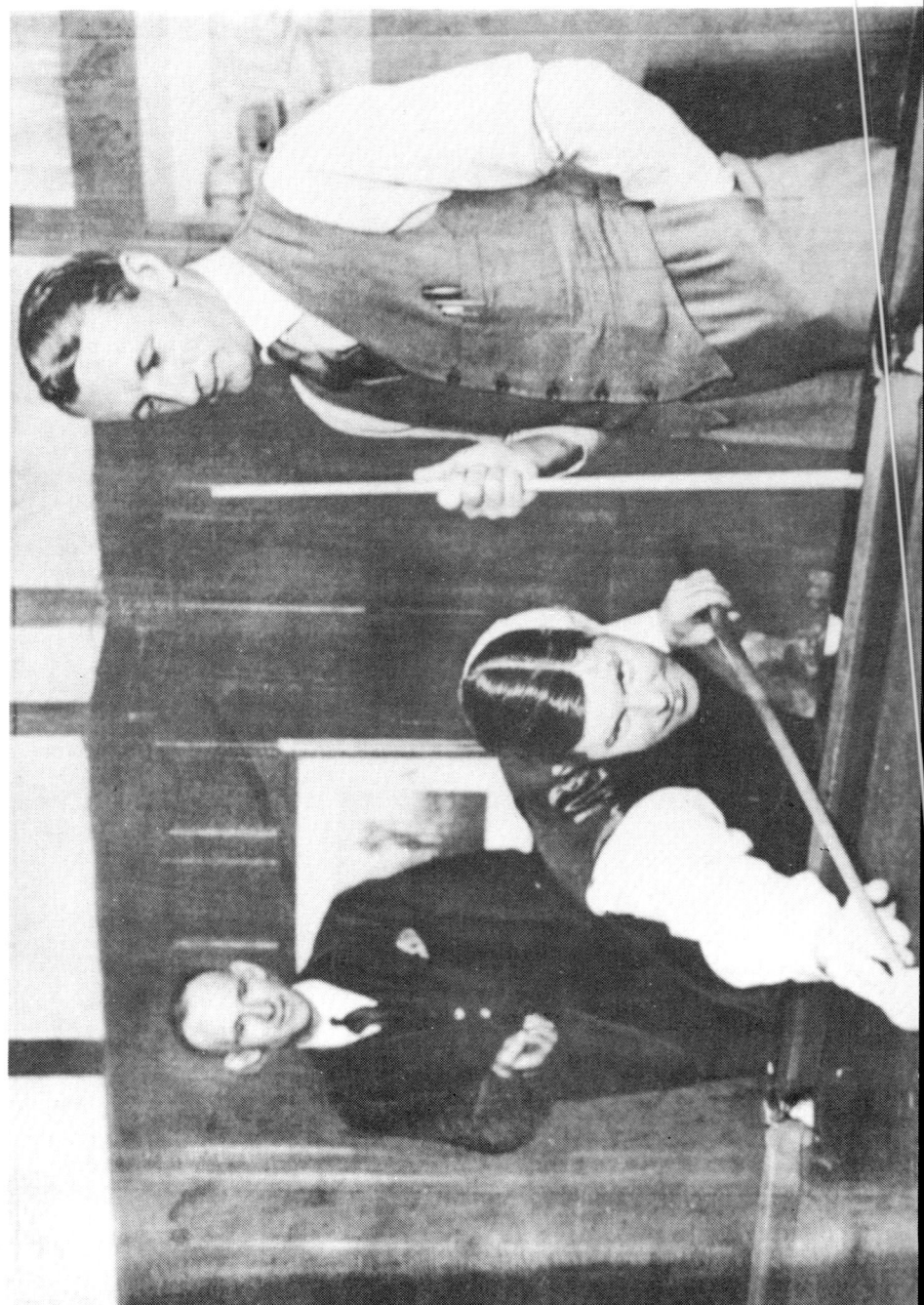

After some accurate top-of-the-table play Lindrum made a run of 58 cannons, and he reached four figures, for the eleventh time this season, with another run of 94 cannons. When the break had realised 1,189 the red ball was left just outside the baulk line and near the cushion. Lindrum played a white loser which brought the object ball into the baulk area, but he made a splendid cushion cannon, which left him with an easy white loser into the bottom pocket to make, and he went on to score with the greatest ease by a variety of methods.

Beginning another run of cannons to the left of the middle of the cushion, Lindrum played the balls to the right corner, reversed the position, and played the balls round to the left middle pocket in a brilliant run of 135 cannons. His positional play was exceptional. Lindrum began another run of cannons at 1,759, and he reached 2,000 in the course of a run of 122 cannons. . . . It seems almost superfluous to remark that Lindrum's play was masterly. When he was not making cannons he scored with the same freedom at the top of the table, in which his judgement in making a series of winners and cannons was splendid. Lindrum had shown before that he has never had an equal as an all-round player, and in this great break he emphasised the point. His resource seems unbounded. As a test of endurance his achievements are remarkable, and it is extremely difficult to estimate how superior in scoring skill he is to his contemporaries. A little before the break had reached 2,300 Lindrum had to make a difficult run-through loser and, a few strokes later, an awkward run-through cushion cannon. The ingenuity with which he secured position for nursery-cannon play was admirable, and almost amusing. Lindrum added other runs of 51 and 48 cannons, and he passed 2,600 with a run of 88 cannons. . . . At 2,949 he began another run of cannons, and when he reached 3,000 he was given an ovation for a most brilliant achievement. (20 January 1932.)

When Lindrum arrived at Thurston's for the resumption of play on the third day he had to battle his way into the hall through an overflowing crowd of spectators. The pavement and stairway leading into the hall were jammed with fans who had failed to gain admittance. The hall doors were locked to exclude the crowd. It was a scene of unprecedented enthusiasm. Lindrum, although outwardly appearing self-poised, was disturbed and distracted by the boisterous crowds. The referee brought the crowd under control and called the scores. Joe Davis said, in an audible whisper, "I think Walter should declare the innings closed."

Lindrum had left himself an awkward opening position, and he appeared to be uncomfortable. He nearly missed several difficult open play shots before he got the balls into good position at the top of the table. (The *Argus.* 21 January 1932.)

Facing page: *Putting the finishing touches to his canvas of Walter Lindrum, is the Australian portrait painter, Sir John Longstaff. The painting was done about 1932–33 and is now the property of E. A. Clare & Son Ltd, Liverpool, England.* (Herald & Weekly Times)

Preceding page: *Walter's return to Australia in 1931 after his second English tour. With him (from left) are Sydney Lee, Tom Newman and Laurie Steeples.* (Dolly Lindrum)

A run of 112 cannons followed amidst 'breathless' silence. At 3484 the red ball almost stopped on the brink of the pocket, hovering before trickling in. There were grunts of anguish from amongst some in the crowd while others immediately reprimanded them with cries of 'sssh'. Lindrum passed 3500 after fifteen minutes of the session, and added the next hundred in three minutes, while he reached 3700 in a further 2½ minutes. He was closing in on his record of 3905. The audience was hushed. The uncanny silence disturbed Lindrum and he anxiously wiped his cue and hands. A bout of open play followed. At 3799 Lindrum asked the marker the score. Apparently he thought he was 100 higher. When he was within a few points of the record the crowd became so nervously excited that it ceased smoking. Finally the previous record was equalled. Lindrum was faced with what appeared to be an easy cannon if he was to break the record. As if he found delight in holding the spectators in one final moment of glorious uncertainty, Lindrum paused, chalked his cue with great deliberation, and grinned to the onlookers before playing the simplest of cannons. It was a world record. Pandemonium reigned. The crowd stood and cheered wildly for some minutes. One Australian in the audience threw his hat and it landed on the billiard table. There were eager cries of Speech! Speech! from some of the spectators. Others shouted No! No! for they were concerned that such an interlude would ruin Walter's concentration. Walter resolved the spectators' conflict by resting his cue on the floor, gesturing for silence and saying:

> I thank you most heartily for your appreciation of my break. I can assure you that it is only possible to make such a break before an attentive audience as you have shown yourself to be. I am proud to have broken the record in London again. *(The Breaks Came My Way,* Joe Davis).

Lindrum resumed and soon reached the 4000 mark amidst further enthusiastic applause. When the score reached 4137 Lindrum was faced with a slightly awkward cannon. He took the short rest to play a cushion cannon with strong right-hand side. Lindrum contacted the object white fractionally thick and missed the cannon by the proverbial 'coat of paint'. It was all over. The break had ended after two hours and fifty-five minutes. Included in the break of 4137 were 1295 nursery cannons. Joe Davis went to the table for the first time in over 1½ sessions. Lindrum expected that his break would affect Joe's morale and confidence. Davis, though, with grim determination, played out the rest of the session with a remarkable reply of 1131 unfinished. The break eventually ended at 1247. It was the first time that opponents had made successive four-figure breaks. After the session Lindrum disclosed:

> Just before I left Sydney, I was offered 3 to 1 against breaking my previous record, a Melbourne man offered me 2 to 1 that I would not exceed a break of 4000, while a Perth man gave me 2 to 1 against occupying any three sessions. I took the lot. (The *Argus,* 21 January 1932.)

The most surprising aspect of the match was that Lindrum, despite his record break, did not win it. At the conclusion of his 4137 break Lindrum trailed Davis by only 1482 points. He had wiped off most of Davis's 7000 points start in less than three days. Lindrum made an additional four breaks over the thousand but the final scores were in Joe's favour by 27 413 to 26 162. The result of the match has faded into oblivion while Lindrum's superb break of 4137 has been entrenched in the record book where it will remain, unchallenged, for as long as the game of billiards is played.

It was not thought, at the time, that Lindrum's new record would survive for very long. As Lindrum and Newman departed from Southampton on the S.S. *Bremen* for Canada, Newman opined:

"I consider it long odds on Lindrum passing the 5000 mark." (*News of the World* 14 February, 1932)

It was not not really a rash statement by Newman. After all, in just over two years Lindrum had lifted the break record from Smith's 2743 to the current 4137, an increase of 1374 points or almost 50 per cent. There seemed no reason why Lindrum could not increase the record by another 863 points to reach 5000. Indeed Lindrum firmly believed that he would reach the 5000 mark. He could not foresee that during his absence from England the nursery cannon craze would reach such epidemic proportions that the B.A. & C.C. would have to finally take stock of the situation. The resultant rule change would effectively place a 5000 break, even a further 4000 break, beyond the capabilities of the genius of Walter Lindrum.

Lindrum and Newman were accompanied to Canada by the promoter, Bill Camkin, who was given the responsibility of negotiating with the leading American players in an effort to arrange a special challenge match. Camkin approached the two champions, Willie Hoppe and Walter Cochran, through an intermediary but negotiations could not be finalised until an American promoter could be found who would finance the contest. The local promoters seemed indifferent to the idea and so the project had to be shelved. Part of the difficulty in finding a promoter was because the trio had brought samples from English manufacturers who were keen to break into the American market. Sections of the American trade boycotted the tour and one of the avenues most likely to provide sponsorship and promotion was thus closed to the players.

The tour opened with matches in the Canadian cities of Montreal, Toronto and Winnipeg. The duo also played a match at Detroit and in early April made their way to New York. In a daring move they opened up on Broadway but it proved an expensive experiment for only moderate crowds turned put to watch two fine artists of English billiards. Lindrum did his utmost to capture the public's attention by making a break of 2711 but it failed to overcome the fundamental reason for poor attendances — the public were not interested in a form of billiards that they did not understand.

After the final session of the match Lindrum was approached by a well built young man who asked, as he shook Walter's hand:

"Mr Lindrum, do you play snooker?"

"Yes, occasionally", replied Walter.

"Well, I challenge you to play me twelve games of snooker for $500, aggregate scores to decide the winner", said the stranger.

Lindrum excused himself on the pretext that he wanted to find out if Newman had made any arrangements for the following afternoon, when the stranger wanted to play the match. Lindrum explained the proposal to Newman who said:

"No one in New York knows the first thing about snooker; accept his challenge for $1000 and I'll be half in it."

Lindrum went back to the stranger to clinch the deal and arrange a venue. The young man agreed, much to Lindrum's astonishment, to play on the table on which he had and Newman had just finished playing. The stranger also guaranteed that a good crowd would be in attendance and that Lindrum could have the whole of the gate takings. The only stipulation that the rash challenger made was that he be allowed twenty minutes practice on the table prior to the match. Lindrum could not shake hands quickly enough on the deal. Newman echoed Lindrum's thoughts when they returned to their hotel: "Well, laddie, that looks to be the easiest money I've ever seen".

The following afternoon Lindrum arrived early at the venue for his opponent to have the agreed twenty minutes' practice. Lindrum opened the case containing the set of snooker balls and the challenger took the cue ball and placed it on the table. He then asked Lindrum to scatter the balls around the table. Having done so Lindrum sat down with Tom Newman to see how the young man shaped. The debonair-looking young fellow banged down a red from a difficult angle. Lindrum sat up and nudged Newman. Ball after ball disappeared into the pockets until the table was cleared. A bewildered Lindrum sat speechless and watched as the young man retrieved the balls from the pockets and scattered them around the table. He chalked his cue nonchalantly and proceeded to sink every ball again. Wearing the same serene smile the young man sauntered over to a dazed Walter and said: "Mr Lindrum, the table is fine, and the balls O.K. I'm prepared to start when the boys arrive". Lindrum would have been happy to call the match a draw before commencing. He decided that he would have to rely on safety play to counter his opponent's superlative potting.

A capacity house saw Lindrum win the toss and break off for the first of six frames which were scheduled for the afternoon session. Lindrum sliced off the second last red in the bunch and left the cue ball against the bottom cushion. With a glorious shot his opponent cut in a fine red to commence a break that ended after the fifteen reds as well as the yellow, green and brown had been potted. Lindrum's opponent had made a 97 break on his first visit to the table. Lindrum disgustedly potted the blue, pink and black. The large number of onlookers was some consolation for Lindrum as they would cover the side wager which he felt certain he would be paying. Tom Newman offered some sympathy: "Laddie, he can't keep it up; bang him the way you have been treating me lately". (*Sporting Globe*, 9 July, 1938.)

Lindrum retrieved the situation with an unexpected but most welcome break of 93 in the second frame. This break had the effect of steadying the play and breaks of 40 and 50 were the order for the rest of the session. At the end of the first six frames Lindrum trailed the dashing youngster by 25 points. Lindrum conferred with Newman in an endeavour to find a counter to the young American's game. They agreed that Lindrum's opponent seemed to play better on one side of the table than the other.

In the evening session Lindrum played to the young man's weak side with good effect. While keeping his opponent quiet Lindrum rattled in two breaks in the 90's and two in the 80's to clinch victory. Lindrum collected his winnings from his elegant opponent who had remained jovial and sporting throughout the match. Lindrum had almost recovered from the ordeal of the match when the young man offered him a hefty fee to play him six games of snooker for each of three nights. Lindrum readily accepted although he did not favour the venue, a saloon on Broadway where his opponent could back himself.

The following evening Lindrum arrived at the venue, an underground theatrette, and was surprised to find it contained a beautiful English table. When his opponent announced to the crowd that he would back himself for $50 he found several takers. The smaller pocket openings on the English table were to Lindrum's advantage and he won the first three games. His opponent had little knowledge of the smaller pocket openings and his shots continually wriggled in the jaws and came out again. Lindrum was perturbed to see his opponent peeling off bills to settle with several shrewd gamblers. He looked for a way to cut his opponent's losses and cleverly lost the next two frames. He was bluntly warned by one gambler that non-triers were not welcome in the club. Lindrum's opponent reassured him: "I want you to go at high pressure all the way, Mr Lindrum; I'm enjoying it immensely". (*Sporting Globe*, 9 July, 1938.)

Lindrum felt uncomfortable for the duration of the match and was relieved when it finally ended. He had won by 13 frames to 5 and his opponent had lost around $2000 on the match. Despite his loss the young man insisted on taking Lindrum and Newman to the Hollywood Restaurant for a lavish supper. Finally the good-humoured sportsman revealed that he was Marcelle Camp. The name conveyed nothing to Lindrum but he later learnt that Camp was the man who had toured the States as the 'Masked Marvel'. He played matches all over the country under contract to the Coca Cola Company. He always wore a mask and proved a huge success as an advertising medium. It was the end of a remarkable episode which left Lindrum convinced that Camp was, apart from being a great sportsman, one of the best snooker players that he had ever seen.

The prospects of a challenge match with Hoppe and Cochran had suddenly improved with the famous boxing promoter, Jimmy Johnson, showing interest in staging a contest at none other than Madison Square Garden. Lindrum, Newman and Camkin travelled to Detroit to meet the two American champions. After four hours of negotiations they reached agreement on a set of rules for the contest. Lindrum & Co. returned to New York and told a delighted Johnson to draw up contracts. At the last minute a hitch developed about the American's percentage and the matches fell through. Lindrum and Newman had come very close to making a breakthrough which could have led to a compromise being made between the two major forms of billiards.

A disappointed Bill Camkin returned to England having failed in the real objective of the tour. Lindrum and Newman journeyed to Montreal for one final match before setting sail. The tour had been a costly experience for the duo and they returned to England, convinced that it would never be possible to bring English and American billiards together. Lindrum took some consolation from the fact that Mr Ben Singer, managing director of Brunswick-Balke Company, presented him with a choice billiard table valued at £500.

Upon their arrival in England, Newman and Lindrum found that the air was thick with the nursery cannon problem. The situation was the direct result of the efforts of Clark McConachy who had, by meticulous practice, dramatically improved his close-cannon play. McConachy specialised in strings of nurseries along the top cushion. When the corner pocket was imminent he would reverse the balls and proceed to play another string of cannons back to the other corner pocket. On 18 February, McConachy made a run of 297 cannons which included nine strings along the top cushion. The sequence was an unparalleled performance and caught the attention of the billiard world. More significantly it awoke the B.A. & C.C. from its lethargic dormancy for no longer could it remain detached from the dilemma that nursery cannons had created. This was exactly what McConachy had set out to do. He openly stated:

> My recent world record of 297 close cannons, made against Joe Davis, was compiled on a new principle that I was the first to exploit. Instead of manipulating the balls past the top pockets, I executed a turning movement, and took them nine times backward and forward along the top cushion. Why did I do this? Because I wanted to demonstrate that close-cannon play has reached a point where further limitation is necessary in the best interests of English billiards. I do not want to do anything to put a stop to a fair proportion of scoring by means of this exquisite 3-ball movement, but feel that we ought to avoid a surfeit of it. *(News of the World,* 28 February, 1932.)

McConachy had thus placed the responsibility for dealing with the cannon problem firmly in the hands of the Control Council. To ensure that the governing body did not neglect its duty, McConachy accentuated the situation with further runs of 424 and 464 close cannons. The public wearied of this intricate, but repetitive scoring method. The billiard enthusiasts were so anaesthesised by the time that McConachy and Davis met for the Championship that only thirteen paying spectators saw the opening session of the match. To highlight the predicament even further, both Mac and Davis were preoccupied with cannon play throughout the fortnight's play. Mac, from the outset, predictably worked away at his cannons. Davis had a penchant for 'sitting-in' on his man, of adopting his opponent's scoring methods, and he was soon cannonading with increasing frequency. So much so that of the 25 161 points that Joe scored in winning the event, over 11 000 came from close cannon sequences of 30 or more. Similarly, Mac scored 8000 of his 19 259 by this method. This meant that in excess of 43 per cent of the points scored in the match came from nursery cannon play. The other feature of the match was that it was played on the Janus cloth. The controlling body had at last seen fit to allow trade firms, other than Thurston's, to be involved with the staging of the Championship.

The ease of Davis' win in the championship was most unexpected. Mac's phenomenal runs of cannons and his overall fine form suggested that he had a strong chance of winning the coveted title. Davis went into the final well aware of this possibility for Mac had beaten him in two of their three preliminary matches.

During the first of these matches McConachy made a brilliant break of 1943 which, as it turned out, was to be his lifetime record. The reason for the

New Zealander's defeat in the Championship was his methodical execution of the nursery cannon. Despite the fact that he held the world's record for cannon sequences, Mac was not really a specialist. He was better suited by the all-round game and his great strength lay in his ability to deal with abnormal positions by producing extraordinary recovery shots. His weakness lay in the slowness of his methods as compared to Lindrum, Davis and Newman. Therefore, by rigidly adhering to his pre-planned method of scoring, McConachy found himself disconcerted by Davis's 'sitting in' and domination of the nursery cannon play. He thus lost the initiative and also a golden opportunity to win the Championship. It remains, though, to McConachy's credit that he of the 'Big Four' who played nurseries took the first positive step that led to the restriction of nursery cannons.

Walter Lindrum was not in favour of limiting nurseries. He was, after all, the father of the nursery cannon. He had adopted it out of its neglected infancy, caressed and fostered it through a brief childhood, then cultivated and developed its latent potential in its youth. However, the proud father, blinded by devotion and love for his creation, could not see that it had matured into an overly conspicuous monster that, by its very presence, threatened to help destroy the game of billiards. In doing so the nursery cannon would necessarily destroy itself and ultimately promised to seal the destiny of its ingenious, but short-sighted, father.

Indeed, it seems surprising how long it took the professionals to realise the threat that nursery cannons posed to the game of billiards. Of course, Willie Smith was the notable exception. He refused to adopt the nursery cannon game, claiming that the 'cushion crawlers' would not provide entertainment for the spectators who were an integral part of the game, for without them the game could not survive. Smith's views were supported by several members of the press, the most outspoken of these being Riso Levi who decried the monotony of the close cannons. Lindrum could not conceive that nurseries were boring for he found them a continual challenge. After Levi had first denounced nurseries he was warned that Lindrum was in a sour mood towards him. Levi, though, was not one to hide behind the power of the pen. At the first opportunity he joined a group of enthusiasts who were enjoying a quiet drink after a session of a Lindrum–Newman match. Walter was in the group, along with Tom Newman and his wife. It was not long before Levi and Lindrum were involved in a heated argument over Levi's press articles. Finally, in a state of agitation, Lindrum said: "Do you know that you are doing your best to ruin the popularity of billiards by the kind of articles you are writing for the Press?"

Following a further exchange, Lindrum added: "You're the most foolish writer I have ever come across".

Levi thought it was timely to remind Lindrum of the set of billiard balls that he had given to him, bearing the inscription: "To Riso Levi, the world's greatest billiard writer".

While this heated argument was taking place Tom Newman sat silently, only speaking to verify the truth of some minor incident that Levi recalled. It seems strange that Newman did not come out in support of either man for Levi's claim had just as much relevance for him as it did for Lindrum. It was not until May of 1932 that the 'Big Four' held a meeting, at the Victoria Club,

London, to discuss the problems of nursery cannons and the future of billiards. It would have been in their best interests if the players had made an agreement among themselves to cut down on close-cannon play. Lindrum was a stumbling block for any such move, believing it was designed to deny him his supremacy at billiards.

The fundamental problem with nursery cannons was that very few spectators could appreciate their beauty and finesse. At times the ball movements were so infinitesimal that the referee had to stand right over the play to see if a cannon was actually being scored. Imagine the spectator who was trying to watch the play from the back row of seats! Additionally, because nurseries were played on a restricted part of the table, there were occasions when spectators, whose vision was obstructed by the player's body, would miss seeing a run of fifty cannons. Joe Davis clarified the problem when he acknowledged a few years later: "Unfortunately the kind of game we play is a hidden science."

The future of professional billiards was on the rocks. It was the duty of the Control Council to make the necessary rule changes and prevent the demise of the game. It can be argued that Lindrum & Co. had already sealed the fate of billiards because they had mastered the game and made it look too easy. Whatever the situation was, there is no doubt that the imminent rule change would influence the life span of professional billiards.

Walter Lindrum left England around 12 May. He returned to Australia for two months in which time he took a break from the demands of his profession. In his hometown Melbourne Fred Lindrum senior called a little family gathering. The venue was the Windsor Hotel in Albert Park where Fred junior ran the billiard room. Apart from Fred senior, Fred junior and Walter, young Horace was also present. It was a quiet evening in the hotel and not many of the guests realised what a formidable array of cueists was present. One of them certainly didn't — an elderly Englishman who, during the course of the evening, asked Fred junior for a game of billiards. Fred junior accepted and ran out an easy winner before his opponent had scored. The visitor then challenged Fred senior with a similar result. Young Horace was next, and when he too had run out, the visitor doggedly refusing to lie down to a beating, singled out Walter.

"Surely, he said, "I must be able to score against someone tonight!"

But with Walter as an opponent it was all over in a matter of minutes. The dumbfounded visitor, shaking his head, took out a £5 note which he offered as payment for the best night's entertainment he had ever had. The elder Lindrum handed it back with a smile, and introduced his family, explaining just where they all stood in the hierarchy of billiards.

"Well," said the visitor, "I'll have something to tell them when I get home. In one night I've played four games of billiards without making a single score. I've played against four champions on equal terms."

10 Lindrum's Rule

> Lindrum is so far in advance of his contemporaries that his superiority cannot be fully estimated. For a reason which is not easy to explain he has developed the game to an extent not quite understood before.
>
> *The Times*, 21 January 1932

Walter Lindrum arrived back in England on 24 September, 1932 following his journey on the *Orama*. It was the fourth consecutive season in which he had visited the home of billiards, and it was to be the last. Lindrum had been involved in a number of controversies during his previous trips and this fourth trip was to be no exception. The source of the conflict was the new rule which had been introduced by the B.A. & C.C. in an endeavour to restrict nursery cannon play. The new rule, which became known as the baulk-line rule, read: "The cue ball shall be made to cross the baulk-line at least once in each hundred points in a break."

The rule was to be given a four-month trial and then reviewed. By requiring the players to cross the baulk line the rule would necessarily interrupt the long bouts of close-cannon play. It seemed a very roundabout way for the Control Council to counter the nursery cannon invasion. In previous times when first the spot stroke and then the losing hazard were exerting an unhealthy domination of the game, a specific limit was placed on sequences of each stroke. In both instances the rules proved successful in restoring balance to the game. In introducing the baulk-line rule the controlling body chose to ignore the success of previous experiences. It seems apparent that the members of the B.A. & C.C., several of whom lacked an understanding of billiards that playing of the game would have given, were given outside advice on the problem. The question is, by whom? The available evidence suggests that it was Tom Newman. Of all the leading professionals, Newman was the one who remained in relative harmony with the controlling body. After the baulk-line rule was introduced he was the first to voice support for the change. (There was also endorsement from Willie Smith but he never enjoyed a harmonious relationship with the Control Council.) In his regular column in the *News of the World,* (4 September, 1932), Newman said:

> In my opinion, the governing body has taken the first step towards the most beneficial reform billiards has seen since Rimington-Wilson simplified fouls and limited successive games.
>
> Whatever comes of it, Mr. John Bisset and his colleagues on the Control Council deserve the thanks of all lovers of billiards for making an honest endeavour to prevent the game from falling into a rut.

Lindrum disagreed with Newman's view. His immediate reaction was to denounce the rule but, following a meeting of the leading players at which it was decided to give the rule a fair trial, he restrained from making public comment. Lindrum did declare that he expected to make a thousand break after two or three weeks of play under the rule. Apparently Lindrum had a few problems in adapting to baulkline billiards for in his first four weeks of play under the rule he failed to make a solitary thousand break, his highest being 869. Clark McConachy was not experiencing much difficulty with the rule which he thought was a 'really splendid one'. On 1 October Mac clearly won the honour of the first four-figure break of baulkline billiards with a 1321 against Davis. Incidentally, Mac made the 1321 with a cue belonging to Miss Thelma Carpenter which he had brought away from Bournemouth by mistake.

The baulk-line rule was amended by the B.A. & C.C. and now required a crossing once in every 200 points. Lindrum responded immediately by making four thousands and a 996 in a match with McConachy. The second highest of these breaks, 1566, contained only 197 close cannons — an indication that the line rule was changing the methods of scoring and adding variety to the play.

The question of the start that Lindrum would concede to the other players had to be reviewed in light of the line rule. In his first match under the rule Lindrum conceded 2500 start to Newman over a fortnight. Lindrum had overhauled Newman by the end of the first week, so the match was called off and a second encounter commenced. Newman received another 2500 start for the one week match, meaning that he had received a total of 5000 start in the fortnight's play. After further matches with Newman, Davis and McConachy, it became the practice for Lindrum to concede 6000 start over a fortnight or 3000 start for a one-week match.

The major event planned for the 1932–33 season was a Gold Cup Tournament, sponsored by the *News of the World*. It was to be run on similar lines to the highly-successful tourney of the 1930–31 season. The 'Big Four', Lindrum, Davis, Newman and McConachy, all agreed to contest the Event. Willie Smith was also invited to compete but he failed to reply and so remained in his self-imposed exile. On 30 October the 'Big Four' met at the offices of the *News of the World* to finalise the conditions for the Gold Cup. They decided to ignore the line rule, instead preferring to play under terms which allowed the scoring of 75 consecutive cannons. This was completely against the wishes of the Control Council who, fearing rejection of the baulk-line rule, made official representation to the players prior to the meeting. It was an obvious sign of the power that the professionals could wield, provided they acted as a unified body.

The first open dissent from the line rule came from Claude Falkiner, in early December, when after three sessions he refused to continue playing under the rule in a match with Lindrum. Falkiner declared: "The public does not get the breaks it is entitled to expect".

The two players agreed to finish the match under the former rules. The line rule probably had more effect on Falkiner's game than it did on any of the other players. His greatest strength was his nursery cannon play in which he ran a close second to Lindrum. Thus he had every reason to fight for the retention of rules which did not restrict the close cannon game. Falkiner's comment illustrates just how difficult the situation had become. With the introduction of the line rule, and the resultant decline in the size of the breaks being made, would the game lose its appeal to the public? Certainly spectator interest was already waning but the line rule, although intended to open up the game and add variety to the play, may drive away a public with an appetite for big breaks. On each occasion that Lindrum appeared likely to break the world record the spectators turned up in droves to bear witness to the feat. The sheer magnitude of the break was adequate compensation for the repetitive play that was an essential ingredient in the compilation of such mammoth scores. The plain fact was that the cannon-craze had continued unchecked for far too long. The result was that the public had grown accustomed to the large breaks that nursery cannons facilitated and now expected, as a matter of course, to see these breaks being made.

After playing under the line rule for almost three months Lindrum made his first public criticism of it. He said:

> The new baulk-line rule is the world's worst idea. I have given the experiment an extensive trial and no one has gained. Attendances have fallen considerably and every leading professional was down hundreds of pounds in comparison with his receipts last year, when records were being smashed. The public want to witness first-class billiards and particularly the making of big breaks. When I return to England next year I will not play baulk-line billiards. (The *Argus*, 23 December, 1932, from the *Daily Herald*, 22 December.)

Lindrum later added:

> In my opinion the line rule tends to destroy the beauty and science of billiards. It removes from the game scores of delightful and scientific strokes, and offers in place a crude shot demanding the executional skill of an average amateur.
>
> It is a reversion to the cramp game of our forefathers. The public certainly do not like it, and the experience I have had with it convinces me of its complete undesirability in the interests of English billiards. *(Billiards for All Time,* Riso Levi.)

The Control Council did not respond to the criticism of the line by Lindrum & Co. The rule had already been amended so that the players were required to cross the baulk-line once in every 200 points but, whereas the former 100 point rule had proved a harsh limitation, the extension to 200 points allowed the players to operate with too much freedom. For example, if a player crossed the baulk line with an early stroke he could then score the best part of four hundred points before he needed to cross the line again. Lindrum was, though, still unhappy with the rule. The controlling body had ignored the substance of his complaint. The 200 point rule still forced the players to make a crude shot and so destroy ideal position. Lindrum would have been happier if the rule simply set a specific limit on cannon sequences.

A novel contest was the 'Test Match' played in December of 1932, with Australasia being represented by Lindrum and McConachy while England's players were Davis and Newman. The sessions were of 90 minutes' duration with large crowds witnessing Australasia's defeat of England by 28 644 to 25 348. Davis made the only four-figure score (1009) while Lindrum made a run of 139 close cannons — a record under the new rules.

Lindrum soon obliterated this cannon sequence from the records with an incredible effort in a heat of the Gold Cup. Lindrum forewarned his opponent, Joe Davis, that he was about to do something which would cause great concern to those who guided the destinies of billiards. He was, of course, referring to the members of the Control Council.

Lindrum proceeded to make a run of 529 cannons, so pacing his break that he crossed the baulk line at least once in every 200 points. Lindrum took the balls around the table two and a half times in his amazing run. Joe Davis watched increduously as Lindrum ignored simple in-offs and played difficult screw cannons to maintain his run. It was an outstanding example of the genius of Walter Lindrum. The most basic precept of nursery cannon play was to conserve cushion space and so maximise the scoring potential of a given length of cushion. In order to circumvent the baulk-line rule, which was designed to eliminate long runs of nursery cannons, Lindrum abandoned that fundamental principle of conserving the cushion space. He continually shunted the balls well ahead so that for each cannon scored he covered as much distance as possible. By deliberately wasting the cushion space Lindrum was able to travel the balls around the table with sufficient rapidity to comply with the demands of the line rule. It was a grand gesture of defiance on the part of Lindrum to show the B.A. & C.C. that he could overcome any rule it chose to introduce. Lindrum defiantly declared: "It won't make any difference. I'll play under any rules — under the three-card trick rule if you wish".

There is no doubt, despite Lindrum's assertive stand, that the line rule did have a marked effect on his scoring power. The rule served, in the short term at least, to make a 2000 break beyond Lindrum's reach. There was no question that he was still the best and he continued to compile many thousand-plus breaks; but to a lesser degree so did Davis, Newman and McConachy. This showed up clearly in the Gold Cup matches when Lindrum, conceding 6000 start to the other three players, failed to record a win. Without an occasional break of at least 2000 he could not make up the leeway that he had to concede. The Gold Cup was won by Newman who defeated McConachy in the deciding game. The Tourney was a far cry from the highly successful event of 1930–31. The spectator interest was limited and it was apparent that the future of professional billiards was in grave doubt.

The popularity of the Janus cloth had also declined markedly. The cloth was not as durable as the traditional woollen fabric and with continual use it became very greasy. Willie Smith proved this conclusively when he fitted a Janus cloth to one of the busiest tables in his saloon, only to find after a few months of constant use it was virtually unusable. Smith also maintained that the playing properties of the cloth were inferior to the woollen cloth. An interesting comment by Smith for Walter Lindrum made his break of 4137 on the Janus cloth. One can only speculate on the size of break that Lindrum might have made if during his English matches he was playing regularly on woollen cloths and had not been hamstrung by the introduction of the baulk-line rule. The makers of the Janus cloth, Reddaway & Co., had by obtaining the services of top professionals and skilful promotion, made inroads into the market. The product that they offered simply did not have the necessary quality to hold that market.

One result of the introduction of the line rule was for Willie Smith to return from oblivion with a challenge to Lindrum, Davis, Newman and McConachy for a £100 a side match. Smith considered that the new rule would effectively restrict cannon play, thus encourage his open style of play and give him every chance of defeating the other professionals. Only Lindrum and Davis attempted to arrange matches with Smith.

Lindrum offered to play Smith a series of six matches, three under the old rules (in which Smith was to receive 20 000 start), and three under the line rule (in which the start was to be 15 000). The only unusual condition for the match was that the daily sessions be of three hours duration each instead of the usual one-and-three-quarters or two hours. Smith thought these terms were generous and he agreed to play the matches. The side wager had grown from the original £100 to a sizeable £300. At the time Lindrum had £303 to his name, so a loss to Smith would leave him virtually penniless. Lindrum was prepared to offer Smith generous terms and risk all his finances on the outcome — why? The terms that Lindrum had agreed to were not quite as reckless as they appeared at first glance. It was Lindrum who stipulated that each daily session be of three hours duration. He reasoned that Smith, because of his open style of play and the amount of walking associated with it, would tire towards the end of each session. On the contrary Lindrum, with his powerful physique (his back rippled with muscles that were developed by the long hours of practice), would still be playing strongly at the end of each session. Gradually, over the fortnight's play, Lindrum expected to simply wear Smith down. Lindrum was the consummate judge on matters relating to the billiard table and it would be an impertinence to question his assessment of his capacity to concede Smith such huge starts. Indeed Smith himself may have have had second thoughts about the conditions for he pulled out of the matches after refusing Lindrum's obvious right to a major percentage of the gate.

The negotiations between Smith and Davis, although more protracted and at times very heated, had more fruitful results. They eventually met in a series of three matches to decide the pecking order among the English players. Smith had for almost ten years held an unusual position in the billiard world. He had first won the Championship in 1920. He refused to enter the 1921 event, arguing that the 'Tom Thumb' dimensions of Thurston's were no longer suitable for staging the championship. He reasoned that a larger hall would allow for greater financial return and also that seating at a cheaper rate could be provided for the working class or rank-and-file enthusiast. In 1922 Smith was a non-entrant for similar reasons. In 1923 Smith returned to the fray partly because the controlling body had seen fit to permit the players to organise the running of the championship. The players made the most of the opportunity and staged the event at a tidy profit. Smith duly won the championship, beating Newman after a close battle. Smith was never to win another championship as he never competed for it again. In 1924 the Control Council, for reasons best known to itself, again assumed control of running the event. Smith took offence at this move and declared, in his usual forthright manner, that he would not contest the event again until the players were given some degree of financial control. However, in 1924 Smith had second thoughts on the matter and made a last minute attempt to lodge his entry.

Smith had a seemingly endless argument with the Control Council. There were times when he was guilty of an irrational outburst but he often had grounds for questioning the actions of the controlling body. Many of Smith's criticisms revolved around the basic inequity which existed in English billiards — that the B.A. & C.C., which was run by a group of amateurs — should be in a position of such power that it could make decisions that could threaten the livelihood of the professional players.

Smith's confrontations with the Control Council served to reinforce his popularity with the rank and file of billiard enthusiasts. Smith never forgot his early years as a linotype operator and retained an acute awareness of the plight of the working class. By the use of his column in the *Empire News* to advance his case against the controlling body Smith was seen to be suffering similar inequities to those which plagued the working class. Consequently Smith formed an emotional bond with the working class which increased the status he had established as a player.

Smith and Davis offered a complete contrast in attitude and presentation to the billiard world. Smith, as explained, was the champion of the ordinary man, having risen from their ranks to the top flight of his profession while maintaining a strong link with them. On the other hand Davis was, first and last, a professional cueist. Despite being champion at both billiards and snooker he found it tough going in the late twenties. However, he decided that life as a cueist was far more congenial than the only other prospect that had been open to him, that of a coal-miner. Davis was the complete businessman, thoroughly efficient and reliable. He was engrossed with advancing himself to the top of the billiard-snooker ladder. He was a dominating personality who commanded the respect of all and sundry. One of the junior professionals of the time stated that one was always aware of the presence of Joe Davis. He surrounded himself with an aura that could not be ignored. Thus Davis, by his very nature, became the champion of the upper crust. When Davis and Smith finally met in the showdown for local honours, it was also a confrontation between the champion of the upper class and the champion of the working class. Herein lies the paradox of the situation. Despite being the official champion Davis was only earning a bare income. The hero of the elite was, in fact, a real battler. Contrarily Smith, by virtue of a contract with Burroughes and Watts which gave him £60 per week, was living a very comfortable life. The champion of the working class was anything but a battler.

The end result of the Davis-Smith confrontation, although conclusive, was disappointing. Davis was a clear-cut victor in two of the three matches played and he established, once and for all, his standing at the head of the English scene. Smith displayed rather indifferent form during the matches and did little to raise the hopes of the scores of people who had backed him to beat Davis. Smith had been absent from the rigours of competitive play for too long and he was only a shadow of the great player that he had once been.

In March of 1933 Walter Lindrum was joined in England by Miss Patricia Hoskin. Pat had been Walter's secretary for some time and hailed from the small country Victorian township of Violet Town. More relevant was the fact that Pat and Walter had been engaged for over six months. It was a closely guarded secret that few of Walter's friends knew. To complete the intrigue Walter and Pat were married at the Registry Office in Henrietta Street

London on 9 April with only Mr and Mrs Clark McConachy and two other friends present. It was a low-key wedding for such a well known sportsman but undoubtedly Walter had his own reasons for preferring a quiet ceremony. It is accepted that Walter was an unpredictable man, doing things that were difficult for others to understand. He did not respond to certain situations in the way in which the majority of people would have been expected to respond.

Lindrum had an individualistic way of life and he could be described as a non-conformist inasmuch as he did not believe in maintaining the status quo simply for its own sake. Certainly Lindrum led a carefree life which at times bordered on the casual. Such an outlook did not endear him to the likes of Joe Davis, a very methodical and deliberate fellow who sought success, and found it, in both personal and financial terms. Lindrum seldom bothered to keep a record of his appointments and, on occasions, he simply forgot to turn up for exhibitions and other engagements. It was not his deliberate intention to not fulfil arrangements that had been made in complete sincerity. Lindrum was just a very unorganised person; the epitome of an absent-minded genius. It is not surprising that Davis described Lindrum as 'hopelessly erratic in money matters' and unpredictable. Davis recalled another occasion that showed how unpredictable Walter really was:

> After an evening session we went out on the town and it was well into the early hours by the time we got to bed. Just before the party broke up we met a gentleman who had an interesting business proposition to put to us and who invited us to lunch with him the next day. I arranged to collect Walter from the Strand Palace Hotel where he was staying and was as good as my word. But when the receptionist telephoned his room to tell him I had arrived he received only a faint reply asking me to go up to see him. On entering Walter's room, I discovered him lying on the bed with a cold towel wrapped round his head.
>
> "What's the matter?" I asked.
>
> "Cancel the lunch, Joe, and this afternoon's match as well. I'm too ill to do anything."
>
> "You can't do that," I told him. "You're in play with 800-odd unfinished and we'll have a packed house waiting to see you make a thousand or more. I'll tell you what I'll do: I'll go and keep the lunch appointment and pick you up this afternoon. You'll feel better in a couple of hours."
>
> He looked no better when I rolled up after lunch but we applied more cold towels and I somehow managed to get him to Thurston's in a taxi. Walter began play with a 'Full House' board outside, as predicted, and reached 1,000 in no time. Finally he took the break to 1,300 and left me an impossible position. I missed the shot and did not get an opportunity to play another one all afternoon; Walter went to the table and ended the session with over 1,200 unfinished. This was quite unbelievable to me, knowing how terribly off-colour he was. But there was just no holding Walter when a cue was in his hand. *(The Breaks Came My Way,* Joe Davis.)

Walter Lindrum's night out on the town with Joe Davis was an exception rather than the rule. During the early part of his career Walter was a teetotaller. In his book, *Billiards*, published in 1930, Lindrum said: "The inner man is better without tobacco and alcohol: I never take neither but drink tea at all hours".

Lindrum was not prepared to allow anything to interfere with his billiards ambition. Gradually Walter relented from total abstinence — as Joe Davis verified — indulging in both alcohol and cigarettes. Scotch-and-water became Walter's favourite drink in later years.

Sydney Lee recalled another occasion when during an afternoon session the tip almost came off Walter's cue. After the session Walter asked Sydney to accompany him to his hotel and re-tip his cue for him. Arriving at the hotel Walter decided to have a cup of tea in a room which had an open view of the street. Walter sat sipping his tea and watching the lovely young ladies of London walk by. The minutes slipped away and, before Walter realised, it was time to head off to the hall for the evening session of his match — without having replaced the loose tip. Walter resumed play and proceeded to score a break in excess of 1000 in the session with the tip hanging flimsily on his cue.

The B.A. & C.C., in announcing conditions for the forthcoming 1933 World Championship, displayed a welcome change of attitude towards the contestants. The players were permitted to decide the venue for the Event and the make of table and cloth to be used. The controversial baulk-line rule was to be in force. The players elected to move the Championship from the hallowed precincts of Thurston's to the more spacious Dorland Hall in Lower Regent Street, London. Walter Lindrum's name was amongst the entries for the event. He was at last free from any obligations to a trade firm which had been allowed to thwart his earlier endeavours to win the Championship.

The other three entrants for the event were the defending champion, Davis, and Newman and McConachy. In his semi-final against Newman, Lindrum set a Championship record break of 1578, under the current rules, in winning by 21 470 to 20 252. Lindrum's opponent in the final was to be Davis who had earned his place with a 20 136 to 16 110 win over McConachy. The final was an exciting tussle with Davis holding the lead for the first ten days of play. On the second Friday Walter staged a dramatic, although predictable, comeback to enter the last day within a short margin of Davis. Hundreds of spectators had to be turned away from the Dorland Hall on the last day as the enthusiasts thronged to witness the result of the tense struggle. Lindrum managed to dominate the play and take the title by 21 815 to 21 121. His best breaks were 1492, 1272 and 1013 with an average of 92.

Walter Lindrum had, at last, fulfilled his one remaining ambition. He was now the world champion — officially. It was one thing to be regarded as the greatest billiardist in the world, as he had been since his first trip to England. It was quite another thing to be the official world champion. The joy that Lindrum experienced in winning the championship was not shared by all in the billiard world. Of course Joe Davis was disappointed at losing the crown

Facing page: *Walter Lindrum with Bill Camkin and Tom Newman at Bonaventure Station while travelling on* The Montrealer *from New York, 1932. (Dolly Lindrum*

Overleaf: *Walter Lindrum receiving the Championship Cup from Mr J. C. Bissett Chairman of the B.A. & C.C., 1933. Looking on (from left) are the Hon. Lionel J. Hill, Agent-General of South Australia, Joe Davis, Arthur Goundrill (referee) and Mrs Lindrum. (BBC Hulton Library)*

Walter being congratulated by Joe Davis after playing out an entire session to lift his break from 701 to 3151 unfinished. The break finally ended at 4137, made in 2 hours and 55 minutes. It was a world record and the highest break of Lindrum's career. Note Walter's glazed appearance — a sure sign of fatigue — as compared to Joe Davis' 'fresh as a daisy' appearance. (Central Press Photos Ltd)

Walter signing one of his cues in the early 1930s. (Dolly Lindrum)

which he had held for five years, even if for the last three years the championship had not been contested by the bulk of the leading players. There were many Englishman who regretted seeing an 'outsider' win the title which had been held by one of the fold since its inception in 1870. In a much broader sense the occasion was sad for it marked the last occasion that the 'Big Four' were to compete in the one event. Few could have envisaged that possibility at the time but neither could Walter Lindrum foresee that he would be involved in a bitter controversy over the championship which left him so disillusioned and disenchanted with the way things were done in England that he refused to return ever again.

Indeed, despite winning the world title, Lindrum's fourth trip to England had been a difficult one. The billiard season had been unduly hampered by the introduction of the baulkline rule — the most controversial rule in the history of the game. Lindrum was never happy playing under the rule and he voiced his opinion openly. No one seemed to want to listen. Riso Levi was one exception. Levi was regarded by some as being too acerbic in his writing but perhaps that was because his criticism was too uncompromising in its intent. Levi made the following observations on the line rule after Lindrum had declared his opposition to it.

> After such a scathing denunciation of the rule by the world's greatest player, a wise governing body would have called our leading cuemen together and asked them whether they desired the rule to remain in force for further trial, or whether they thought it should be wiped off the slate altogether there and then. Had Lindrum had the courage to decline to play any longer under the rule, there is little question that he would have been supported in his revolt by most of his brother professionals. The 'line rule' would have received its death blow, and have had to go. The Australian, however, apparently caved in afterwards. At any rate he played for the rest of the season and the Championship under the rule.
>
> The quick end of Lindrum's defiance must have emboldened the members of the Council and stiffened their backs, because again they remained silent. Even when the championship was over they made no move, and it was not until just before the beginning of the 1933-34 season that they again took up the matter, and informed a surprised billiard world that they had decided not to leave the rule any longer on trial, but instead to enter it in the statute book.
>
> If the B.A. & C.C. had not neglected to seek the opinion of the professionals, the rule would have undoubtedly been thrown out. By refusing to consult our great players on the matter, the Control Council did not act in the best interests of the game. Indeed, it is not too much to say that they showed their incompetence to do so. (*Billiards for All Time,* Riso Levi.)

There was at least one reason why Lindrum did not lead the professionals in a virtual strike over the line rule. The simple fact was that Lindrum's earnings on the tour were so mediocre that he could not risk any disruption to his matches. Tom Newman was, at this stage, still loyally supporting the line rule, so that there was not unanimous support for strike action. By the end of the year Newman had changed his opinion and echoed the protests of Lindrum, Davis, Falkiner & Co. However, it was then too late to do anything about the line rule. Lindrum and McConachy had returned to their dis ant homelands, so the professionals lacked the necessary unity and co-ordina ion to force the issue. Why the Control Council stood so resolutely behind the ine rule, despite the widespread disapproval of players and spectators alike, was most confusing at the time. Why had it ignored the obvious solution to excessive cannon play, that is, to set a limit on the number of cannons that could be played in succession? In retrospect, it appears as if the line rule was intended to restrict more than just close-cannon play. It was the nursery cannon which Lindrum, and then the other professionals, had established as the fastest and most reliable scoring medium. For some years, though, the top of the table game had also been a highly developed and somewhat repetitive mode of play. The Control Council could, by framing the line rule as they did not only eliminate long bouts of cannon play but also force the players to open up the top of the table game. The line rule allowed the controlling body to simply 'kill two birds with the one stone'. Such an interpretation of the intent of the line rule gives an easy explanation of the reason for the Council's implacable stand on the issue. Although there was an alternative method by which nursery cannons could be restricted there was no simple means by which the winning hazard–cannon routine at the top of the table could be harnessed.

During the final days of the English tour Walter Lindrum was the guest of the English Jockey Club for the running of the Derby, the blue riband of the turf, at Epsom Downs. Lindrum previously had established a friendship with Lord Derby, the 17th Earl of Derby, who revealed that he had a fine colt entered for the Derby. That colt was Hyperion, a pint-sized dynamo of horseflesh which captured the affection of the racing public in winning the Derby of 1933 by four lengths in course record time. Lindrum, having taken £8 to £1 about Hyperion, cheered him on to victory. Hyperion went on to a highly successful stud career, being champion sire six times and leading brood-mare sire on two occasions. Hyperion has made an indelible mark on Australian racing through the deeds of his grandson, Star Kingdom, which established a siring line that dominates, and should continue to dominate for many years, the Australian breeding industry.

Walter Lindrum sailed from England for the last time on the *Arundel Castle*. He was accompanied by his wife, Pat, and Mr and Mrs Clark McConachy. In late June the ship berthed at Capetown, South Africa. Lindrum and McConachy disembarked for a visit. They managed to secure bookings for exhibitions at a few of the Capetown clubs but these proved only moderate successes. The response at East London was a little better. At Port Elizabeth the spectators showed real enthusiasm for billiards and the duo made a tidy profit from their exhibitions. At Kimberley the Lindrums and McConachys were shown over the famous De Beers Diamond House. While at Kimberley Lindrum received a telegram from Alan Prior, the South African billiards champion who had won the World Amateur Championship in 1927. The telegram read: 'Frank Ferraro will play you at Johannesburg with 5000 start for £500.'

It was welcome news for Lindrum for his tour to date had been fairly disappointing. Ferraro's £500 would turn the tour into a profitable venture.

Lindrum offered McConachy a half-share in the wager and the big New Zealander readily accepted. Lindrum was puzzled by Prior's role in arranging the match. Prior had seen Lindrum in England but apparently he was not overly impressed or else expected the local conditions to trick Lindrum. The £500 had to be lodged with a Johannesburg newspaper. Lindrum lodged his money only to find that Ferraro's backers had pulled out of the match. Someone had told them that Ferraro did not stand a chance with 5000 start in a fortnight against Lindrum. After waiting a week for Ferraro to lodge the £500 Lindrum realised what had happened. Lindrum was not pleased at having his plans thwarted. In the heat of his annoyance he declared that he would get Ferraro to the table by offering him 20 000 start. Poor Mac looked closely at Walter, wondering if he was all right.

"Walter," he said, "I know you're a good player, but do you know how many noughts there are in 20 000?"

Lindrum glared furiously at Mac, offended by Mac's lack of confidence. McConachy quickly added:

"If you can play better when you're ruffled than you do when you're calm, I still want to be half in the bet if you give him 100 000."

Lindrum then headed to the Victorian Club where Ferraro was reputed to spend much of his time. Sure enough, Ferraro was there. Lindrum bowled up to him and said:

"I'll give you 20 000 start in a fortnight's play for £500."

"You couldn't do it, but I'll take 10 000 start from you," said Ferraro.

Lindrum refused to listen further. Instead he went off to a leading morning newspaper, issued his challenge and lodged the £500. It was a move that would get the desired result and quickly. It was said that Lindrum was conceited and had more money than sense but all he wanted was Ferraro's £500. Ferraro's backers did not hesitate to accept the extravagant terms. The basement under Woolworths was fitted out with seating for 800 people. The incredible terms of the match had captured the public's imagination and on opening night the room was packed. The first obstacle was over. The next assignment was to find out how good Ferraro was at billiards. Lindrum had given 20 000 start to someone whom he had not seen play!

The moment that Ferraro placed his bridge hand on the table Lindrum knew that he was an above average player. In reply to Ferraro's safety break Lindrum scored a 32 break. On his next visit to the table Ferraro compiled a stylish 297. Lindrum had seen enough in that break to realise that, unless he could unsettle Ferraro's confidence, he was in for a tough fortnight. The smirks of delight on the faces of Ferraro's backers confirmed Lindrum's thoughts. Inside he knew that he had been reckless in giving such a huge start. However, he had no intention of letting Ferraro gain the moral ascendancy. He heard Ferraro say to Prior:

"I'll beat this chap level."

Lindrum went to the table, fully determined to throw back a big break at Ferraro. He decided to play a high-speed break with the intention of putting the pressure back on Ferraro. By firstly using the top of the table game, then switching to nursery cannons, Lindrum strung together a break of 890 in only 25 minutes. The referee, Len Chambers, was literally gasping for breath as the break drew to a close. It was the faces of Ferraro's backers that gave

Lindrum the most satisfaction. Gone where those smirks of delight and in their place were gaping, incredulous stares. Lindrum moved quickly to the player's seat, intent on watching Ferraro's next break to gauge the effect of his lightning play. Ferraro made a 40 break in which the balls were scattered all over the table. Lindrum breathed a sigh of relief.

> It takes a lot of will power to sit out and watch a big break and then come back strongly. I had stolen Ferraro's thunder in one hit. I knew he was mine. (*Sporting Globe*, 13 August, 1938)

Lindrum played relentlessly throughout the first week of the match. At the end of the eleventh session the difference in the scores was only 5704. Lindrum conferred with McConachy and they agreed to offer Ferraro an extra 5000 start. Ferraro readily agreed for he knew he had no chance of beating Lindrum. The extra handicap kept the match alive and another week of good crowds was some compensation for Ferraro. Lindrum proceeded to whittle this start away. He wanted to give Ferraro even more start but McConachy insisted that Lindrum should make sure of the match. Lindrum agreed and when the match ended the scores favoured Lindrum by 39 195 to Ferraro's 33 523. Lindrum had made seven breaks over the thousand, including a 2269, which established a South African record that still stands. Lindrum thus held both the billiards and snooker records, for a few weeks earlier he had made a snooker break of 113 at the Matabeland Tattersall's Club.

Strangely, what had started out as a real needle match between Lindrum and Ferraro turned into a most enjoyable game. Ferraro was a jovial fellow who took his defeat in the best possible manner. Ferraro, a well known owner and trainer of racehorses, derived great pleasure from Lindrum's big breaks. He amused himself by making wagers with bookmakers as to the size of Lindrum's breaks. Having made the bet, Ferraro would discreetly tell Walter how big a break was required. Lindrum duly complied.

The sheer size of Lindrum's win brought an abrupt end to his South African visit. There was no one prepared to play him, regardless of the match conditions. Lindrum and McConachy decided to take a short holiday before departing from South Africa. Mr Hunt, the manager of a motor company, placed a car at their disposal. They travelled to Rhodesia, observed the wildlife in Kruger National Park, gave an exhibition for the Rhodesian governor and then returned to South Africa. At Durban they played one final exhibition match before sailing for India via the East Africa coast.

The captain received a wireless message near Zanzibar, asking for Lindrum to perform there. The captain, being a billiard-lover, held the ship up for a few hours while Lindrum and McConachy gave an exhibition for the entire British population of Zanzibar — 27 in all. Further along the coast, at Mombasa, the captain agreed to another request for a billiard performance. The occasion was a memorable one with the playing conditions among the worst that Lindrum ever experienced. The billiard table was patched and holey. The lighting consisted of a kerosene lamp. Suspended perilously above the table were several big spiders. Thousands of little insects dropped onto the table during the play only to be squashed by the balls. After a tedious struggle for over an hour Lindrum scored a break of 120, a break which he considered one of the hardest in his life.

Lindrum rejoined his ship and travelled on to India, arriving in mid-October. Lindrum had previously visited India in 1929 when he was on his way to England for the first time. He had, on that occasion, given an overnight exhibition at Bombay. Lindrum was surprised by the popularity of billiards in India despite the climatic conditions. Most of the billiard rooms were cooled by punkahs and occasionally the billiard balls were caught in the draught of the punkah and ran off course. Lindrum liberally used eau de cologne to keep his hands and forehead free from perspiration. He also developed an unquenchable thirst and consumed large quantities of Vichy water. In his first match with McConachy the Australian made a break of 983. Lindrum would have made the first four-figure break in India but for forgetting that he had recently crossed the baulk line and breaking down when attempting to cross the line again. His 983 broke the previous record of 870 which had been made in 1920 by Clark McConachy. At the Parsee Club, Bombay, the duo performed before an audience of almost 1000 people in a very elegant setting. Lindrum was besieged with offers for his cue that evening and was concerned that he might lose it. Money could not buy the cue that he had used to make hundreds of four-figure breaks. After that incident Lindrum was careful to play his exhibitions with any cue of about the same weight and length as his old favourite. He could then give the cue away to a happy spectator at the end of the session. Other Indians were anxious to obtain some form of memento of Lindrum's visit. At practice one morning, Lindrum placed his cake of chalk on the table. The chalk quickly disappeared into the pocket of an enthusiast who left 50 rupees in its place. "I'm sure you won't mind, Mr Lindrum." said the enthusiast.

One keen amateur offered 300 rupees to play Lindrum for an hour and a half. He spent most of the time pulling the balls out but he thought it was great fun. Lindrum spent time with some other Australians, Alex Higgins, Jimmy Munro and L. H. Hewitt and also attended a race meeting at the beautiful Bombay racecourse. He was bemused by the bookmakers who walked among the spectators, with neither stands or tickets. Billiards was mostly played in private clubs. One very popular game was Indian billiards, a combination of snooker and billiards. The six coloured balls were place on the table, the yellow placed about 33 centimetres from the baulk cushion and counting double points. The various colours had to be potted in certain pockets and after three pots the sequence had to be broken with a cannon or losing hazard. Lindrum tried his hand at Indian billiards and made one run of 500 unfinished.

Lindrum's visit to India was shortened by a smallpox scare. In Ceylon he played William Perera, a very popular identity, who had beaten every notable player to visit its shores. Perera always received a start from the visitors and usually had the playing conditions in his favour. The visiting players would lose their touch during the boat trip to Ceylon. Perera would run out the winner before the visitor had found his touch. Walter Lindrum was only too aware of what a sea voyage could do to a player's touch. He explained: "I will be telling a secret for the first time when I admit that on boat trips I practise every day, putting three balls on my bed and knocking them about for hours with a cue. By that means I never lose the feel of a ball striking the tip. I doubt if another player in the world does that." (*Sporting Globe*, 20 August, 1938)

Perera, an uncrowned king with his countrymen, and immensely popular with Europeans, always played in evening dress and with a comb in his beautiful black hair. He was the manager of the billiard room at the Grand Oriental Hotel. He had plenty of backers who believed he could defeat Lindrum with 600 start in the 1000 up match. Perera was capable of making 200 breaks but Lindrum never gave him a chance, going out in only two visits to the table. The Lindrums and the McConachys sailed for Australia on the *Cathay* and celebrated Christmas Day on the boat.

11 End of an Era

Walter Lindrum arrived in Melbourne on December 29, 1933 after being abroad for sixteen months. After disembarking from the S.S. *Cathay* he was interviewed by reporters. The following day the *Argus* (30 December 1933) carried detail of the interview, part of which follows:

> Mr Lindrum brought with him the handsome cup which was presented to him by the British Billiard Association when he won the world championship. It was the first time for sixty years that the title and cup had left England. Mr Lindrum said that there would be a challenge match for the Cup in Melbourne during the Centenary Celebrations. It was hoped that the English champions would visit Melbourne. Invitations would be sent to Davis, Newman, Smith and others by the Australian Billiard Control Council.

Lindrum's outline of the arrangements for the 1934 Championship seemed clear-cut. Yet, within a couple of weeks Lindrum was at the centre of a controversy over the championship. It was to prove the most bitter controversy in the history of billiards. Lindrum claimed that he had been given assurances by John Bissett, chairman of the B.A. & C.C., that the championship could be staged in Australia. Bissett more or less denied this but Lindrum, with the possession of the championship cup as a point of leverage, resolutely stood behind his 'right' to defend the title on his home soil. Lindrum came under fire for his stand on the matter. He was, and still is, portrayed by English writers as being the guilty party in the episode. These are the English views on the situation, views which have been arrived at without a full and impartial evaluation of the circumstances. It is not intended to present a blind defence of Walter Lindrum in his stand over the championship. Hopefully, a balanced account of the happenings can be presented (for the first time) and readers can form their own opinions on the matter.

Before going into a detailed report of the championship controversy it is appropriate to make mention of a dispute which occurred during Lindrum's absence from Australia. That conflict was during the M.C.C.'s tour of Australia in 1932–33 when a type of bowling, which became known as 'bodyline', was used as a means of dismissing the Australian batsmen. Bodyline was a new form of bowling attack, an adaptation of leg theory, which had been developed specifically to curb the prolific scoring of the master batsman, Don Bradman. The tactic was successful in reducing Bradman's run rate, even though he still managed to top the averages for the series. Inevitably other Australian batsmen fell victim to bodyline. The essence of bodyline was for the fast bowler to pitch the ball well short of the batsman on or outside the line of leg stump. With the ball lifting towards his head or chest the batsman could duck underneath the delivery or scramble out of the way. If the batsman attempted to move inside the line of the ball and play it on the leg side he would risk hitting a catch to the packed cordon of fieldsmen. It was not always possible to get out of the path of the lethally directed ball. Batsmen were struck painful blows. Some were felled to the ground.

The situation reached crisis point during the Third Test in Adelaide when Woodfull was hit over the heart. Bert Oldfield, the wicket-keeper, glanced a short-pitched delivery from his bat into his face. The spectators became very vocal and vented their hostility towards the English players. Police armed with batons and automatic pistols were said to have been sent to the ground for fear of an imminent full-scale disturbance. On the 18th of January, during the Adelaide Test, the Australian Cricket Board of Control dispatched a cable to the Marylebone Cricket Club. The cable read:

> Body-line bowling assumed such proportions as to menace the best interests of game, making protection of body by batsmen the main consideration, and causing intensely bitter feelings between players, as well as injury. In our opinion it is unsportsmanlike, and unless stopped at once is likely to upset the friendly relations existing between Australia and England. (*Sydney Morning Herald*, 19 January, 1933).

In reply the M.C.C. deplored the cable and the suggestion of unsportsmanlike play. The use of the world 'unsportsmanlike' was at the crux of the dispute for it, in effect, challenged the imperial tradition that Britain set the standards for civilised behaviour. The altercation quickly spread beyond cricket circles with discussions taking place at the highest political and diplomatic levels. The dispute raged in the press and on the radio in both countries with, predictably, the Australian newspapers condemning the tactics and the English scribes incensed by any suggestion of unfair play. The crisis reached such intensity that politicians expressed the fear that it could damage the imperial ties between the two countries. Certainly the remainder of the M.C.C. tour was in grave doubt. It was only on the eve of the Fourth Test in Brisbane that the crisis was averted. A conciliatory cablegram from the Australian Board of Control assured "We do not regard the sportsmanship of your team as being in question . . .". The dispute was defused — at least at the official level. The issue was far from resolved in the mind of the general public. It continued to be a source of fierce debate for several years. An indication of how volatile the controversy remained can be gauged from the comments of Joe Davis upon his arrival in Australia at the end of June 1934. It was some fifteen months since the bodyline tour by the M.C.C. had ended.

> Even the Press failed to come up trumps. When we put in to Port Adelaide and later Sydney the newspaper boys came on board all right but although I tried hard to promote the idea of the wondrous matches that Walter and I would soon be playing to the delight of millions, all they wanted to talk about was cricket, in particular what the English thought about Jardine, Larwood and bodyline bowling . . . But I kept a low profile and commented merely that the English cricketing public

thought it deplorable . . . I had enough to worry about without getting caught in cricketing crossfire. (*The Breaks Came My Way*, Joe Davis.)

When, in January of 1934, Walter Lindrum became involved in conflict with the B.A. & C.C., the issue immediately spread beyond the billiard context. It served to rekindle the fires of the bodyline series. The dispute became Australia versus England all over again and the question of fair play and justice were again at the heart of the argument. With the bodyline crisis providing such an acrimonious background it was inevitable that the Lindrum versus the B.A. & C.C. conflict was charged with emotion. The Press in both countries rallied behind the opposing causes in a way that made a rational settlement of the dispute very difficult. Emotions over-ruled reason as the newspapers succumbed to a squabble over the issue. Misrepresentation of the truth was the obvious consequence when the reporters allowed their emotions to influence their writing. Once inaccuracies are perpetrated in print they are bound to refurbished in later writings. Consider what Joe Davis said in his autobiography, published in 1976:

> Anyone who knew Walter as well as I did, having been in such close contact with him, could not honestly have been amazed, therefore, at the news that came from Australia late in 1933 to the effect that having got the billiards trophy on his sideboard he was now adopting a 'come and get it' posture. (*The Breaks Came My Way*, Joe Davis)

It is not difficult to draw the inference from this passage that Davis, prior to the arrival of Lindrum's message at the end of 1933, had no idea that Lindrum was going to adopt such an attitude. This seems to suggest that Lindrum had employed clandestine manoeuvres to get the championship trophy out of England. Such was not the case. Lindrum had been quite open in expressing the view that it was the right of the champion to defend the title on his home soil. The various comments on the matter by John Bissett, chairman of the Control Council, gave no indication that he was not previously aware of Lindrum's attitude. Much more explicit evidence was the exchange between Lindrum and Stanley Thorn, secretary of the Council, which took place in August 1930. The *Sydney Morning Herald* (15 August 1930) reported:

> The secretary of the B.A. & C.C. (Mr Stanley Thorn) referring to Walter Lindrum's statement that if he won the championship he would insist on the next championship being played in Australia said that the suggestion was not likely to commend itself to the Council. It was not for Lindrum nor any other player to dictate the terms and conditions under which English championships should be played.

Therefore any suggestion that Walter Lindrum acted deceptively to get the championship cup out of England can be dismissed out of hand. The Control Council cabled Lindrum in regard to the championship. An article in the *Argus* on 13 January 1934 explains both the contents of the cable and Lindrum's response to it.

> Surprise was expressed yesterday by Walter Lindrum when he received a cable message from Mr Stanley Thorn, secretary of the English Billiard Control Council, stating that entries for the professional championship of

1934 would close on February 19. Lindrum was further advised that conditions would be the same as when he was successful last year, and that first-class games would commence in April. An additional request to Lindrum was to return the championship cup if he found himself unable to return to England in time to defend the title.

Lindrum is indignant at the turn of events, and is amazed at the attitude of the Billiard Control Council of England. With the intention of defending his title during the Centenary Celebrations later this year Lindrum has already made tentative arrangements for the appearance in Melbourne and Sydney of the English champion, Joe Davis. . . . Until more definite information is received Lindrum is not inclined to regard the present cable message seriously, being of the opinion that trade interests in England are mainly responsible for its despatch.

Lindrum stated that he would not return the championship cup to England until he was defeated in Australia. He contends that champions in most other sports are expected to defend titles only in their own country and he feels that the same should apply in billiards.

Lindrum left no doubt as to his attitude towards the cable and the championship. When he also declared that he had been given an assurance by John Bissett that the next championship could be played in Australia, Lindrum convinced the Australian Press of the merits of his cause. In reply to this claim Bissett said that "he has no recollection of having told Walter Lindrum that he could defend his title in Australia. Indeed he had no authority to do so". (The *Argus*, 7 January, 1934.)

The wording of Bissett's reply is interesting. If he had not given Lindrum any such assurances he could have been expected to be more positive in his denial of Lindrum's claim. It seems unlikely that the chairman of the Control Council would not have recalled precisely what he had said to Lindrum on what was now proving such a provocative topic. Bissett's reply ought to have been an unequivocal yes or no. It was true in the legal sense that Bissett had "no authority" to permit Lindrum to defend his title in Australia. It was similarly true that the Council had no authority to demand that Lindrum must return to England to defend the championship. When the Council stipulated that the 1934 championship must be held in England it only served to confuse the issue. The original cable to Lindrum stated that conditions for the 1934 championship were to be the same as in the previous year. One of those conditions was that the players were to decide the venue for the event. That clause had been inserted in the championship conditions in place of the clause that had stated that the championship would take place at Messrs Thurston's and Co.'s Hall, Leicester Square, London W.C. This change had resulted from 3 years of lobbying by the professionals who believed that the previous clause gave Thurston's a distinct advantage over the other billiard firms. The rule which allowed the players to select the championship venue had been introduced to overcome the lack of independence of the Control Council from the billiard trade. That rule was now being applied in a much broader sense and in a different context from the situation which existed when it was introduced. The Control Council moved quickly to correct the error in its first cable to Lindrum when it announced that after entries closed on 19 February, it would be left to the players to decide the venue.

Lindrum's basic contention was that, like champions in most other sports, he should have the right to defend the title in his home country. He maintained that it was unreasonable that overseas players should have to return to England each year to defend the title. The Control Council had, apparently, never considered the implications of an overseas player winning the championship. There was no mention in its constitution of the procedure to be adopted if an overseas player won the championship. There was little clarification of the rights of the champion, be he an English or non-English player. It was an area of weakness in the constitution which had never previously caused concern, for in the sixty-year history of the professional championship it had never been won by an overseas player.

Sporting Life made the following comments on the confrontation: "Lindrum is either a confirmed leg-puller or he has no idea of procedure. He holds the British, not the Empire or the world's title. There has never been a British championship contested overseas." (The *Argus,* 15 January 1934.)

It was a very feeble argument to advance. Lindrum repudiated the claim by quoting from the *Billiard Player,* the official organ of billiards, which carried an advertisement in May of 1933 referring to the "world's professional billiard championship". The claim that no British championship had ever been held overseas was a falsehood. The amateur billiard championship was known in 1934 as the 'British Championship', even though it was effectively a world championship. There existed at the time a completely separate event for amateurs which was known as the 'English Championship'. The title 'British Championship' was dispensed with in 1951 in favour of 'World Billiard Championship'. The right of the champion in the amateur game was clearly defined with the holder being permitted to defend the title in his home country.

There may have been some merit in Lindum's claim of his 'right' to defend the championship in his home country. However, the manner in which he confronted the B.A. & C.C. with an ultimatum was not likely to draw a favourable response. Such tactics only served to get the Control Council's 'back up' with the result that it became more intransigent than ever. Lindrum's ultimatum to the controlling body was a reaction to the first cable sent to him. Lindrum was, by nature, a modest and reserved person but he possessed a highly-developed sense of justice, which at times prompted him to become aggressive and forthright.

Consider the pro-Lindrum case in regard to the championship controversy. Lindrum claimed that he had been given assurances that he would be able to defend his title in Australia in 1934. He felt that the Control Council had made an about-face on the matter, probably as the result of trade pressure. Recall Lindrum's earlier experiences when he had, on two separate occasions, been denied entry in the championship by the selfishness of the trade and the inflexible attitude of the Control Council. Recall also the later controversy over the iniquitous baulkline rule which the Control Council insisted on retaining despite widespread protests from players and spectators alike. Is it any wonder that Lindrum did not hold a very high opinion of the B.A. & C.C., a group of amateurs who could exert great influence on the livelihood of professional billiardists? Could Lindrum be excused for believing that some people had done their utmost to prevent him winning and holding the world title? Could he be excused for feeling persecuted? If so, was it only natural that he had to reach a breaking point and react, rationally or otherwise? Lindrum had certainly been involved in a number of controversies during his English tours. The cable from the B.A. & C.C., telling him to return the cup, if unable to return to England to defend it, was the last straw. Lindrum denied the Council's edict and stood up for his 'rights'. Whether Lindrum was justified in doing so is left to the reader to decide. There may be two answers to the question, one based on legal grounds, the other on moral grounds.

The cables continued to flow in from the irate Control Council. The secretary, Mr Thorn, said: "if worst comes to worst, and he still refuses to return the Cup, we will have no option but to take drastic steps to recover it. Naturally, nobody wishes anything of that nature to happen." At the height of the battle the Agents-General for Victoria (Mr Linton) and South Australia (Mr Hall) entered the arena on Lindrum's behalf. The B.A. & C.A. agreed with reluctance to allow the 1934 championship to be played in Australia under the auspices of the Australian Amateur Billiard Council. Walter Lindrum duly lodged his entry for the championship before the closing date of February 19. Entries were also cabled to the Control Council by Horace Lindrum and Fred Lindrum junior. However, for reasons unknown, the Council did not include the names of Fred and Horace when the nominations were announced. There were only three entrants declared: Walter Lindrum, Joe Davis and Clark McConachy.

Of the three entrants, both Lindrum and McConachy were in favour of playing the championship in Australia. Davis had also expressed interest in the proposition in conjunction with an Australian tour. Thus a majority of the entrants favoured playing for the title in Australia. As Lindrum had indicated on his return from England, the championship would be held in Melbourne, during the centenary celebrations. It was almost as if the numerous cables, the demands and the threats by the Control Council, had been unnecessary.

As a consequence of the Championship controversy, and its decision to allow the event to be staged in Australia, the Control Council introduced a new billiard event, known as the United Kingdom Championship, which was restricted to the native-born. The first winner of this new event was Joe Davis who defeated Tom Newman by 436 points after a gripping struggle. Davis thus confirmed his standing as the leading English player and it was appropriate that he was to represent his country in the World Championship in Australia. Prior to his departure for 'down under', Davis sent cables in an endeavour to secure guarantees covering all the expenses of his Australian tour. Davis delayed his departure as he vainly sought the guarantees before finally embarking on the *Orsova* in May.

It is interesting to note the attitude of the English Press in regard to financing of Davis' trip to Australia. It was felt that the player could not be expected to finance himself to Australia in an effort to win the world title. It seemed the Press overlooked the fact that both Walter Lindrum and Clark McConachy had to finance trips to England, the ultimate objective of which was to win the Championship. Lindrum would not have agreed with the claim by the Press that whereas the financial prospects of billiards in Australia were doubtful, those in England were satisfactory. Neither would McConachy have agreed that England was a happy-hunting ground for a professional billiard player. Mac's many English tours never returned 'as much money as he would have liked' and at the end of one tour he had to borrow money from Claude Falkiner to pay his fare to New Zealand. (When he next returned to England, McConachy, being the man of integrity that he was, immediately tracked down Falkiner and repaid the loan).

Joe Davis arrived in Fremantle, Western Australia, on 27 June. He immediately made a phone call to Melbourne to inform Lindrum of his arrival and find out what arrangements had been made for matches and exhibitions. Davis was stunned to learn that there were no definite engagements arranged. This situation was not entirely as Davis suggested, the result of Lindrum's vague attitude. Approaches had been made to various sponsors with the Sydney sporting goods firm, Mick Simmons, showing great enthusiasm for staging matches. These negotiations fell through, perhaps because of the lingering doubt and confusion caused by the Championship controversy or because Mick Simmons was not prepared to give Davis the financial guarantees which he sought prior to leaving England. Davis took stock of the situation and, in his usual efficient way, organised a venue and a series of pre-Championship matches between himself, Lindrum and McConachy.

The matches were arranged to be played at the YMCA match room in Sydney. Davis met McConachy in the first of the 'Test Matches', a title which was attached to the contest as a means of stimulating public interest. Billiards, however, was no longer attracting the throngs of spectators as it had during the visit of Willie Smith in 1929. Both the predictability of the play and the impact of the Depression were factors that influenced the decline in numbers. Davis won the first Test Match by a clear margin over McConachy. He opened the second Test Match (against Lindrum) in fine form, making an 1122 break on the first day. Davis proceeded to win the match by 22 269 to 21 691 against a Lindrum who was described as being 'below his best form.' There were times when Lindrum seemed more interested in how the Australian cricketers were faring in the Test in England. Much to Davis' consternation, Lindrum left the room on several occasions to hear the latest radio reports on the Test Match. When Lindrum was absent from the room Davis was under some pressure to remain in play for it could have been embarrassing if Davis broke down and there was no sign of Lindrum.

A very similar incident occurred in a later match between Davis and Lindrum, only this time it was Joe Davis who was absent from the room. Davis, though, was not in the hallway listening to the Test Match scores; he was not even within cooee of the YMCA hall. A youthful Jim Collins, later to become New South Wales amateur billiards champion, and an administrator of the State Association for over forty years (and who was recognised with membership of the Order of Australia in 1980), was a witness to a remarkable incident. Jim Collins is not certain of the exact date when the following events transpired. It may have been during the first week of the third Lindrum/Davis match, played in Sydney from 11–23 September, 1934. During that week Lindrum made a break of 1909, a personal best under the baulk-line rule, and only 18 points short of Clark McConachy's record break of 1927 (made in Brisbane a couple of months previously). Lindrum's 1909 break ended most unexpectedly — the balls had been spotted after touching (as required by the rules) and he missed the long loser from hand! It was prior to an afternoon session of play that Jim Collins observed Joe Davis draw Walter Lindrum to one side. In a state of considerable agitation Joe informed Walter that a hitch had developed with some business matter which needed his personal attention — immediately. This meant placing the session of play in jeopardy.

"Well, what can we do Walter?" asked Joe desperately, "Can we cancel the session, or defer it for an hour or so?"

"Don't worry about it Joe," assured Walter, "As I'm in play, I'll hold the fort for a while. It'll work out somehow."

With that assurance Davis hastened off to attend to his business, after warning Walter that he could be absent for an hour, perhaps even longer. The session of play commenced with a moderate number of spectators watching Walter resume his break. The player's chair, where each player retired after his visit to the table and waited for his next visit, was conspicuously empty. After an hour of play the player's chair was still empty. After an hour and a half Davis had still not taken his place on the player's seat. Lindrum was still at the table, building one of his customary breaks and, apparently, oblivious to the fact that Davis had still not returned to the Hall. With less than twenty minutes of the session remaining Davis quietly slipped into the player's chair, trying to convey the impression that he had just returned from a brief visit to the washroom. As Walter walked around the table to play his next stroke he acknowledged the presence of Davis with a brief glance. After playing a few more strokes Walter broke down, allowing Davis his first visit for the session.

What a classic illustration of the absolute mastery of Lindrum! He seemed capable, when the situation required, of holding the table, almost indefinitely. He had the capacity to rise to the occasion — the sign of a true champion. A number of Lindrum's most notable performances were made in response to the demands of the situation. His two largest breaks of 4137 and 3905, were made in very demanding circumstances. Walter Lindrum admitted that there were very few occasions in his career when he was fully extended. He regarded the toughest match that he ever played as being the final of the Gold Cup in 1931 when he conceded 7000 start to Tom Newman. At a crucial stage of that match Lindrum rattled off successive breaks of 2835, 451, 1796 and 2583. Lindrum's capacity to lift his game, when faced with a demanding situation, raises a question. What sort of performances would Lindrum have made if there was another player who could have kept him fully extended? Jim Collins, A.M. seems to answer this question when he opined: "I don't believe we ever knew just how good a player Walter Lindrum *really* was".

The 1934 Championship, the first to be staged outside England, commenced on 24 September at the Railways Institute Building in Flinders Street, Melbourne. Lindrum met McConachy in a heat of the Event with the winner to play Davis in the final. It was Lindrum who advanced to the final when he defeated Mac by 21 903 to 20 795, scoring a break of 1065 in the process. The final commenced on 15 October and was opened by Prime Minister Lyons who was in Melbourne to participate in the city's Centenary Celebrations. Lindrum devised a strategy for the final as a means of making victory that much easier. Davis, as Lindrum knew only too well, had a strong penchant for adopting his opponent's game, of 'sitting-in' on his man. It was a tactic which Davis had used with great success in many matches for it quite often disconcerted his opponent and allowed Davis to establish psychological supremacy. In the final, though, Lindrum decided to exploit this facet of Davis' game, allow him to hold an advantage for the first week of play and turn this to a disadvantage in the second week. The plan, as Lindrum reveals, worked from the very start:

> Fate could not have been kinder to me than when Davis, in choosing balls for the match, decided on a heavy set. The weight of the balls varies from 5 ounces to 5 ounces and 20 grains, and to the championship player, making his shots with mere fractions of inches as margins, 10 or 15 grains can make a great difference.
>
> My plan was to make Joe play top of the table and open billiards in the first week, so that he would develop a rather heavy touch, which, in the type of shot he usually plays, takes the edge off the sense of cue delivery for nursery cannon play.
>
> Following my lead, when the match started, Davis, with his lighter cue, had to hit the heavy balls harder. He struck his best form right away. I was tired after the game with McConachy, and many days of making arrangements for the series, and I could not score with anything like the freedom shown by Davis.
>
> Joe was obviously pleased with the way he was running along. He commented freely, too, on the feeble showing I was making — with the idea, perhaps, of worrying me into an introspective frame of mind that would break my game up completely.
>
> Of course, I was as pleased as Joe himself that he was cracking them hard and liking it, because the more he played himself into that heavy touch, the easier I expected would be the job of beating him. (Melbourne *Herald,* 17 December, 1934).

At the end of the first week of play Davis led clearly by 12 111 to 11 097. The best breaks by Davis were 824 and 728 which, as it turned out, were to be his highest breaks in the entire match. Lindrum scored a break of 1013 on the fourth day of play but he took a laborious 50 minutes and 53 seconds to compile it. It was probably the slowest thousand break which he ever made and was an indication of the amount of open play which he was deliberately playing.

Lindrum decided to work his change on the Monday of the second week. Switching the game to nursery cannons he went all out to score at a fast rate. Lindrum reached the thousand mark in 34 minutes and 12 seconds on the way to a break of 1353. Lindrum commented:

> To say that Joe was puzzled by this sudden switch is only brushing it lightly. But, true to his inclination to "sit in", he changed over too. Where was that light touch so necessary for close cannons?
>
> Joe was rather worried, as his comments to me on the second day proved.
>
> "It's funny, Wally, how you got right into form after your weak efforts of last week," he said.
>
> "Just the luck of it," I told him. "I'm feeling better and things went my way."
>
> His failure to follow the close cannon game upset him completely. There was not the slightest indication that Joe jad suspected the plan to switch the game, and I think he left for home without guessing at it. (Melbourne *Herald,* 17 December, 1934.)

The lead alternated in the first three days of the second week but on the Thursday Lindrum, with the aid of a break of 1475 (made in 63 minutes and 50 seconds), swept to the lead and was not headed again. The final scores were Lindrum 23 553, Davis 22 678. Davis later conceded that Lindrum was "just too good for me in the Melbourne final" and the *Argus* said: "Lindrum's margin was 875, but had he desired he could have won by many more points". The championship had been staged at a moderate profit due to Melbourne's Centenary Celebrations and also to Lindrum's drawing power in his home town. It was generally a very difficult time for the professional billiard player. Typical of the times was an exhibition that Davis and Lindrum played at Wagga Wagga in New South Wales when they shared a profit of £1. Davis had experienced the same financial difficulty throughout his Australian tour and at this stage had not cleared sufficient money for the cost of his voyage back to England. This problem was resolved when Davis won a snooker match with a £100 wager attached, against young Horace Lindrum. The match was the result of a heated verbal exchange between Davis and Horace's mother, Violet. Joe grew tired of what he regarded as extravagant claims by Violet and finally challenged her to support her claims with some hard cash. The result was a 63-frame match, with a £100 wager, to be played at the Tivoli Saloon in Melbourne. Young Horace proved no match for Davis who won by 42 frames to 22.

Horace then issued a challenge to Fred Lindrum junior for the Australian Billiard Championship and in a match at the Tivoli Saloon he took his uncle's title by a margin of 18 754 to 9143, with best breaks of 1129 and 1086. Horace Lindrum and Joe Davis were two of the pioneers of professional snooker, making many tours and playing scores of matches. Davis was the first player to make 500 century breaks at snooker in public appearances while Horace was the first to make 1000 centuries in public. Despite Horace's record and his great ability he did not seriously threaten the supremacy of Joe Davis. This was because, in the words of Joe Davis, Horace "was temperamentally more of an exhibition player than a competition player". Horace Lindrum did possess a superb repertoire of trick shots. Apart from the more standard type of trick shots Horace had a unique display of 'finger spins'. Horace could impart an incredible amount of spin on the ball with his fingers and make it drop into the pockets from all angles. As if this wasn't enough, Horace would then repeat these finger spins, using a dummy hen's nest-egg in place of the ball. Horace's finger-spins became so famous that a dubious Alex Higgins, on an Australian tour in the early seventies, sought out Horace and had his own personal exhibition. Only then was Higgins convinced that the finger-spins were actually possible. Horace Lindrum had a special attribute which facilitated these incredible trick shots: he was 'double-jointed' in all fingers. Ever-smiling Horace performed his unequalled array of trick shots with great enthusiasm. This most amicable man ranks as a truly great entertainer.

Although not realised at the time the departure of Joe Davis for England marked the end of the 'Golden Era of Billiards', that remarkable period when the game developed at a rapid rate and evolved into the highest possible form. Walter Lindrum was responsible for the final, and most dramatic stages of this evolutionary process. His arrival in England in 1929 denotes the start of

Walter and his fiancee, Pat Hoskin, after the announcement of their engagement in London, March 1933. (Dolly Lindrum)

Walter with the Championship Cup at the height of the 1934 controversy when he declared he would fight any move by the B.A. & C.C. for the Cup to be returned to England. (Melbourne Age)

Harriet Lindrum proudly displays the Gold Cup won by her son, Walter in the 1930–31 English season. The cup contains 84 ounces of pure gold and is stored in a Melbourne bank. (Dolly Lindrum)

A rare shot of Charlie Chambers (left), doyen of referees, outside Thurston's Hall, Leicester Square, London with Horace Lindrum, taken 1935–39. (Norman Clare)

that final, dramatic period of evolution. Lindrum's arrival at the home of billiards was to have a number of consequences, in both the short and long term, for the game. In 1929 the future of billiards in England was somewhat uncertain. This uncertainty had been evident for a number of years and was a consequence of the prowess of the leading players. The following article appeared in a London newspaper in 1925:

> In London billiards are not as popular as they used to be. It is contended that the main cause is that the great professors of the hour are too accomplished. They string up big breaks with such ease that play becomes monotonous, so that people in search of excitement are not as prepared to patronise the game as they formerly did. Someone has suggested that Newman and Smith should betake themselves on a foreign tour for two or three years, and give the game a chance to settle down to a more normal environment, and restore the old competitive atmosphere. (Reproduced in the *Referee*, 1 April 1925.)

Smith and Newman did not follow the advice offered in the article. Instead they made bigger and bigger breaks at ever-increasing frequency, and by 1929 there was some degree of complacency in the public's attitude towards these breaks. The future of professional billiards was not at all clear. Along came Walter Lindrum, waved his magic cue, and the uncertainty was swept away, almost over night. He captured the imagination of the public with his prodigious scoring and breathed a new life into billiards which saw it enter probably its most popular period ever. Lindrum's billiards, with the nursery cannon as the ultimate scoring weapon, caused a rapid transformation in the method of play. The other professionals worked feverishly to integrate the close cannons into their games, reasoning that if they were to have any chance of competing with Lindrum, they would have to adopt his methods. Of course, Willie Smith was the notable exception who, from the outset, believed that nursery cannon play was not in the long-term interests of billiards. Smith was proven all too correct with the spectators rebelling against the repetitiveness and the obscure refinements of the close cannons. Joe Davis eventually realised the problem and tried to convince Lindrum to adopt a more open style of play. Lindrum refused to curtail or reduce his cannon play. Davis, although wanting to play the type of billiards that appealed to the public, did not reduce his cannon play for he feared that Lindrum would be left with a clear advantage. In 1935 Davis made an interesting comment, following a break of 2002, made in 113 minutes under the line rule:

> I am beginning to realise the astonishing fact that my biggest breaks are made without the use of the close-cannon game. Possibly the strain of close cannons, which is infinitely greater than it appears to be, has something to do with it. Today I deliberately kept the game open.
> (*Billiards for All Time*, Riso Levi.)

Davis had realised that there was perhaps a feasible alternative to the nursery cannon game. But it was too late for any attempt to save billiards. By 1935 billiards as a spectator sport was, in Davis' own words, 'as dead as mutton' It seems unlikely if anyone, or anything, could have saved billiards from its demise. There were many factors which influenced its decline and it is impossible to consider any one factor in isolation from the rest. Certainly the prevalence of nursery cannon play had its effect, as did the overall high standard of performance by the professionals. In most other sports a higher standard of performance will attract larger numbers of spectators. Such was not the case in professional billiards in the thirties. The players made the mistake of becoming too proficient with the result that play became too predictable for the spectators.

The game of billiards also suffered from the management of the B.A. & C.C. The Council seemed to lack the strength, and independence from outside influences, necessary for sound leadership. It seemed, at times, to isolate itself from the reality of the situation and failed to consult the players when this appeared the obvious thing to be doing. Some of its decisions were ill-advised, the introduction of the iniquitous baulk-line rule being a prime example of the Council's failure to appreciate the substance of a situation.

Trade interests also played a part in the decline of billiards. Petty jealousy between trade firms caused uncertainty and disrupted the smooth running of professional billiards on several occasions. It seemed as if some sections of the trade were more intent on preserving their own interests than thinking of the long term future of the game. This short-term outlook ignored the fact that the trade was somewhat dependent on the state of the professional game for its long-term future.

The Depression of the thirties also affected the popularity of billiards. Although it initially had a positive effect in providing recreation and escape, as time wore on and the economic conditions intensified, people had to tighten their budgets. Billiards, whether played or watched, was one expenditure curtailed. The Depression may have affected the popularity of billiards in another way: it may have altered the outlook of people towards life itself and this could have been reflected in their attitude towards billiards. The game of billiards has always had an abstract, intangible quality about it. The player, if he was good enough, could literally go on forever. There is a certain elegance and uncertainty about the game which contributes to its leisurely nature. It seems as if the game of billiards reflected the lifestyle of the pre-Depression days. That may be one reason that billiards was such a popular form of recreation. The Depression may have changed all that. Having experienced the trauma and trepidation of these harsh times, which shook the very foundations on which their lives had been built, people were no longer content to live in that leisurely, almost casual style of the pre-Depression days. There was a desire for a more secure lifestyle, an urgency for a more finite aspect to life. This desire may have carried over into the recreational side of life. Billiards was not suitable to this new approach to life. It was too abstract and uncertain. An alternative was sought which offered finite, positive dimensions. The game of snooker offered these features. When the game commenced there was a total of 147 points that could be scored (barring fouls), and that had to be scored in a definite way (each red followed by a colour, and then the colours in sequence from the yellow to the black.) There is also a definite crisis point in snooker when one of the players requires a snooker to win the match. Snooker was indeed a very suitable replacement for billiards.

Perhaps the Depression did cause such a change in attitude towards life that influenced the demise of billiards. Perhaps it did not. Certainly the mid-thirties saw a rapid increase in the popularity of snooker and a corresponding decline in the popularity of billiards.

In his analysis of the reasons for the decline of professional billiards in *The Story of Billiards and Snooker,* Clive Everton states: "But possibly worst of all was that Lindrum, having retained the Championship after a struggle, was disinclined to put it at risk again". (pp.53–4.)

This statement is not strictly correct. Lindrum was quite prepared to defend his title, but only in Australia. He believed, rightly or wrongly, that it was his right as champion to defend the title in his home country. Any of the overseas players had the option of coming to Australia to challenge Lindrum for the championship. The problem was that the financial prospects for professional billiards were very bleak in Australia, so there was little incentive for Davis & Co. to visit the Antipodes. The situation in England was much the same. Who could blame Lindrum for not wanting to return to England to defend his title, and probably suffer financially as a consequence? There is no doubt that Lindrum was reluctant to return to England but the reasons for this reluctance have not been fully explained previously. Lindrum was not happy with the way billiards was run in England. He was tired of having to submit to the whims of the Control Council. He was also disturbed by the unhealthy influence which sections of the trade seemed to be able to exert on the game. He was also disappointed with his financial returns from his various trips to England. His earnings could be described at best, as moderate. Considering that he was the hottest billiard property to have walked on earth it is more appropriate to describe his earnings as mediocre. There were a number of factors that contributed to this situation — the Depression, poor management by the trade of Lindrum's first tour, and Lindrum's own lack of business acumen. It was the response of the billiard firms to Lindrum's deeds which was disappointing. Some sections of the trade did see fit to give financial incentives to Lindrum for breaking records etc. Other sections of the trade, though, were conspicuous in their parsimony. Lindrum did far more than merely re-write the record books: he gave billiards a new image. No longer was billiards looked down on as the game of disreputable layabouts. It became fashionable for men to wear evening dress to the evening sessions and it was now sociably acceptable for women to attend billiard matches. Lindrum's Command Performance for King George V and Queen Mary was the ultimate seal of approval for the game. As Lindrum said a few years later: "I am irritated when I hear people say that proficiency at billiards is the sign of a misspent youth. If such was the case, do you think I would have been invited by the late King George V to give a command performance at Buckingham Palace?"

Such was the popularity of billiards in the early thirties that the English billiard trade was somewhat insulated from the grips of the Depression that swept the rest of the economy. It was the exploits of Walter Lindrum that were largely responsible for this insulation. He was a virtual 'meal ticket' for the trade. But as the thousands of pounds poured into their coffers sections of the billiard trade saw no reason to reward the genius who had made it all possible.

According to Clive Everton, author of *The Story of Billiards and Snooker,* "He (Lindrum) left England owing large enough sums for goods purchased within the English billiards trade for these debts to be advanced as an important reason why he never returned." When challenged to name the source of this information, Everton's reply was: "My information about Lindrum's debts came from many figures in the English Billiard trade, past and present." Such a vague and non-committal answer was most unsatisfactory. The assistance of Mr Norman Clare, of the billiard firm E. A. Clare & Son Ltd, Liverpool (England) was sought as a means of clarifying the detail of these alleged debts. Mr. Clare was in an excellent position to check out the allegations for he has close links with a number of the English trade firms, as his reply indicates:

> I can definitely say that there was no money owing to ourselves (E. A. Clare & Son of Liverpool), or to our associated companies Thos. Padmore & Son Ltd; of Birmingham with whom Walter Lindrum did have many business and promotional arrangements, neither was there any money owing to Thurston & Co. Ltd., of London.
>   . . . when I contacted our remaining associated company namely: Peradon & Fletcher Ltd; of Andover, they were able to provide me with quite conclusive evidence that Mr. Walter Lindrum did owe quite a large sum of money to the original Peradon Co; dating back to the time when he left U.K. in 1933.

So there is was, Walter Lindrum did owe money to one trade firm when he left England for the last time. That debt was described as being 'large' but what qualified in the thirties as being a large debt remains unknown. From the scant information available it seems likely that the money was owing for the purchase of trade goods, probably a consignment of cues. Mr. Norman Clare, after confirming that Lindrum did leave a trade debt in England, further revealed that " . . . it is only because I am the Chairman of Peradon & Fletcher Ltd. that I have been able to obtain this information from them and I am definitely able to say that Clive Everton certainly did not obtain his information from that source."

Where, then, did Clive Everton obtain his information on Lindrum's trade debt/s? Surely it was not hearsay that was the basis of Everton's serious allegation that trade debts were an important reason that Lindrum never returned to England after 1933? Mr Norman Clare may well be the only person who has access to documentary evidence which confirmed the existence of a trade debt. He has also supplied proof that this debt was later liquidated by Walter Lindrum. In a letter dated 30 October, 1947, Lindrum wrote:

> Dear Mr. Peradon,
> This will serve as a binding contract for you to manufacture any cues bearing the name of Walter Lindrum for the British Empire, except Australia.
> No royalty is required to me for any cue you manufacture. In appreciation of many kindnesses. This contract is for ever.
>
>   Walter Lindrum

This letter was not the gesture of a man who had refused to return to England because he owed money in that country. It was the touching and sincere gesture of a man who, despite having no obligation to do so, chose to settle an old debt in a most generous manner. Lindrum did not take the legalistic view of the situation and refuse to settle a debt that was absolved by the statute of limitations. He preferred to honour the debt, and honour it he did in a most sincere manner. The closing sentence of that letter, "This contract is for ever", epitomises the warm-hearted, spontaneous being that was Walter Lindrum.

During the heights of his triumphant tours Lindrum had enthusiastically declared that Great Britain was the finest country in the world. The popularity and acceptance that he enjoyed there prompted him to place Great Britain above his native Australia. When Lindrum left England for the last time, in 1933, he had lost his infatuation for the mother country. Lindrum was seeing through the shallow handshakes and the cosmetic friendships that overlay ulterior motives. Everybody wants to know a winner, for one reason or another. Walter Lindrum left England, a disillusioned and deeply hurt man.

12 A New Lifestyle

The quiet little man is Walter Lindrum, the man whose skill in his own field is so great that he is forever doomed to sit in unapproachable loneliness and watch the feeble attempts of ordinary folk to follow where he leads.

South West Pacific (magazine, late 1940s)

The years from 1935 to 1939 can only be described as a transition period in Walter Lindrum's life. He had vowed that he would never return to England, the scene of so many triumphs. When Lindrum opted to discontinue his English tours he was effectively cutting himself off from a way of life. No longer would he experience the same degree of glamour, the public exposure, the adulation and the press coverage that had been part of his life. And no longer would he have to undertake the arduous hours of travel, the heavy schedule of matches or be at the centre of controversy, which had all been part of his English tours. Lindrum had chosen to withdraw from that lifestyle and he was, inevitably, suffering withdrawal symptoms. He was undergoing an enforced adjustment to his way of life — just as many champions have done over the years — and, like other champions, he took time to make the adjustment. In his period of re-adjustment Lindrum yearned for a return to active competition and for matches with his world title at stake.

There were offers from England — including one for £5000 and organised by Joe Davis — made to Lindrum for an English tour. They were for a series of snooker matches between Lindrum and Davis. Snooker did not appeal to Lindrum and consequently he rejected a number of lucrative invitations.

In May 1935 Lindrum travelled to New Zealand, via Sydney. He toured the Shaky Isles with Clark McConachy, his old friend and foe. The two decided to visit Canada and spent several months in that country in an attempt to popularise English billiards. Lindrum returned to Melbourne on 29 February 1936 after his voyage on the Matson liner, *Mariposa*. It was Lindrum's last overseas tour for twenty years and the last time that he toured with an opponent.

Lindrum's services were still in demand for exhibitions at clubs and for commercial organisations. In May of 1936 Lindrum was engaged to perform for the leading retailer, David Jones, at the firm's premises in George Street, Sydney. During the exhibitions news came from London that Joe Davis had made a record baulkline break of 1784 (the baulkline rule had been tightened to stipulate that a crossing must be made every 180-200 points.) A few days later (10 June) the Sydney papers announced that Lindrum intended to break Davis' record. That Lindrum competitive streak was as keen as ever! Two days later Lindrum made a break of 1796. The break was verified by Claude Spencer, the referee, who was associated with a number of Lindrum exhibitions and who also reported on billiards for the *Referee*. Apparently there was some confusion in Australia on the interpretation of the latest amendment to the baulkline rule. Although Lindrum first crossed the line at 194, and crossed it an additional seven times before he reached 1600, he did not follow the strict letter of the rule. The break of 1796 thus never received any official recognition.

Lindrum continued to hold hopes that there would be matches for the world championship. The papers reported on several occasions Lindrum's declaration that he was prepared to defend his world title, but only in Australia. There was no response from the English professionals. However, the New Zealand champion, Clark McConachy, showed interest in playing for the championship. Lindrum and McConachy organised to play a match in Sydney in February 1938 and intended it to be for the world title. However, the B.A. & C.C. did not ratify the match and thus it could not be for the world championship. Lindrum won the match by a clear margin of 18 349 to 14 121. It was a sad moment for the billiard fraternity, although nobody realised its significance at the time, for it was the last occasion on which Walter and Mac played each other. When they were first pitted against each other in 1916 both players still had a relatively rudimentary knowledge of billiards, particularly McConachy. Few could have envisaged how proficient they would become and what an integral part that each would play in the billiard revolution of the late 1920's and early 1930's. Walter was undeniably a far superior player, but McConachy did have the honour of recording more victories over Lindrum off scratch than any other of the leading professionals.

During the transition years, 1935–39, Walter Lindrum established two new businesses. He entered the billiard trade and specialised in the re-covering and general servicing of billiard tables. This business, which employed one experienced hand, continued on a small scale for most of Walter's life. Lindrum's other venture at about the same time was to open a billiard room in the town of Red Cliffs, situated near Mildura in the Sunraysia district of Victoria. Lindrum took over the lease of a billiard room which had been rebuilt after being extensively damaged by fire. The room contained four tables with an adjoining refreshment room which fronted onto the street. Lindrum's became a popular retreat for both billiard and snooker players and as a place to go after the pictures for a cup of coffee.

The Red Cliffs district had been developed in the early twenties for fruit-growing. Irrigation from the Murray River turned an arid region into an oasis of vines and citrus trees. Most of the early settlers were Diggers from the War and each was allotted about six hectares. The district became a hive of activity in February each year when the harvesting of the fruit crop commenced. With the influx of seasonal workers for the harvest the town's social and economic life enjoyed a boom for a couple of months. Lindrum's Saloon was very busy during this period, making a healthy profit, which helped carry it through the quieter months of the year.

In February of 1939, after only a few days of the fruit harvest, heavy rains wiped out most of the crop. One Saturday afternoon, when the shops were open for late shopping, several hundred disgruntled itinerant pickers gathered in the streets. A few of the frustrated pickers started a brawl and there were soon hundreds of pickers and townspeople involved in a wild melee which has since become known as the 'Red Cliffs Riot'. The riot was eventually quelled by the fire brigade who used hoses to gun down everybody in sight — including rioters, pickers, townsfolk and police. The loss of the fruit crop, which indirectly led to the riot, had serious repercussions for the business life of Red Cliffs. Lindrum's Saloon was one of many businesses that suffered a decline in patronage. Despite this setback the saloon may have been able to survive but for the outbreak of war some seven months later. With the exodus of the youth out of the district and into the services, Lindrum's Saloon lost its main source of business. It was a fate that many other saloons, which had struggled on through the Depression, also suffered. Lindrum's Saloon at Red Cliffs closed in the early 1940s. The room had been managed first by Walter's brother-in-law, Horace Morell, a local identity, Henry Beaton, and finally by Walter's nephew, Bill Dunn.

The closing of many public billiard rooms, enforced by the outbreak of World War II, was part of a general decline in the number of venues for billiards. One type of the venue that suffered its demise in the pre-World War II years was the Mechanic's Institute or School of Arts. In 1833 the Reverend Henry Carmichael opened the first Mechanic's School of Arts in Sydney. These premises originally consisted of a library of technical books for the education of adult workers. Gradually the concept of the Institute was broadened to cater for the leisure of the workers and, of course, included billiards. The Institute billiard players were the true, unadulterated lovers of the game for gambling was strictly prohibited: those players who had a predilection for gambling thus tended to frequent other billiard rooms. The Institutes were gradually phased out, with a number of them being converted to serve as a town libraries.

Another type of venue which flourished in the 1920s and 1930s was the local fire station. During the early decades of this century many firefighters worked extraordinarily long hours. The firemen virtually lived at the station, going home only for a quick meal or for rest. When they were not attending fires the firemen had little work to do, apart from the regular maintenance of equipment. A billiard table was installed at many fire stations as a means of keeping the employees occupied. Many fine players were products of the fire station tables and a number graduated to state championships. The shortening of working hours, and the introduction of shift hours, heralded the decline of the stations as a venue for billiards and snooker. There are, though, still a few stations that maintain a billiard table for the men.

One of the finest products of the fire station tables was Anthony William ('Nick') Winter who could be generally described as a 200-break player. Winter was an all-round sportsman whose achievements in the fields of athletics, tennis, soccer, Australian Rules football, golf, cricket and roller-skating earned him the description of the most versatile sportsman in Australia. In the 1924 Paris Olympics, Winter won the hop, step and jump with a leap of 50 feet 11 3/16 inches (about 15.55m). Winter once rode a bicycle for ten miles (16 kilometres) seated on the handlebars, facing the rear of the bicycle, to win a bet with a friend. He had exceptional muscle development and could perform remarkable feats of strength. At billiards Winter was more interested in setting himself challenges than in playing the orthodox game. For example, on one occasion he scored 165 points in consecutive short jennies off the red ball. Winter revelled in trick shots and possessed one masse stroke that was unique. When Walter Lindrum saw

Nick Winter perform the masse stroke he conceded, after several attempts, that the shot was too difficult for him. The masse stroke, played from a heavily snookered position and off two cushions, may have been facilitated by Winter's great strength and finely-tuned body.

The outbreak of World War II, in early September 1939, saw Australia adjusting and gearing up for a supreme effort. Many were to make the ultimate sacrifice in foreign lands and those who remained at home underwent voluntary and compulsory restraints. Thousands of women joined the Land Army to replace the men who had joined the armed forces. The essential food supply was maintained with the invaluable help of the Land Army volunteers who left the comfort of city life to drive tractors, drove sheep, pick fruit — anything at all to keep up production.

Walter Lindrum was ready to offer his services in any way that they could be used. He quickly became involved with various fund-raising efforts and appeals that were to occupy his time fully for the duration of the war and overflow into the post-war years. The war was the start of a new chapter in Lindrum's life. It effectively completed Lindrum's transition from serious match play and overseas tours. Previously Lindrum had written himself into the record books with his mastery of billiards. Throughout the war Lindrum gave unstintingly of his prowess to raise funds and by so doing etched himself a place in the hearts of many unknowing grateful Australians. Many a Digger was to enjoy the diversion of a cigarette that had resulted from Lindrum's 'Fags for Fighters' campaign. Such was Lindrum's humility that he never sought to equate his efforts with the heroic deeds of the active servicemen. Yet his campaign on the home front was so remarkable that it was later claimed that 'no other individual has ever equalled his lone effort.'

Lindrum's first involvement was with the Racing Patriotic Appeal Fund. The men of the Victorian turf requested help for their Fund and Lindrum responded by offering his services to them free of charge. At Lindrum's suggestion a match was organised between himself and ten of the leading Victorian amateurs. Among his opponents were Tom Cleary, current Victorian champion and a future Australian and World Champion: Jim Long, a future Australian champion and Stan Wood, a prominent amateur and family friend who has for many years given lessons on Walter Lindrum's own table. Other players were Frank Freston, D. D. Dinley (bookmaker), E. N. Bracey, R. Mousally, W. H. Carter, F. F. Hancock and C. E. Norman. Each amateur played two sessions of two hours duration and received 2000 start from Lindrum. The amateurs each took a turn at refereeing one day's play. As Dave Dinley, the bookmaker, refereed one session he called the scores in a monotone voice as Lindrum built up a break. However, it reached a high pitch when he made a correction after calling the scores: "398, 400, 2, 4, 6-to-4-on — sorry, I mean 406".

In a later session Lindrum stopped several times when about to make a shot while there was a hubbub of noise in an adjoining room. He appeared a little upset but soon brightened when the sound of an orchestra playing 'The Blue Danube' drifted into the room. Lindrum skipped lightly around the table in making a break of more than 1000 and his cue appeared to keep time with the music. When the bass notes of the music were heard Lindrum played his all-round game, but when there were lilting notes he kept time with a series of nursery cannons. The final scores for the match were 36 352 to 27 988, in Lindrum's favour, with his best breaks being 2466 and 1859. Proceeds for the match were around £400.

Walter later played a fortnight match with brother Fred, again for the Racing Men's Fund. The first week went very well with good crowds in attendance. Joe Connell, the Fund's chairman, became concerned when the crowds started to dwindle in the second week. Walter agreed with Connell: "We're not getting enough people. I'll tell you what we'll do. I'll make a break of 2,000 tomorrow and the next day which means they'll come along in the hope of seeing me break a record".

Walter did just as he promised and sure enough the crowds flocked back to the match. He did not make a record break, though, somewhat to the crowd's disappointment — but to Fred Lindrum's relief. During the war years Fred had the dubious honour of sitting through several large breaks by Walter. The first of these was a 3361 break, made on 31 July 1940 at the Flinders Lane Saloon.

The 'Fags for Fighters' drive commenced in the early months of the war and continued on for several years. One of the first areas that was selected for raising funds was the Dandenongs. Radiating out from the railhead at Ferntree Gully were fifty kilometres of hilly country excellent for growing fruit. Lindrum's first move was to contact a local identity to help organise a venue, handle publicity and, most importantly, find a sponsor. All proceeds were to go direct to the Fund. Harry Price was a local councillor and a member of the R.S.L. The veterans of World War I were only too pleased to be part of such a familiar cause. Price approached Gilbey's, of gin fame, and they agreed to meet the sundry expenses of the evening. Lindrum always gave his services free. Gilbey's even appointed their sales manager, Keith (the Horse) Horsely, to assist in organising the occasion. It was agreed to combine the Lindrum exhibition with a monthly meeting of the R.S.L. in their Ferntree Gully Hall.

On the afternoon of the show Lindrum arrived to prepare for the evening. As there was no table in the hall Lindrum brought one along and also two assistants to help erect it. It was not a full-sized table, which were so cumbersome to handle, but a smaller, American table. It was soon obvious to Harry Price just what a perfectionist Lindrum was. Every detail — the location of the table, the levels, the lights, the seating — had to be perfect and nothing was overlooked. When all these factors had been dealt with and the helpers were expecting to adjourn for a drink, Lindrum called for a brief rehearsal of the programme. Even the seemingly impromptu, spontaneous challenges, invitations, wagers — and collections — were slotted into a schedule. Price had the arduous task of collecting and accounting for all moneys — entrances, donations, etc. — and filling in the forms for the Fund. When he was certain that the performance was completely mapped out, Lindrum consented to cross to the pub for a quick meal.

As he reached the door, Lindrum stopped to survey the layout. A wry smile curled around Lindrum's lips as he noted the unlined walls of the small weatherboard hall. "Well Harry", he laughed, "she's a bit rough, but she'll do". Price was quick to explain that when the hall was built by World War I veterans and volunteer labour they had stopped work on the inaugural day to sample the contribution of the local publican. Thereafter the interior remained uncompleted and somehow the members liked it that way. A member once complained that the hall was draughty but the issue was permanently settled when one veteran, known affectionately as Old Matt, said: "Struth, Mr President, if you make the joint too comfortable the bastards will never go 'ome".

Lindrum entered the packed hall at 8 o'clock and was welcomed by the President of the branch and the local Member of Parliament, George Knox, who later became Sir George and Speaker of the State House. The 'Brig', as he was fondly called, was an immense and popular figure with all political parties. He was never opposed in his electorate and was always ready to take up the cause of an ex-digger who had suffered hardship. The local R.S.L. members were there to a man, drawn from their diverse ways of life by their common interest. They were predominantly orchardists, small farmers (as George Knox was), railway men, council employees, casual labourers, shop-keepers and a spattering of professional people. Many had served in the first war and now joined the Volunteer Defence Corps.

After the formalities of introduction were over Walter moved into his programme. Initially he demonstrated the losing hazard game before advancing to his top-of-the-table play and then the intricacies of the nursery cannon. Lindrum cast a spell over the audience as he moved through his routine at great speed and with perfect control that could be matched by no other. As he hastened around the table he maintained a running commentary of pointed anecdotes that kept the audience in high spirits. Having demonstrated his skill at the formalised game Lindrum turned to the light-hearted, but more important, trick shots. After a few elementary and successful tricks Lindrum suddenly, unaccountably, missed. Immediately (as planned) a spruiker went into action:

"Hello, what's happened here? Not an easy one, is it Walter?"

Walter stood nonplussed before settling down over the table, with exaggerated deliberation, for another attempt at the shot. Again he missed. The spectators looked on in anguish. The spruiker took Walter's dilemma to the spectators:

"Well, it looks as if this one's got the champ beat. Who'll give ten bob for Walter to make the shot with the next go?"

"I will", was the immediate reply from Harry Price. "Make that a quid", came a voice from the body of the hall. "Thirty bob, two quid, three quid, four quid, a fiver" were offered in rapid succession. With some hesitation Walter took up position for a further attempt at the difficult stroke. There was hushed silence in the hall. Lindrum played the stroke and, amazingly, was successful. The hall echoed with enthusiastic applause. Without hesitation Lindrum moved on to other trick shots. He was successful with a couple of shots but then missed by several centimetres. With little need for prompting the offers flowed in for a successful attempt. Lindrum duly obliged and a happy spectator contributed to the fund. After another trick was successfully performed Lindrum again met with failure. Lindrum paused, and addressed the audience:

> Gee, I'm playing badly tonight. I remember when I gave an exhibition at the Royal Automobile Club in London. It was one of those nights

where everything went right. I made a thousand unfinished at billiards and cleared the table in a frame of snooker. My trick shots all worked first time and I was most satisfied with the evening. As I was about to leave a little man in the front row pulled my sleeve and asked: 'What do you do for a living?'

The audience roared. The spruiker called, "Right, who's going to give a quid for the champ to have another go at this difficult shot?" The offers poured in and Walter, of course, made the shot. Out came the wicker basket for more trick shots. Lindrum failed with some shots and more donations were extracted for the Fund. When the exhibition came to an end a substantial amount had been contributed to the 'Fags for Fighters' Fund. The billiard table was dismantled in speedy fashion and loaded back onto the truck. After refreshments, during which the talented R.S.L. members performed their familiar acts with undiminished zest, Walter Lindrum set off on the journey back to town. It was a routine that he was to repeat at scores of venues over the next few years. On occasions the local club or organisation had its own table and more often Lindrum provided the only form of entertainment for the evening. He continued to perform his act to the rustle of notes and the jingle of silver. As the months went by, and the travelling home in the late hours continued, the physical and mental strain must have been considerable. Yet Lindrum always remained the debonair artist and seldom, if ever, questioned the exacting demands he made of himself. When Lindrum returned home after the evening exhibitions he would take his cue, sets of balls, basket and other equipment to his billiard room. In the room was a long, padded seat. Walter was often found on this seat, sound asleep, the next morning, and still wearing his evening dress. He was, apparently, so fatigued that he had succumbed to the lure of the padded seat in preference to the comfort of his own bed which was only a short walk away. By the end of the 'Fags for Fighters' campaign Lindrum had seen four million cigarettes sent to the active services.

In early February, 1941 Walter Lindrum commenced exhibitions at Anthony Hordern's Fine Art Gallery in Sydney. Hordern's, the *Daily Telegraph* and Tooheys Limited sponsored the exhibitions which were for the Lord Mayor's Fund and the Red Cross Appeal. At the same time a book by Walter Lindrum, *Billiards and Snooker*, was released with the proceeds from sales also going to the Lord Mayor's Fund and Red Cross Appeal. One of the driving forces behind these Sydney exhibitions was Eric Callaway, then the General Manager of Tooheys Ltd. Callaway, who was one of Walter's closest friends, later became President of the N.S.W. Billiards and Snooker Association, and is now an Honorary Life Member of that body.

Lindrum's opening match of the exhibition was played against the Lord Mayor, Alderman Crick, who received 95 start in 100-up. Lindrum broke down on four occasions, which prompted a call for the stewards, before Crick won by 101–52. One of the terms under which Lindrum played the matches was that, if he defeated his opponent who received 95 start, a donation of £1 to the Appeal was expected. Although the Lord Mayor was not obliged to do so he gave £5 to the Appeal. Lindrum often produced 'rabbit' billiards and allowed his opponent to win. He miscued, missed balls hanging over the pockets and muffed simple cannons. His opponents usually entered into the spirit of the cause and gave the £1 donation, and more. Celebrity comperes were a regular part of the programme. One was the English actor, Edwin Styles, who quipped: "It's easy to play Walter Lindrum; all you need is an Anthony Hordern's armchair, a glass of Tooheys beer and a *Daily Telegraph*".

One who played Lindrum was Cyril Oswald-Sealy, a competent player who has for many years been closely associated with the administrative side of billiards. Oswald-Sealy has been both President and Secretary of the N.S.W. Association, is an Honorary Life Member of both that body and the Australian Council, and is also patron of the Australian Council. Oswald-Sealy had made a bet with an accountant friend, by the name of McAndrew. "I'll bet you a fiver", challenged Oswald-Sealy, "that I can beat Lindrum with less start than you can". McAndrew agreed to the bet and went to the Hordern Gallery to arrange a time when both he and Oswald-Sealy could play Lindrum. It was agreed that they would play in the following week. McAndrew was the first to play Lindrum and with 95 start managed to defeat the maestro. Oswald-Sealy, prior to commencing his match, asked Lindrum if he could play him with only 94 start. Lindrum readily agreed. Oswald-Sealy broke off, putting the red ball in baulk and the white ball at the other end of the table. Lindrum, instead of playing his shot, walked over to the microphone and asked: "Who will give £5 if I make 100 in less than five minutes, before my opponent scores his required six points?"

When Lindrum had secured a sponsor he commenced playing. He rattled up the 100 points in around three minutes, without allowing Oswald-Sealy another stroke. Oswald-Sealy could not believe his luck, knowing that Lindrum usually gave his opponent a chance to go out. Although stunned, Oswald-Sealy walked over to shake Lindrum's hand and thank him for the game. As they shook hands Walter could contain himself no longer. Breaking into a broad smile, he said: "I'm sorry, Cyril. This joker (McAndrew) put me up to this last week".

Another of Lindrum's opponents was a keen eleven-year-old by the name of Eddie Charlton. The previous day young Eddie had watched Lindrum play for five hours and sat open-mouthed while Lindrum made a break of 109 at snooker. After receiving forty points start Eddie won a game of snooker by 67 points to 23. The lad readily admitted: "Mr. Lindrum didn't fool me, I could tell he was running dead". This did not prevent the cool-headed youngster from obtaining a signed statement of defeat from Walter Lindrum. Mixed in with the light-hearted matches were individual demonstrations at both billiards and snooker. On 20 February Lindrum, in three consecutive visits to the table, made 1000 unfinished at billiards, cleared the table for a 123 break at snooker, and then compiled another 1000 unfinished at billiards. "I've never been in better touch", Lindrum enthusiastically declared. In slightly over a fortnight since the exhibition had begun Lindrum had lost seven kilograms. He had shed all his surplus weight and was down to his ideal 'match-weight' of 73 kilograms. The proceeds of the exhibitions at the Anthony Hordern Gallery totalled £4545. They were equally shared by the Lord Mayor's Fund and the Red Cross Appeal.

In May of 1941 a billiard match commenced at the Lindrum's Saloon in Flinders Lane between Walter and Fred Lindrum junior. The match was originally scheduled to last a fortnight but it eventually ran into five weeks. Walter conceded 7000 start and only counted his breaks of more than 700. It was a remarkable match for Walter scored a total of 31 breaks in excess of 1000. These included breaks of 3735, made on 15–16 May, and 3752, made on 31 May. A few frames of snooker were played at the end of the sessions. Walter made numerous century breaks, including two breaks of 135, the first of these being a full table clearance after Fred had broken the balls. On 5 June the evening session of the match was cancelled because Walter and Fred were appearing at the Angler's Club in aid of the St Vincent's Hospital Appeal. Due recognition has not been given to the charity efforts of Fred Lindrum and also Horace Lindrum. With Walter giving such a staggering number of charity performances the generosity of other members of the Lindrum family has been completely submerged with the passing of time. Fred Lindrum junior was accustomed to playing the supporting role to his more illustrious brother. It was a situation which he tolerated with somewhat mixed emotions. In the broad sense Fred was extremely proud of Walter's exploits. This pride was apparent from the glowing terms Fred used when talking about his brother. At the same time Fred was envious of Walter's privileged position in the billiard world, a position which Fred would have dearly loved himself. Fred's envy occasionally got the better of him and resulted in an inopportune remark which caused embarrassment to both Walter and himself.

During one of their matches in the war years at the Flinders Lane Saloon Fred caused a slight amount of embarrassment and a great deal of hilarity with one of his comments. Walter was in play, building one of his customary breaks. A frustrated Fred was waiting impatiently on the player's seat for a chance to show his skill. Unbeknown to Fred, Robert Menzies came into the room during the progress of the break. Menzies managed to find a vacant seat; a few rows from the front, and close to where Fred was parked on the player's seat. Fred, though, was obscured from Menzies' view. After watching Walter continue for more than half an hour, without even looking like missing, Menzies enquired of the person sitting next to him: "Where's Walter's opponent?" From his obscured position Fred Lindrum turned around and in frustration declared: "He's just about to go to the Plaza bloody pictures". It was only then that Fred realised who had asked the question.

Although Walter Lindrum was a special favourite of Menzies, who was an avid follower of Australian sport and sportsmen, it would be a gross exaggeration to claim that Lindrum had more than a mild interest in politics. Yet it is true that Lindrum once influenced the progress of some legislation through Parliament. It was during one of his Canberra visits that Lindrum fell in with a plan engineered by Menzies, which involved playing billiards with the Labor member for East Sydney, Eddy Ward.

Menzies and Ward were arch enemies and had may heated exchanges in the House. It was a clash of two strong personalities that went beyond the fact that they belonged to opposing political parties. The duo represented a complete contrast in style and presentation. Menzies was a superb orator with his use of repartee, insult, the smooth word and ridicule. He could use the pause with great effect to change the direction and emphasis of his speech. He was justifiably proud of his ability as a speaker and debater. Ward was, in contrast, a user of simple language but delivered his speeches with great speed and emphasis. Menzies described Ward as having "the foulest tongue that has ever been unleashed in this House" and once said "I do not propose to enter into a hopeless competition with a man with such mastery of the argot of the gutter".

Ward described Menzies as "this military genius who a high military officer in this country said would have had a brilliant military career had it not been for the outbreak of the last war". Ward really touched a sore spot with this biting remark. After the outbreak of World I, Menzies' older brothers enlisted in the forces. Bob decided to stay at home and take care of his ageing parents and family responsibilities. Similar decisions were not uncommon at that time. Menzies, however, was not allowed to forget his supposedly unpatriotic act by certain sections of the populace, and by wily politicians such as Eddy Ward. When World War II began Menzies was anxious to reintroduce universal military training. With his sensitivity to his own military record, and the general community dissension in mind, Menzies decided to 'fly a kite' on the issue. After many weeks of careful planning an overflow meeting was held in the Melbourne Town Hall. Only two speakers addressed the meeting — Vinton Smith, a prominent Melbourne stockbroker and member of the Young Nationals, and Walter Sykes, a notable party member. Among the handpicked audience were members of the Victorian Amateur Boxing Association who were to deal with any protesters who attempted to disrupt the meeting. It was the unanimous verdict of the meeting that the Federal Government be asked to reintroduce universal military training for home defence. The story was splashed across the front page of major newspapers throughout Australia. Menzies 'acceded' to this popular demand.

It was Eddy Ward who nick-named Menzies 'Pig Iron Bob'. In 1938 wharf labourers at Port Kembla refused to load 23 000 tons of pig iron for Japan on the grounds that it would be used to make bombs and shells for use against China. Menzies, as Attorney-General, used the Transport Workers Act in an attempt to force the loading of the pig iron. The result was that the whole port became idle. After two months of stalemate the watersiders agreed to load the 23 000 tons of iron provided that there were no further consignments.

In early September, 1939, after the declaration of war, Menzies' government introduced the National Security Bill into the House. It was a lengthy piece of legislation and its progress had been continually hampered by Eddy Ward. It was not that Ward opposed the general principles of the Bill but he did object to any infringement on civil liberties. With the necessity to curtail severely the domestic use of essential resources, and so maximise the war effort, there was no alternative but to infringe on the freedom of individuals. As the Bill was in the final stages of passing through the House, Ward declared his intention to oppose every remaining section. Menzies was, by this time, extremely unsettled at having to endure Ward's speeches. It was the belief of some of Menzies' colleagues that Ward for many years 'had the wood' on the Prime Minister. It was not until the early 1950's that Menzies, with a scathing attack, finally broke Ward's hold. Ward was never again the same in debate with Menzies. On many occasions Menzies walked out of the House when Ward followed him in debate. In this instance, because of the importance of the legislation, Menzies had no choice but to stay in the House and endure Ward's 'gift of the gab'. Menzies wanted to fly out that night to an important meeting in Perth. Although the government had the numbers, Menzies did not want to depart until the vital clauses were disposed of. If Ward fulfilled his promise the Bill could not possibly be passed until the following day.

Menzies was desperate to make his flight. He knew that Ward often spent the recesses over the House's billiard table. Walter Lindrum happened to be in Canberra on one of his visits. Menzies went to Lindrum with his dilemma. He asked if Ward could somehow get involved in a game of billiards with Lindrum and so be kept out of the House. Lindrum in turn sought the assistance of Walter Sykes who was in Canberra to discuss business with his partner-in-law, Harold Holt. Lindrum and Sykes adjourned to the billiard room. It was the luncheon recess and there was Eddy Ward, playing on the table. It was an obvious suggestion for Walter Lindrum to give an exhibition. Lindrum indicated that he would enjoy playing a game against one of the members. Eddy Ward, who fancied himself as a billiardist, needed little encouragement to play the legendary Lindrum. The table was, of course, dominated by Lindrum but he managed to jaw the occasional ball and allow Ward a chance to show his ability. Ward made a few handy breaks that were greeted with enthusiasm by the members. Lindrum added his own words of encouragement.

Eventually the luncheon recess ended and the members began to return to the House. Ward was, by this time, totally enthralled with playing the world's greatest and readily accepted Lindrum's invitation to stay on and see some trick shots. Eddy forgot time and his resolution. From time to time the majestic figure of Menzies flitted past the entrance to the billiard room, noted Eddy's absorption, and gave a veiled signal to Walter Sykes that all was well and to keep Lindrum at his task. This he did and the Prime Minister made his flight on schedule.

William Morris Hughes, Prime Minister from 1915 to 1923 and the longest-serving politician in Australia's history (with 58 years in politics), was another who enjoyed his game of billiards. Hughes' small, sinewy frame was regularly stretched out over the billiard table at Parliament House. During a game one night at the Hotel Canberra, Hughes was constantly distracted by an onlooker who repeatedly asked political questions and received non-committal answers. At last, quite piqued, he said, "Mr Hughes, I think you should give me your attention", and Billy, with and eye on his opponent's shot, merely said, "Why?" "Well, I voted for you at the last election". Billy chalked his cue, deliberately sighted his shot, straightened up, and answered, "Listen brother, I won by thousands last time, and I'm not going to allow your one vote to spoil my billiards". (*Pedals, Politics and People*, H.F. Opperman)

Walter Lindrum's War Drive continued at a relentless pace. In early 1942 with Tom Cleary, the fine amateur player, as his off-sider, Lindrum set off on a tour of South Australia. The tour was in aid of the Red Cross and the A.C.F. (Australian Comfort Fund, which was formed to help all the Services.) The

Facing page: *Walter with leading amateur, Tom Cleary, during an exhibition match in Melbourne. (Melbourne* Age)

Overleaf: *This cartoon, published after Lindrum's 3262 break in 1929, portrays the attitude of the public to his complete mastery. (All Sports, 28 December 1929)*

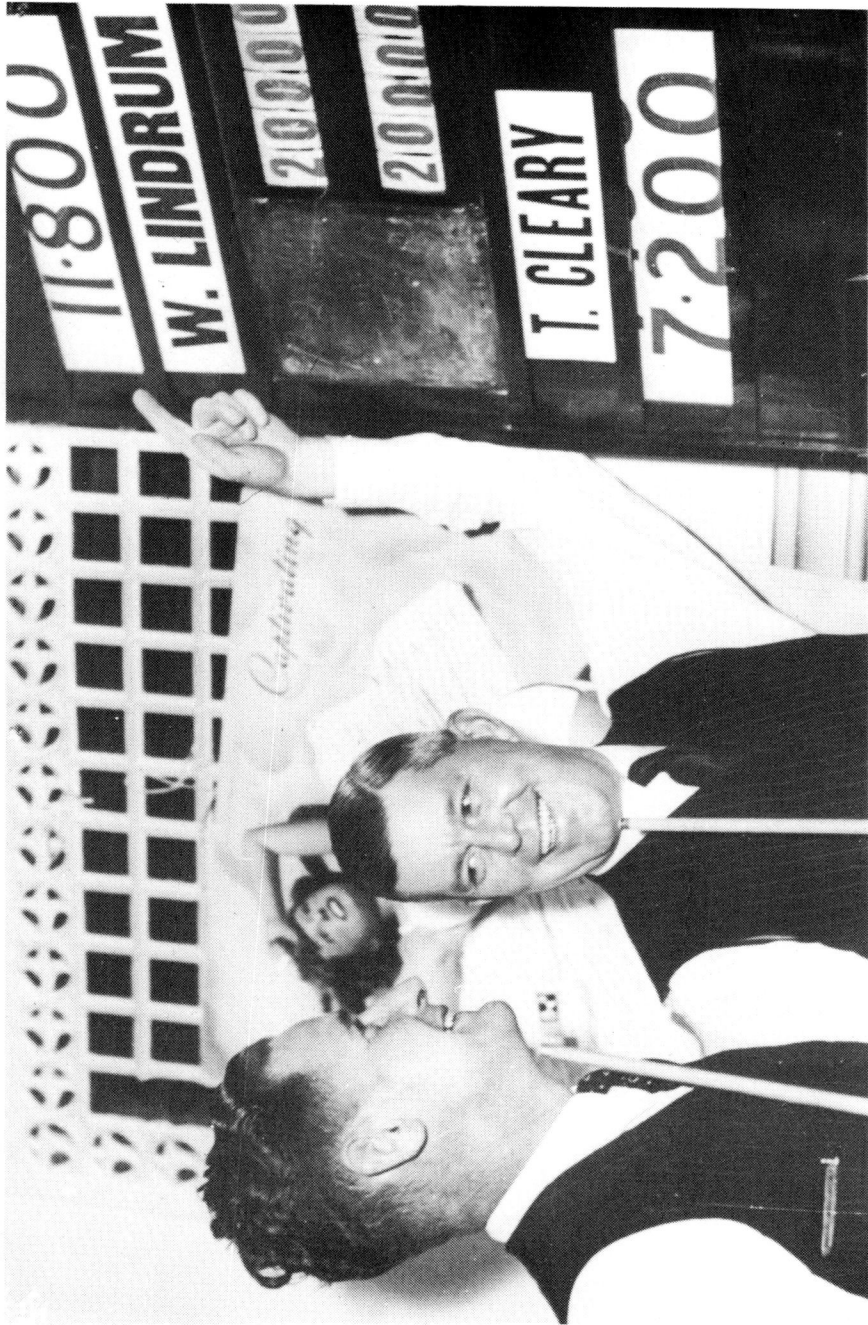

11·80 U W. LINDRUM 20 000 20 000 T. CLEARY 7200

WALTER LINDRUM

MAKING A BREAK OF 62

MAKING A BREAK OF 262

MAKING A BREAK OF 1262

MAKING A BREAK OF 3262

LIKE GOLF, POSITION IS EVERYTHING WHEN ADDRESSING THE BALL

WALTER LINDRUM
AUSTRALIA

JOE DAVIS
GREAT BRITAIN

CLARK McCONACHY
NEW ZEALAND

THE REACTION OF THESE BILLIARDS ENTHUSIASTS TO AN 800 BREAK BY A CHAMPION IS NOT QUITE AS DEMONSTRATIVE AS THAT OF A CRICKET CROWD WHEN A BRADMAN SCORES A CENTURY.　　Drawings by Brodie Mack.

The decline of interest in professional billiards is clearly illustrated by this work of Brodie Mack in July 1934. (The Sydney Mail)

Air Force had offered to fly Lindrum between venues but he preferred to travel by the slower, and lower, means of transport. The journey from Melbourne to Adelaide was made by train. Cleary soon began to realise what a fanatic Lindrum was. Walter asked him to check his gear and to get the set of billiard balls down from the luggage rack. Cleary watched in amazement as Lindrum reached for his cue and started practising on the carriage seat. Cleary did not realise that Lindrum was merely keeping 'in touch'.

The tour opened in Port Pirie, situated on the eastern shore of Spencer Gulf. There was trouble almost immediately when Walter's set of strip rubber cushions, being carried separately by Brady & Son, failed to arrive in time for the exhibition. Lindrum told an astonished Cleary that he would not play on the table which was fitted with block rubber cushions. Lindrum had an abhorrence for block rubber cushions which he found were less responsive to side. Consequently he found it impossible to play certain shots while other shots had to be played with greater strength. The result was that Lindrum did not have the same degree of control over the balls. He could not perform with his usual artistry and perfection. Tom Cleary, though, was probably not very interested in the reasons for Lindrum's intransigence. Cleary knew that a good crowd was waiting expectantly for the start of Walter Lindrum's exhibition but the star of the show was adamant that he was not going on. Cleary was in for a further shock when Lindrum insisted that he go on in his place. Cleary's role on the tour was to act as the spruiker — and he hadn't even bothered to bring his cue with him. Lindrum offered his cue to Cleary who reluctantly borrowed it and set about entertaining the crowd. On his very first visit to the table Cleary made a break of 375! Cleary's trepidation was short-lived for the Brady & Son truck arrived with the cushions. They were fitted during a short interval and the maestro was then ready to appear. Lindrum did not disappoint the spectators who had patiently waited for his appearance, for he immediately produced a 1000 break at his first hit. The usual trick shots were performed, after the customary failures, and Tom Cleary collected the notes and the silver. The Port Pirie exhibition netted £400.

The duo travelled to Port Augusta where the local skating rink was hired as the venue. Lindrum scored the customary thousand break at billiards and made 124 at snooker. The huge crowd present responded generously to the trick shots and £4000 was raised for the night. In the latter part of the tour Lindrum was feeling the strain of the heavy schedule. When the strip rubber cushions failed to arrive Lindrum's spirits dropped even lower. Cleary agreed to substitute for the entire session. He raised £1200 for the night! When he returned to the hotel and broke the news, Lindrum was so thrilled that he gave Cleary a kiss. After five arduous weeks of touring South Australia a very weary duo returned to Melbourne. They had raised a considerable amount for the A.C.F. and the Red Cross.

As the war continued Lindrum visited every state of the mainland in a seemingly endless programme of exhibitions. He performed at the Royal

Facing page: *Walter Lindrum with the ten amateurs whom he played November/December 1939 in aid of the Racing Men's Fund. Back row, from left: W. H. Carter, F. F. Hancock, D. D. Dinley, F. Freston, J. Long, E. N. Bracey. Front row, from left: T. Cleary, R. Mousally, Walter Lindrum, C. E. Norman, S. N. Wood. (Dolly Lindrum)*

Empire Show, in private homes, clubs, etc. — anywhere that would help the war effort. He visited the camps to entertain the troops. Often he gave an around-the-clock display, playing for twelve hours straight with only a five-minute break each hour. At one camp, after twelve hours at the table, Lindrum gave a personal twenty-minute exhibition for one soldier who had just finished guard duty. The endless travelling and exhibitions drew heavily on Lindrum's reserves of stamina. At one stage a doctor ordered that he take a fortnight's rest. The diagnosis — exhaustion. Lindrum refused to obey the doctor and played on. It was not only Lindrum's health that suffered from his heavy schedule. His prolonged absence from his wife, Pat, was a contributing factor in the disintegration of their marriage.

By the end of World War II Lindrum had raised a vast amount for a variety of funds and organisations. Estimates of the amount he did raise are many and varied. The highest figure suggested was three million pounds. That does seem to be an exaggeration. A conservative estimate is £500 000. There are numerous factors that make difficult any accurate assessment of Lindrum's exhibition takings. For example, during one series of exhibitions in April 1945, a total of £75 000 was raised for the Third War Loan. What credit should Lindrum be given in the raising of that sum?

There will probably always be disagreement as to the amount Lindrum raised during the war years. There is surely no dispute, though, that Lindrum's selfless deeds must rank as a most remarkable contribution to the welfare of his nation.

13 The Latter Years

Walter Lindrum was one of the most outstanding Australian sportsmen and philanthropists.

Sir Norman Brookes in the *Sporting Globe*, 1960

With the cessation of hostilities in the Pacific on 15 August 1945, World War II was finally over. The armed forces were gradually demobilised and the civilians began returning to their peacetime occupations. For Walter Lindrum there was no respite from the heavy demands of the war years. There was a constant stream of requests for his services by various charities and other organisations.

In 1946 the R.S.L., anxious to replenish funds depleted during the war, engaged Walter Lindrum for an exhibition tour of Victoria. The tour commenced in the Gippslands, the fertile east-Victorian district, bounded in part by the Great Dividing Range and the coastline. Walter was assisted on the tour by his nephew, Bill Dunn, the son of his sister, Florence. The tour covered 90 towns in as many days, excluding Sundays. Very few centres were by-passed with towns as small as Heathcote (population of 1200) included on the itinerary.

The programme for each day followed a regular pattern. In the morning Walter and Bill would travel by car to the venue. The billiard table and seating, which followed by truck, were erected in the afternoon by Dunn. After a shower and dinner the Lindrum exhibition commenced with Dunn acting as marker. A large crowd always pleased Walter who would comment to Dunn: "Nice crowd here tonight, Billy. We'll have to make a 2000 break for them". Walter would commence with the balls set up in a drop cannon position and proceed to make the 2000 break. Occasionally he failed to reach that objective — but only occasionally. A 100 break at snooker followed. Walter would issue a challenge for a member of the audience to place the billiard balls in a position from which he could not score. If Walter scored from the position, the spectator was required to give a £10 donation. Walter would invariably miss the shot at his first attempt. After commenting on how tough the shot was Lindrum would then ask if there was anybody who would give £20 for a successful attempt. When he had secured a sponsor Lindrum would score the shot and collect the £20. When the show concluded the table and seating were dismantled and loaded onto the truck in readiness for an early departure the following morning.

The erection of the billiard table posed problems in some places. The most difficult time was when the hall had a sprung dance floor. Extra care had to be taken to arrange the table and seating evenly around the centre of balance. The table was then levelled. However, these careful arrangements could be ruined if there was an unequal distribution of spectators around the table. If there were 50 more spectators seated on one side, the table would tilt slightly and Lindrum would have to make adjustments to compensate for the roll of the balls. Undoubtedly the most trying experience of Lindrum's career occurred in January 1946. The venue for the exhibition was the visiting aircraft carrier, H.M.S. *Implacable.* The billiard table was erected on the deck, then lowered into the hull on the aircraft lift for the crew to have a better view. *Implacable,* belying its name, lurched and swayed throughout the performance. It was a perilous task for Lindrum to control the balls, which continually rolled off course. It was one occasion when a player could be excused for attributing his failures to the roll on the table. It was an experience Lindrum vowed never to repeat.

An amusing incident occurred at the town of Swan Hill, on the Murray River, 345 kilometres by rail north-west of Melbourne. Lindrum was to give an exhibition in the evening for the local hospital. To fill in time in the afternoon Lindrum and Bill Dunn walked down to the local billiard room. As they stood watching, two young lads playing billiards started arguing. The lad who was getting the worst of the argument turned to Walter, in desperation, and pleaded: "Do you know anything about billiards, mate?"

After more than three months of touring Lindrum and Dunn wearily returned to Melbourne, having raised a substantial sum for the Victorian R.S.L.

It was in 1946 or 1947 that Lindrum was engaged to give an exhibition for the Lord Mayor's Fund, in aid of charity. It was a gala social occasion with some invited guests and a £2 admission fee. Amongst those attending was Hubert Opperman (now Sir Hubert) who was there as part of the general audience, not by special invitation or arrangement. Sir Hubert recalled:

> Lindrum gave his usual friendly run up address to a very large crowd, and said 'I'd like to open up with a bit of competition' and as his eye lit on me, 'Good! Here's Oppy. I'll play him a hundred up and give him 95'. There was great applause and loud laughter by all but me. I was quite embarrassed and said quietly, 'Walter, I'm a terrible billiards player'. 'O.K.' he announced at once, 'I'll break them up,' and left the red right over the pocket to give me at least three. But, quite inadvertently, I cannoned off the red and unforgiveably sank his white. The crowd roared and Walter clapped a hand over his face in mock anguish. I apologised profusely and hypocritically while I faced an easy red pot with 99 on the board. I missed it, Walter came back on the table and ran up his usual astronomical score within the usual amazing short time. I said to Walter, 'What would you have done had I potted the red?' He laughed and said, 'I would have challenged you to give me 95 miles in 100 on bicycles. But I wish you had, we would have made some good paper coverage for the next exhibition.' (Correspondence, 11 January 1980.)

In the immediate post-war years Walter Lindrum established his own billiard room at 323 Bourke Street, Melbourne. It was a small room which took on the atmosphere of a club. The patrons had the option of receiving lessons from the master. Walter had left the Flinders Lane room because he found it could not support the whole Lindrum family. Fred (Walter's brother) also made life difficult for everyone in the billiard room when he had been on one of his drinking sprees. At these times he was short-tempered and unpredictable. Harriet Lindrum (Walter's mother) died in 1951, aged 87 years. Her husband, Fred, had predeceased her, dying in 1943, at 77 years. Following his mother's death Walter returned to take over the running of the Flinders Lane room.

During the post-war period the leading United States manufacturer, Brunswick-Balke Co., became interested in the Australian market. Apart from billiard tables and accessories they also manufactured ten-pin bowling equipment. Brunswick-Balke sent one of their vice-presidents, Russel J. Bowell, to investigate the potential Australian market in both these areas. One of Bowell's first tasks was to renew the acquaintance between his company and Walter Lindrum which had first been made on Lindrum's trip to the States in 1932. During that visit Lindrum had been presented with a beautiful table by Ben Singer, the president of Brunswick-Balke. The American company needed a representative to handle its Australian operations. Bowell approached Walter Sykes who had met the American by chance on a trip to the United States. Although Sykes was heavily involved with his own business commitments he agreed to take charge of Brunswick-Balke's Australian operations.

As a means of promoting their range of billiard equipment Brunswick-Balke hoped to stage a series of matches between Walter Lindrum and the great American champion, Willie Hoppe. Of course, there were differences between the two games — American billiards being played on a smaller table and consisting entirely of cannon play. Still the basic principles of the English and American games were similar enough for some form of contest to be possible. Russ Bowell and Walter Sykes worked assiduously to formulate a series of rules that would be a fair compromise between the two games and allow both champions to use their specialities. The proposed matches thus took on a wider significance with the merging of the rules of the two billiard games possibly being the forerunner to the establishment of a truly international game of billiards. After formulating a contract for the matches Bowell and Sykes submitted it to the governing bodies of both games for approval. Both bodies signed.

The stage was set for an exciting contest with matches to be played across Australia and the United States. As the final stages of planning were being reached Walter Lindrum's enthusiasm for the matches began to dissipate. It was because there was so much at stake, in terms of status, that Lindrum lost interest in the contest. A long lay-off from rigorous competition and a more indulgent lifestyle had dulled the sharp edge of Lindrum's acutely-developed skill. Lindrum preferred to rest on his impeccable record rather than risk losing prestige in what was virtually a world championship. He was reluctant to present his lessened powers to the scrutiny of the public eye. The decline in Lindrum's billiards was not nearly as pronounced as it may sound. He was still capable of a brand of billiards that had to be seen to be believed. However, being the perfectionist that he was, Lindrum's self-esteem would not allow him to injure his immaculate record with an inferior performance. In choosing as he did Lindrum was by-passing the wealth that the Hoppe matches would have given him.

Walter could certainly have used that money for he never could have been described as being financially secure. This was due partly to the fact that he was a poor businessman and because he never sought to accumulate wealth.

Walter was probably his own worst enemy in money matters. He was very generous in donating his services to charities or any other worthwhile cause when approached. He refused to accept any payment for his services. There was a short period, around 1950, when Jack Rohan, of the *Sporting Globe,* acted as Lindrum's manager. Rohan ensured that Walter received a reasonable fee for his services. However, for the most part Lindrum donated his services to a host of causes who unwittingly imposed on the limited resources of an unstintingly generous man. Occasionally a group for which Lindrum had given an exhibition would forward him a cheque in the mail. Although he had refused any such payment at the time of his exhibition Walter was very grateful for a cheque in the mail.

So the grand contest between Lindrum and Hoppe never eventuated. Apart from the drawing power of such a unique contest, an opportunity was lost by which English and American billiards may have been fused together. Brunswick-Balke thus suffered a setback in their hopes to familiarise the Australian public with their small-sized tables. The company was also experiencing some problems in gettings its Australian operations underway. It was Brunswick's intention to manufacture locally its range of billiard equipment. However, they found it impossible to produce some items in Australia. These would have to be imported. In the post-war period of rigid import controls it was very difficult to obtain the necessary licences. After exhausting the normal channels by which import licences were obtained the company was no closer to achieving its objective.

The one remaining hope was a direct appeal to the Prime Minister. It was mid-1949 and Ben Chifley was in the midst of the greatest crisis of his years in office — the coal-miner's strike. It was virtually impossible to secure an appointment with the Prime Minister. The New South Wales coal-miners had struck for more pay, shorter working hours and better conditions. Chifley was concerned with jibes that Government was soft on Communists such as those who controlled the Miners' Union. Legislation was passed forbidding organisations, registered with the Commonwealth Arbitration Court, using their funds to assist miners. The miners' own funds were frozen as were part of the funds of the Communist Party. Eight miners' leaders were gaoled and after five weeks Chifley put troops into the mines to replenish the depleted supply of coal. After seven emotion-charged weeks, during which the basic tenet of Labor was in question, the miners resumed work.

The assistance of Walter Lindrum was sought by Brunswick-Balke in arranging a meeting with Chifley during the coal-miners crisis. The Prime Minister agreed to the request from one of Australia's most patriotic sons. Russ Bowell flew in from the States to assist Walter Sykes in putting the case to Chifley. One hour he promised and one hour they were given. As the impregnable Chifley filled ash tray after ash tray with dead matches (without once succeeding in lighting his pipe) and as his expletives grew stronger and stronger as his secretary brought bulletins of the worsening position on the coalfields, Bowell and Sykes put their case. At the end of the hour Bowell, Sykes and Lindrum prepared to leave the Prime Minister's office. Chifley turned to Walter Lindrum and said: "Walter, it's a pleasure to do something for you. You've done so much for this country." The efforts of Bowell and Sykes to obtain import licences were not successful. Brunswick-Balke's attempts to establish an Australian market for their billiard tables and ten-pin bowling equipment were thus thwarted.

"What was Walter Lindrum really like?" is a difficult question, for, like any other man, Walter Lindrum was a many-faceted creature. While some facets of his character may have been readily discernible there were others that were not apparent in the normal course of events. For someone who never knew Walter Lindrum the task of assessing his character is even more difficult and can only be performed through the eyes of those who knew him.

During the post-World War II years Walter Sykes conducted numerous business dinners for interstate and overseas associates. Walter Lindrum was invited as an additional guest to the dinners and fulfilled an important role in the evening's programme — invariably after dinner Sykes & Co would adjourn to Walter's billiard room for an exhibition by the master. Sykes describes the Walter Lindrum he observed at those dinners:

> Always circumspect, always naturally, slight diffident and self-effacing but always dignified and well-mannered, Walter allowed his reputation to flow over and enmesh men who, for all their success, had never conquered all opposition as had this man in his sphere. Quietly, I would lead Walter reluctantly, into telling some of his numerous stories, many against himself, until very soon he had won more ardent admirers. (Correspondence, 21 March, 1979).

Many people had a deep affection for Walter Lindrum, some forming a very close friendship with him. One such person was the late Sir Kenneth Luke, former President of the Victorian Football League. The extent of Luke's affection for Walter Lindrum can be gauged from a letter received from Alf Knightly of Oakleigh, Victoria. Knightly's letter also illustrates Walter's detachment from worldly possessions. In early 1949 Alf Knightly entered a snooker tournament being staged by the Masonic Club in Melbourne. When it was announced that Walter Lindrum was donating a special trophy for the tournament the nominations came thick and fast. It was Alf Knightly who duly won the event and the Walter Lindrum Trophy, a silver tea and coffee service, which he received at a Masonic Club dinner. Due to other commitments Walter Lindrum was not present at the dinner to award Knightly his trophy although they did meet at a later date when Knightly was able to thank Walter for his generosity.

The story behind the silver tea and coffee service unfolded when Knightly met Ken Luke (later Sir Kenneth) who was then President of the Carlton Football Club. Jock Fraser, Luke's chauffeur, arranged to introduce his friend, Alf Knightly, to the 'Boss'. When Fraser explained that Alf Knightly was the bloke who had won the Walter Lindrum Trophy there was an immediate reaction from Luke. Alf Knightly recalled:

> Mr Luke sat straight back and glared at me. I was amazed and asked how I had offended him. With that he told me that he had made the the service for himself, and wasn't it beautiful? I agreed. Then he said: "You know, nobody on God's earth could have got that particular tea and coffee service off me, but Walter Lindrum, and then he had to give it away." (Correspondence, 30 October, 1979).

Luke took some consolation from the fact that a friend of his chauffeur had won the service and, having met Knightly, was pleased to see it was in good hands.

In 1950 Walter Lindrum was challenged by his old rival, Clark McConachy, for his world billiard title. McConachy had been in solid training in New Zealand, putting in up to eight hours every day for several months. He made the sea-trip to Melbourne and issued his challenge to Lindrum, suggesting that the match would create great interest and bring in some 'fruit for the sideboard'. Lindrum, though, showed not the slightest interest in Mac's proposal. Lindrum was lacking in the hard training which he knew was necessary for a championship match. He maintained that it would take him six weeks of solid work to prepare for a title match. By 1950 Walter had lost his passion for billiards. He had conquered the billiard world as no other player had ever done. The one remaining goal for Lindrum was to conquer himself, to break his own records. That is an endless chase for as soon as one goal is reached a new, higher goal is sought. There is a limit to even the most insatiable of appetites. Lindrum had satisfied his objectives. There were no horizons left to conquer. Having declined the McConachy challenge Lindrum immediately announced his retirement in July, 1950. The championship cup, which Lindrum had steadfastly refused to return in 1934, amid the most bitter controversy in the history of the game, was now forwarded without qualm to the B.A. & C.C.

There were other reasons why the competitive edge had disappeared from Lindrum's billiards. Not the least of these was his pre-occupation with helping charities and other causes. Lindrum gave exhibitions for a variety of causes ranging from hospitals, societies for the blind, orphanages and churches, to very small groups such as Boy Scout 'packs'. Lindrum was always ready to help a family or individual who was in desperate need. When hearing of someone's difficulties, Lindrum would say: "Well, we will have to put on a little show for them". The result was often £200 or more. One example was a billiard and snooker night which Lindrum put on to help cover the cost of hospital treatment for one Kevin Fisher, who suffered from haemophilia. There were various 'one-off' appeals which Lindrum assisted, such as the raising of funds to send the 1952 Olympic Team to Helsinki and to send one of 25 boys to the coronation of Queen Elizabeth II in 1953 (the boy was an orphan).

On 1 April 1954, Walter Lindrum was granted a divorce from his wife, Alicia ('Pat'), on the grounds of desertion. It was the end of a marriage which had been marked by difficulties (some of which were Walter's doings) and by attempts at reconciliation. On 28 July, 1956, Walter married for the third time. His new wife was the former Mrs Beryl Russell who had been secretary to Walter for some years.

During a visit to Melbourne for the 1956 Olympic Games Mr Wong Kwok-Leong of Singapore met Walter Lindrum. They became very good friends and an invitation was extended to Lindrum to visit Singapore and play some exhibitions. He readily accepted. The concept of the trip was broadened to embrace a tour of Singapore, Malaya, Hong Kong and Taiwan. The tour was basically a good will mission with any money raised to be donated to charities in the respective countries. It was thus necessary for Lindrum's trip to be sponsored by some government or private body. Mr W. W. (Bill) Hughes became involved with the tour to act as manager and to secure some financial backing. Hughes has been associated with various charities for many years and received an M.B.E. in 1978 for his service to these causes. In the days of pony races Hughes was a successful owner, winning both the Ascot Thousand and Five Hundred in 1915 with Carwelkin. In later years Hughes turned to horse racing and owned a number of winners, the most prominent being Reperio who won the Alistair Clarke Stakes in 1946. It was through their mutual interest in Melbourne charities that Hughes and Lindrum became associated. Hughes secured financial backing from two private organisations, Richmond Breweries and Paddle Shoes. Approaches were made to the Federal Government and a grant came from the minister for Commerce and Agriculture, John McEwan (later Sir John). The expenditure by the Government was justified in the terms of the Lindrum tour creating good will in countries that were likely markets for Australia's primary products.

Having secured the necessary backing, Walter Lindrum left by boat for Singapore on 22 February 1957. He was accompanied by his wife, Beryl, who was still acting as secretary, Bill Hughes (manager), and Cliff Nowland who was Lindrum's marker for most of his exhibitions throughout the 1950's. The ship travelled via Adelaide and Perth. Mr Wong Kwok-Leong greeted the quartet on their arrival at Singapore. Mr Wong proved to be a very efficient organiser and the overwhelming success of this first segment of the tour was largely due to his untiring efforts. He booked halls, arranged for the installation of the billiard table and handled the advertising for exhibitions at Singapore, Kuala Lumpur, Ipoh and Penang. Wong accompanied Lindrum throughout the trip to ensure that everything worked with clockwork precision. The exhibitions proved very popular with large attendances at the Singapore Badminton Hall, the Chinese Assembly Hall (Kuala Lumpur), the Ipoh Club and the San Xavior School (Penang). Attendances were, on occasions, in excess of 1000 people. Mr Wong, apart from his role in organising the tour, also made a generous financial contribution towards the costs of the exhibitions. Mr Tan Seck Kay did similarly.

Lindrum boarded the S.S. *Glenartney*, bound for Hong Kong, arriving on April 4. The following morning Lindrum and Hughes made the rounds of the various business houses seeking donations for the Tung Wah Hospital in return for which Lindrum would use the firm's products during the trick shot section of his exhibition. There was a large attendance at the Macpherson Stadium exhibition. Lindrum spent the first hour on a demonstration of serious billiards and snooker play. The second hour was devoted to trick shots, performed according to a carefully-planned itinerary. At the end of the Hong Kong visit Lindrum was guest of honour at a dinner party given by Mr Peter T. Loong, vice-president of the Chinese Amateur Athletic Federation.

The Lindrum group travelled to Taiwan where 7500 schoolchildren attended an exhibition. The highlight of this section of the tour was on Good Friday when the group attended church in the presence of Madam and General Chiang Kai-shek. They listened to an address given by Madam Chiang Kai-shek. There were suggestions of the group visiting the Philippines and Burma for further exhibitions. However, these plans were dropped because of Lindrum's reluctance to travel by plane (the only choice open at the time). The tour thus concluded at Taiwan. It was to be the last overseas tour that Walter Lindrum undertook.

In the New Year Honours List of 1958 an O.B.E. was awarded to Walter Lindrum for 'continued and unselfish support of patriotic and charitable appeals for which he has, by his own skill and generosity, raised large sums of money'. Lindrum had previously been awarded an M.B.E. in 1951. In late 1957 Walter was informed of his forthcoming New Year Honour. It was privileged information which Walter was suppose to keep to himself. However, Walter was not very good at keeping secrets, especially secrets of this nature. Walter rang his close friend, Frank Williams, and excitedly told him the news. Walter remarked: "Maybe the other one will come next year". He was referring to a knighthood. Walter Lindrum very dearly hoped that he would receive a knighthood. His unstinting service to his fellow-Australians made him a very worthy candidate for such an honour. (As Lindrum was divorced he was not, according to the conditions in force at the time, eligible for a knighthood.) There is, though, something incongruous about 'Sir' Walter Lindrum. Such an easy-going, everyday type of bloke as Walter, would have looked out of place in the ranks of the knights. There was no hint of greatness, or suggestion of privilege, in the ways of Walter Lindrum . . . On second thoughts, 'Sir Walter Lindrum' would not have been so inappropriate after all.

Many other honours were bestowed on Lindrum by organisations which had benefitted from his services. Walter Lindrum was awarded a Life Governship (or an Honorary Life Governship) of many bodies, such as: Royal Children's Hospital, St. Vincent's Hospital, Alfred Hospital, Royal Victorian Institute for the Blind and Ballarat Orphanage. Lindrum was also made a Life Governor of the Crimea Lodge (Freemasonry) and the Freemason's Homes of Victoria. The involvement of Walter Lindrum with Freemasonry was the continuation of a family tradition. In 1867 Fred Lindrum I (Walter's grandfather), acting as Director of Ceremonies for the Freemasons, led the visiting Duke of Edinburgh into Government House, Adelaide.

In 1958 an appeal was launched in Victoria to raise funds for the fight against cancer. Known simply as the Cancer Appeal it involved the whole community which was divided into various groups, each of which was allotted a target amount designed to raise a total of £1 000 000. Walter Lindrum was asked to form a committee of prominent sportsmen with an allotted target of £15 000. A meeting was held in late February to form the committee of sportsmen. Walter Lindrum was elected President. When the Cancer Appeal closed on 30 June, after raising over £2 250 000, the Sportsmen's Committee had contributed the remarkable figure of £57 000. The sportsmen had conducted various fund-raising nights with an exhibition by Walter Lindrum as a frequent feature. They canvassed the entire Melbourne area and the adjacent country centres.

With the closing of the Cancer Appeal most of the specially formed committees were disbanded. There were several members of the Sportsmen's Committee who thought that it would be a shame to disband such a successful fund-raising group. Consequently a meeting was held at Walter Lindrum's home on August 13 to examine ways of retaining the Sportsmen's Committee. The meeting was attended by many prominent sporting identities including Theo Lewis, Doug Bachli, John Coleman, Bill Golley, Keith Lynch, Noel

Graves, Claude Harris, Gordon Hoadley, Frank Harding, Percy Howdood, Alex MacHutchinson, George Oke, Les Roche, Jock Sturrock, Percy Taylor and Frank Williams. The meeting resolved to form the 'Sportsmen's Association of Australia'. The foundation president was Walter Lindrum, vice-presidents were Jock Sturrock and Doug Bachli, secretary was Noel Graves, and treasurer Alex MacHutchinson. The general aim of the Association were to promote sport in all its branches and to assist charitable and other worthy causes.

The Sportsmen's Association held its first official fund-raising function at the St Kilda Cricket Ground on January 18, 1959. A one-day cricket match was played between members of the visiting English team and an Australian Eleven, consisting of present and past Test players. Len Hutton captained the English team and former Test Captain, Ian Johnson, led the Australians. It was arranged that the voluptuous Sabrina bowl the first ball of the match. There were any number of players (batsmen included) who were prepared to coach Sabrina in the art of bowling. The match resulted in £1050 being raised for the Australian Red Cross.

An amusing incident arose out of the one day match. Apparently Len Hutton and Ian Johnson had a disagreement which was unresolved at the end of the match. Walter Lindrum was anxious to settle the difference, hoping to do so at a function at his home that night. As the players arrived by taxi at the Lindrum home the Melbourne skies released a sudden downpour. Walter Lindrum rushed out with an umbrella to greet a taxi which contained both Hutton and Johnson. Walter escorted them to the house. However, he was so pre-occupied and on edge with devising some means of settling the rift between Hutton and Johnson that he forgot to protect the guests with his umbrella. Hutton and Johnson were quite damp when they reached the house. Walter Lindrum was not!

In April of 1959 the Sportsmen's Association held a dinner for the Australian Test Team at the Melbourne Town Hall. The net proceeds of the night, £550, went to the Royal Children's Hospital. During September of the same year the Sportsmen's Association inaugurated the Brownlow Medallist's Dinner at the St Kilda Town Hall. The Brownlow Dinner, at which the outstanding player of Australian Rules football for each year is announced, is now a highlight of the Victorian sporting calendar. As well as raising funds for various charities the Sportsmen's Association makes donations to sporting appeals, notably the appeal for funds to send the Australian contingent to the Olympic Games. There are now branches of the Sportsmen's Association in most Australian states. The movement also spread to Papua New Guinea which was a member state until Independence in 1975. Since that time Papua New Guinea has formed its own association. The Sportsmen's Association continues to flourish, drawing together members from many diverse sporting fields who are united by its common cause.

One of Walter Lindrum's close friends, and a fellow-member of the Sportsmen's Association, was Keith Lynch who was in the hotel trade. It was therefore logical for Lynch to provide the refreshments for the various gatherings that took place at the Lindrum home. One Sunday morning Lynch drove his small truck to Lindrum's home to clean up after a party held the previous night. With Lynch was his six year old son, Patrick, who brought a young friend along for the ride. Lynch arrived at the Lindrum's and began cleaning up. Walter came out into the yard, exchanged a few words with Lynch, then disappeared with the two boys into the billiard room. Lynch finished in about half an hour. He then made his way to the billiard room to see what the boys were doing. He found that Walter was enthusiastically showing the two youngsters how to play various shots.

After watching for a few minutes Lynch said: "Well, thanks very much Walter for taking time to show the boys how to play. We'd better get on our way and let you go about your tasks".

"No problem," said Walter, "I'll just show them a few more shots". Walter showed the boys shot after shot. It was another half an hour before Lynch and the boys finally left the Lindrum's home.

On the way home young Patrick asked: "Who was that man, Dad?"

Lynch replied, with some pride: "That was Walter Lindrum, the greatest billiard player that the world has ever seen".

"Gee," said Patrick, "that was really nice of him to give us that lesson".

The following Sunday Lynch was cleaning in his hotel. Patrick and another young friend were playing a game of snooker on the table. Patrick potted a difficult red and his young friend exclaimed: "Gee, that was a good shot!"

Patrick stood up and asked: "Do you know who taught me how to play that shot?" The young friend shook his head.

Patrick proudly declared: "Why, it was Walter Lindrum, the greatest billiard player the world has ever seen".

The question of Walter Lindrum's attitude towards teaching others about billiards draws widely-differing responses. One school of belief is that Lindrum clung selfishly to his knowledge and would reveal nothing about the game to anyone. A slightly different view is held by Tom Cleary, former world amateur champion:

> To be quite fair to the master, I really do not think that he could impart to others his knowledge of the mysteries of nursery cannons, or for that matter, any other phase of the game. He was a supreme player and so far ahead of others in the game of billiards that I am afraid he did not know where to commence teaching, but I am sure he would have liked to help me.

A similar opinion is held by Stan Wood, who conducts coaching lessons in the billiard room at the Lindrum family home in Albert Park. Wood refutes the suggestion that Walter was deliberately evasive about sharing his billiard knowledge, arguing that Lindrum was such a generous fellow he would help you in any way that he could.

> I think the whole thing was that Walter just realised that he had to have a very good player to be able to pass on his knowledge. I think that Walter did a lot of things that, perhaps, he didn't know how he did them himself — he was *that* far advanced.

The opinion of Jim Collins, A.M., completes the spectrum of views on Walter Lindrum as a coach:

> I wish to give lie to the oft-repeated rumour that he would show you nothing. I found him to be most helpful to those who sought help genuinely, for plausible motives. Perhaps he would not have been overly keen to help some people, that didn't impress him as people. But I always

found him to be one of nature's gentlemen and anxious to help. He certainly helped me, tremendously. I spent a lot of time with him on the intricacies of the game, such as nursery cannons and masse strokes.

In July 1960, Walter Lindrum and his wife travelled to Surfers Paradise in Queensland, for their annual holiday. Walter took his holidays at this time to escape the worst of the Melbourne winter, which played havoc with his bronchial condition. Walter stayed at the holiday home of his close friend, Frank Williams. The Lindrums and Williams shared the house and agreed to each pay half of the phone bill. It was a regular thing each Saturday morning for Walter to spend an hour or more on the phone getting the latest 'oil' from some of his many racing contacts. He would then head off to the local Southport races and have ten bob or a quid on each of his tips. Walter seldom won enough to cover the cost of the phone bill — even when most of his carefully-gathered tips were successful. A bemused Frank Williams recalled how he paid for half the sizeable phone bill which accrued from this unprofitable investment.

One of Walter Lindrum's favourite meals was tripe and onions. Another was steak-and-kidney pie. One night while at Surfers Paradise Walter went to a local club for his evening meal. He elected to have steak-and-kidney pie. Later that night Walter became very sick. A doctor was called in the early hours of the morning. Walter's condition gradually worsened over the next two days. The doctor made further visits and advised that it would not be wise to move Walter to hospital. On the morning of Saturday, 30 July, Frank Williams was planning to travel to the Eagle Farm race meeting. His horse, Summer Honeymoon, was racing in Melbourne and appeared to have a good chance of winning. Williams intended to back Summer Honeymoon with the interstate bookmakers who operated at Eagle Farm. When Frank saw Walter Lindrum that morning he knew that he was decidedly low. Frank decided that he could not leave Walter. However, Walter insisted that Frank go to the Eagle Farm races and gave him £5 to put on Summer Honeymoon. It was a large bet for Walter compared to the usual ten shillings or one pound. Perhaps Walter sensed he was gambling on more than a horse race; he was having a stake in life itself. Williams was still in two minds but finally decided to go to Eagle Farm. He duly placed Walter's £5, along with his own wager, on Summer Honeymoon. He listened to the race which was broadcast over the course amplifier but, after having every chance, Summer Honeymoon finished in second place. Almost immediately Williams was paged over the course amplifiers. There was an urgent phone call for him. The news was that Walter Lindrum's condition had rapidly worsened — there was no hope.

The official cause of death was given as heart failure. This was undoubtedly induced by the days of sickness. Whatever the exact cause of death was, did not really matter. The irrevocable truth was that Walter Lindrum had put his cue in the rack for the final time. The lights over the billiard table would never again shine with such radiance.

14 Lindrum's Greatness

Genius does what it must, and talent does what it can.

Owen Meredith, 1831-1891

If there is a simple answer to why Walter Lindrum was the greatest billiards player of all time it would be in the terms of his remarkable cannon play. It is absurd, though, to attempt to define Lindrum's success in such simple — and finite — terms. It is also an injustice to Lindrum, the man, for just as man is a many-faceted creature, so there were many facets to Walter Lindrum's greatness. As Lindrum said himself, matches cannot be won on close cannon play alone. It is thus pointless to single out Lindrum's nursery cannon play and consider it in isolation from the other facets of his billiards — top-of-the-table play and losing hazards. These were the visible components of the Lindrum success formula, the active ingredients which, when mixed together, were devastating in their results. Just as it is futile to examine the components of Lindrum's physical game individually it is likewise impractical to divorce them from Lindrum's mental attributes — those invisible ingredients which acted as catalysts to facilitate a reaction and ensure that the formula retained its potency.

Like any champion Lindrum had the will to win, referred to variously as drive, determination, ambition, etc. He had a desire to succeed, be it to satisfy his own ego, achieve recognition, or gain approval from others. It may have been a combination of these. Certainly the desire to succeed is essential to a champion's success. Without it he lacks the dedication to undertake the arduous hours of training, which is essential to his rise to eminence in his chosen field. It is the will to win that usually separates a champion from his rivals. It is the one who most needs to win who, almost invariably, becomes the champion. As the need to win intensifies it becomes a pre-occupation. As it intensifies further it becomes an obsession. Walter Lindrum was obsessed with the idea of being a billiard champion, perhaps with being the greatest billiard player of all time. Some of the tangible reasons why Lindrum fulfilled his obsession are explained in this chapter. Perhaps some of the more abstruse reasons can also be discovered.

There is no question that nursery cannons were the hallmark of Walter Lindrum's outstanding game. Most billiard enthusiasts automatically equate the name of Lindrum with cannons. In making close cannons such a formidable scoring force that they held the balance of power in billiard supremacy Lindrum added a new dimension to the game. Although there had been many competent exponents of the close cannon game prior to Lindrum, none had recognised its potential as the ultimate means of scoring. Lindrum was able to make longer runs of cannons at greater speed than any other player. Claude Falkiner, who had opened Lindrum's eyes to the potential of cannon play, was closest to him in the nursery cannon department. Lindrum possessed an extraordinary ability to bunch the balls for cannon play. Apart from gathering the balls from the orthodox 'drop cannon' positions Lindrum could send the object ball off two or three cushions, to the other end of the table and back, with such uncanny judgement of both direction and strength that the ball would nestle with the other balls in ideal position for close cannon play. None of the other professionals could match this ability. Nor could they rival Lindrum's capacity to convert ideal top of the table position into the more lucrative nursery cannon position. Lindrum possessed a superb masse stroke which was essential to regain close cannon position when the inevitable 'cover' occurred. Lindrum's control of the difficult masse was so precise that not only would he score the cannon but he would leave the balls in perfect position to continue his run of cannons.

In top-of-the-table play Lindrum had no superior, perhaps no equal. Lindrum once told Riso Levi, the great billiard writer, that in practice he had exceeded the thousand solely by spot-end play, without any close cannons. It was a claim that Levi did not question for he had seen Lindrum in match-play make in excess of 400 points in this manner. Lindrum was also ultra strong at the losing hazard game, having twice exceeded the thousand solely by this method (1413 out of 1417 versus Stevenson in 1922; 1581 out of 1879 in 1925 versus Falkiner). These two breaks were made in the early part of Lindrum's career before he had woven close cannons into the fabric of his game. Indeed both these red-ball thousands were made after Lindrum had unintentionally potted the white ball. The losing hazard was relegated to a very minor role in Lindrum's highly refined game. It was, though, always at Lindrum's disposal when he needed to regain position or force an opening at the start of a break. The only player who was in the same league as Lindrum in the losing hazard game was his fellow Australian, George Gray. No other billiards player had at his command such a vast repertoire of strokes as Walter Lindrum did.

One way that reporters used to 'explain' Lindrum's domination of the billiard scene was to describe him as a genius — or a wizard, a magician or as an absolute freak. In one interview the reporter quoted to Lindrum a definition of a genius as one who had a gift of the gods, concentration, and an infinite capacity for taking pains. The reporter then asked Lindrum which of these features of a genius he most dearly desired. Lindrum replied, in his usual candid way, "All of them, and I believe I have them all. But the one that I make most use of is concentration." The reporter was hoping to pinpoint the reasons for Lindrum's success. However, with 'a gift of the gods' given as one of the components of genius the reporter was using one abstract term as part of the definition of another abstract term. Just as "genius" defies finite description so does "gift of the gods". Perhaps a close definition of genius is one who possesses a special insight, an instinctive aptitude for a field of endeavour, which he is able to cultivate as no other can. Whatever terms are used in an attempt to define genius Walter Lindrum unquestionably qualified.

Lindrum certainly possessed enormous powers of concentration. He was unwavering in the single-mindedness of his purpose at the billiard table.

Lindrum possessed a powerful physique (his back rippled with muscles developed during the countless hours of bending over the table) and he had great endurance. It was John Wren, the Melbourne sportsman and entrepreneur, who gave Lindrum a piece of valuable advice. Wren said: "You will find lack of concentration your greatest enemy in compiling big breaks. Move quickly between your shots. A second gained is a point added." Lindrum thus realised that of his human resources it was his mental powers of concentration, and not his physical strength, that would show the first signs of fatigue. Consequently Lindrum lifted the tempo of his game and developed his high-speed style of play. Lindrum had always been a fast player. Following Wren's discerning advice he became an even faster player, in order to conserve his powers of concentration. In his book, *Billiards*, first published in 1930, Lindrum stated: "I have been called 'a man without a single human emotion at the billiard table', and while I consider this definition cold and hard, I admit its truth so far as it relates to anything likely to put me off my game". (Page 144).

Lindrum's capacity for taking pains was bordering on the infinite. He was a perfectionist who was never satisfied until he had discovered, and fulfilled, the absolute potential of the billiard table. He was not content with any stroke that he played until he was certain that the resultant position was the one that offered the greatest scoring possibilities. Fred Lindrum junior described Walter as the most correct player who ever lived. Walter Lindrum defined 'correct billiards' in broad terms as playing every position out to the last shot. For example, if a player has top-of-the-table position, he must not break away from it deliberately, he must play top-of-the-table until the position is lost. Moreover, he must play along the lines of least resistance — that is, he must take easy shots in preference to difficult shots. There is, though, one important reservation. If the difficult shot appears to offer better opportunity of continuing the break, then the difficulty must not be shirked. Correct billiards requires that position should be gained with the minimum number of strokes. If a player takes three strokes to gain top of the table position when two would do, he is playing incorrect billiards. The strictness of the Lindrum Method prompted the *Argus* to comment:

> His passion for correct methods has helped to make Lindrum the greatest of all players, but it has rather spoilt his chances as a showman. In showmanship he does not begin to compare with Roberts. (John Roberts junior). He may become a better showman than he is today, but the business does not come naturally to him. For example, there is a 'showy' way of playing top of the table billiards, which is picturesque and also interesting to watch, because of the difficulties it introduces and the greater variety of shots that it calls for. In the opening, although the white is close to the billiard spot, it is on the wrong or baulk side of it. All may go well for a time, but no matter how delicately the player feathers on to the white in making his cannons he will drive the white gradually away from the spot, and presently he will be in difficulties. The spectators derive their pleasure from watching him get out of them. . . . But if Lindrum has to open a top of the table break with the white on the wrong side of the spot he will correct the position at the first

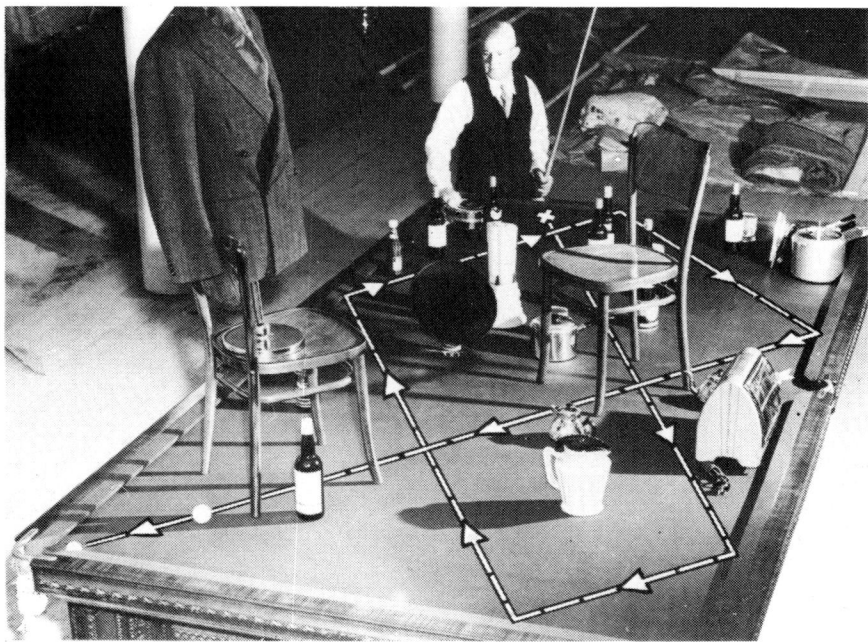

Above: *Walter during a Sydney exhibition in the war years. (John Fairfax & Sons)*

Below: *Prime Minister Menzies at the Flinders Lane saloon during a match between Walter and Fred Lindrum. (Dolly Lindrum)*

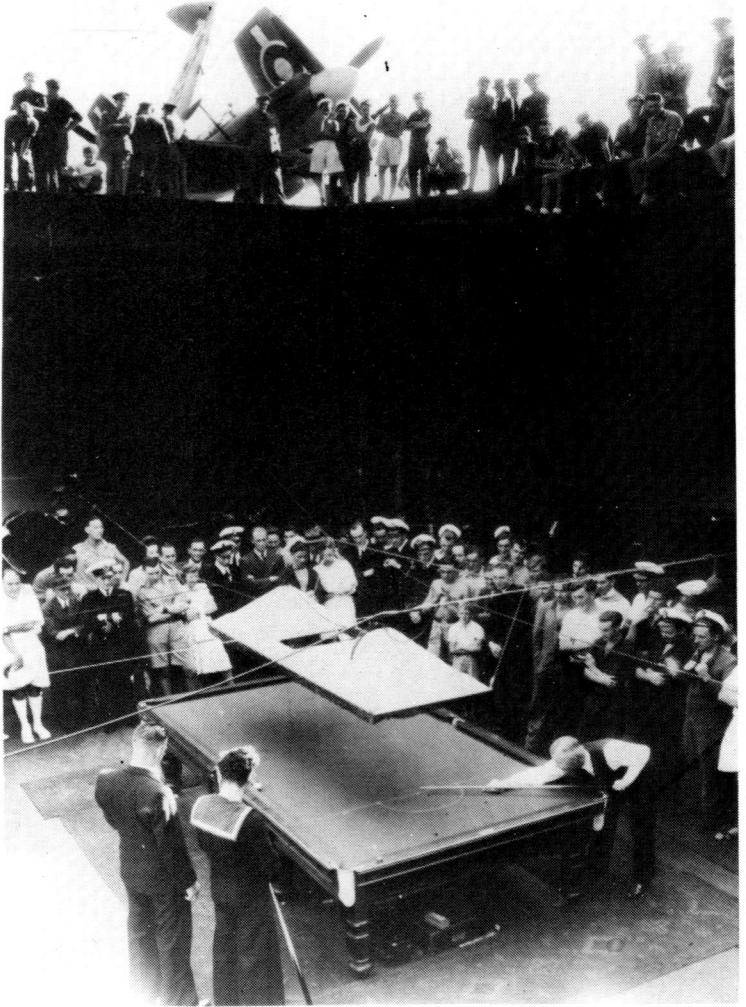

An exhibition on the aircraft carrier H.M.S. Implacable, *January, 1946. It was a trying experience for Walter as the balls rolled about whenever the ship lurched.* (Herald & Weekly Times)

Above: *Walter and niece, Dolly during the 1940s. (Melbourne* Age)

Below: *Two gourmets of the billiard table, Bob Marshall (left), four times world amateur billiards champion and Horace Lindrum, discussing the merits of a different form of table delicacy, 25 January 1954. (Courtesy of West Australian Newspapers Limited)*

Walter being presented with a Life Governorship of the Royal Victorian Institute for the Blind — one of many honours he received for his charity work. (Dolly Lindrum)

opportunity. To do otherwise would be to look for difficulties, and that contravenes one of his cardinal rules of billiards tactics. (30 January 1932.)

These remarks were very true of Lindrum in the early thirties, when he was at the height of his career. He was so single-minded in his intent for billiard supremacy that he was unaware of the real needs of the spectators. Lindrum could be excused for this oversight because, in most fields of endeavour, it automatically follows that the higher the standard of performance the greater is the spectator interest. Billiards, of course, was an exception. Perfection caused the game to appear deceptively easy which resulted in the public's indifference to the game. Once Lindrum had developed his correct billiards technique it was very difficult for him to adopt scoring methods he knew were incorrect, simply for the purpose of entertaining the spectators. He was, after all, an absolute perfectionist. With this approach in mind it is easy to understand Lindrum's intense dislike for the baulkline rule and why he turned a deaf ear to the pleas of Joe Davis and others to reduce his cannon play.

Further examples of Lindrum's perfectionist attitudes were apparent in his preparations for his matches. There are the previously mentioned instances when Lindrum, while travelling by train or ship, would knock a set of billiard balls about on the seat or floor in order to keep his mind attuned to the feel of the cue striking a ball. When a match was in progress Lindrum would often retire to bed between sessions and cover his eyes with moistened pads. He found that the smoky atmosphere and artificial light of the billiard room made his eyes tired and sensitive. By covering his eyes with moistened pads Lindrum rested them for the next tension-packed session. Another method Lindrum used to soothe his eyes was to go for a walk in the clean air of an open park. Prior to a session of play he was often to be found slumped in a chair in the dressing room, half-asleep. Some assumed that Lindrum was merely lethargic. In fact he was undergoing a final stage of relaxation before he was engulfed by the pressure of the session. It was another of the special preparations to ensure him of his supremacy on the billiard table.

A further distinct advantage for Lindrum was that he was totally ambidextrous. Because of the childhood amputation of part of his right forefinger Lindrum had learnt to play billiards with his left hand, his unnatural hand. As Lindrum matured in his youth, and his hands became larger, he no longer had any difficulty in gripping the cue with his right hand. Consequently he devoted many hours of practice to the development of his right-handed play. Lindrum became a very proficient player with the right hand, almost as proficient as he was with the left hand. That missing joint on the right index finger proved to be of benefit to Lindrum. He found that his bridge for some strokes, especially the boucle (looped) bridge, was made

Facing page: *Walter with Geoff Hawksley (Editor of* Sporting Globe*) and Jack Rohan (Director of Royal Children's Hospital Appeal) during a fund-raising campaign. (Dolly Lindrum, copyright* Herald & Weekly Times*)*

Preceding page: *Walter with politicians at Parliament House, Canberra, 1953. From left, Theo Nicholls, Arthur Fuller, George Bowden, Cliff Nowland (marker), Frank Davis, Fred Daly, Arthur Drakeford, Walter Lindrum, Bill Edmonds and Denham Henty. (Fred Daly, copyright L. F. Dwyer, Canberra)*

extremely secure by the strength of the stubbed finger. It was said that the billiard table might occasionally shift but there was no chance of Lindrum's bridge hand moving. It was another advantage, albeit a small one, which Lindrum had over the other professionals. Lindrum would smile wryly when he said that he did not recommend aspiring champions to chip off their forefinger joint.

Lindrum had an uncanny ability to read a billiard table in one stroke. After he played just one shot Lindrum knew the speed of the table, the reaction that the balls would take on the cloth and so on. Lindrum's capacity to analyse the playing conditions was so acutely developed and his billiard skill so readily 'on tap' that if a shot did not turn out exactly as he planned he knew it was due to some variation in the playing conditions and not in himself. On some of his exhibition tours Lindrum was accompanied by his nephew, Bill Dunn. It was Bill's task to erect the table and act as marker for his uncle. On a rare occasion, when Bill had failed to level the table correctly, Walter would walk past him after the first stroke and say, quietly, "You've made a lovely job of this today, Billy".

One of the stories that gives a clear illustration of both Lindrum's knowledge of the billiard table and his unique ability was often repeated by his close friend, Eric Callaway. On one of his Sydney trips Walter phoned Eric, as was his habit, only to find Eric was concerned with the quality of a new cloth which had been fitted on his table by a billiard firm.

"I specified the type of cloth that I wanted, the one that you recommended to me, but I'm not at all sure that they've given me that cloth," said Eric, "I want your advice on the matter".

Lindrum travelled out to Callaway's home and after a meal they adjourned to the billiard room. After a brief look at the cloth, Lindrum said: "Yes, this is what we call the 'pepper and salt' cloth. Strangely, the ball tends to take an irregular path but, funnily enough, it generally ends up at the intended destination. I'll show you what I mean. Before I start, I want to say, here and now, that you should get in touch with these people and ask them to remove this piece of junk and give you the cloth that I specified".

With that Walter threw the balls on the table and commenced playing in order to demonstrate the numerous deficiencies of the cloth. As he played, he was continually talking and explaining the various faults of the cloth. Finally Lindrum stopped playing: "Well that's enough of that. I really don't enjoy playing on this sort of cloth". At the time Lindrum had compiled a break of over 700 points, without a single miss. Such a deed needs no further comment.

Few, if any, have ever loved the plaudits of his fellow-man as much as Walter Lindrum. Yet as Lindrum stood and accepted the applause of the spectators, as he did on so many occasions, an onlooker could be excused for thinking that he was somewhat indifferent to the whole proceeding. Nothing could be further from the truth. Lindrum's apparent aloofness at the billiard table was once attributed to his remarkable powers of concentration and his unaffected bashfulness. Behind the impervious expression of Lindrum, the billiard player, was a sensitive man who hungrily absorbed and savoured the acknowledgement of others. In later years Lindrum was more open in showing his delight and pleasure in receiving the audience's applause.

To gain some understanding of Lindrum's desire for acknowledgement from others, and perhaps comprehend one of the key factors which carried him to billiard supremacy, it is necessary to examine the influences in his childhood that helped to shape his character. Walter's early years were mostly spent in an environment of billiard saloons, hotels, gold miners and gambling. It was a rough and tough environment to grow up in and, sensitive as Walter was, he may have resented the coarse ways of that life. Maybe Walter had ambitions of escaping from such an existence. Perhaps billiards proficiency was one means of escape. Probably it was the only means of escape. Whatever the exact reasons, Walter channelled his energies into billiard practice. The long-term consequences of this rigorous practice, in terms of success at billiards, are written indelibly into the history of the game, but there possibly were repercussions in other ways. The immediate result of the long hours of practice was that Walter became isolated from other children. When he should have been enjoying the carefree existence of a child (especially in his out-of-school hours) he was undergoing the disciplined training of an adult. Walter's childhood development was stunted and his education confined to one narrow field — billiards. In adult life Walter was very aware of the limitations of his education. When he was confronted with conversation on a broad spectrum of topics Walter often became uncertain. He seldom gave opinions on subjects that he felt were outside his limited range. Instead he would look to a friend, whom he regarded with deference, to take his place in the discussion. Walter regarded that friend as having a far better education than himself and therefore he concluded that the friend's opinion (and the friend himself) was superior. The inevitable result of this line of thinking was that Walter at times felt insecure. The one place where Lindrum felt totally secure was on the billiard table, for there he could prove his infallibility. Walter's insecurity helped to feed his obsession for domination at the billiard table. Lindrum expected to be treated with deference at the billiard table, regardless of the stature of the match. If, for instance, an opponent managed to upstage Lindrum during a match — there were a few occasions when this actually happened — he would become most irate and would seek revenge at the first opportunity.

Mr A. J. Chown, O.B.E., former President of the Billiards and Snooker Association of New South Wales, and now patron of that body, recalled one time when Lindrum was upstaged. It was during an exhibition at the Union Club in Sydney. Lindrum's opponent was the fine amateur, J. R. Hooper, who was in receipt of a sizeable start. Hooper happened to be in top form and made a break of 185 before leaving the balls in a safe position. Lindrum missed the difficult shot, became annoyed by Hooper's tactics and eventually lost the match, which was an exhibition of no great significance. Lindrum, though, regarded the loss as a dent on his status and disliked Hooper securing a small slice of glory at his expense. Sometime later Lindrum was engaged for an exhibition at the Royal Automobile Club and Hooper again was to be his opponent. Lindrum was bent on revenge and ruthlessly annihilated Hooper in a merciless performance. He had restored his status. Of course, it was only Lindrum who felt that there was any need to restore his status. No one seriously questioned Lindrum's licence on the game of billiards. Lindrum did not seem to understand that the spectators who attended such exhibitions were interested in seeing both players in action. He did mellow in later years and, provided his opponent showed that he regarded Lindrum with due deference, he was given favourable openings by the master in which he had every opportunity to display his prowess.

One other consequence of Lindrum's isolated childhood could have been that he was starved of human contact and thus developed a desperate need for the companionship of others. Supremacy at the billiard table was one way of gaining the friendship and adulation of others. There were undoubtedly other factors that fed Lindrum's obsession for billiard greatness. It does seem, though, that the limitations of his childhood and the isolated nature of his billiard training were partly responsible for Lindrum's burning ambition for recognition as a champion billiardist.

Lindrum's need for acknowledgement by others was something every champion desires — to some extent, at least. All champions surely seek to raise their self-esteem by their performances. Nothing lifts that self-esteem higher than the acknowledgement and praise of others. Despite the enormity of the ego which a champion strives to satisfy he is seldom content solely in his own knowledge of his achievements. An essential part of the success formula is recognition from others.

Walter Lindrum was known to say, not egotistically: "I don't think that there will ever be another billiards champion as good as me. I sometimes practised for up to twelve and fourteen hours a day. Who the devil is going to do that nowadays?"

It was a pertinent comment by Lindrum even if he did only mention one of the multitude of factors contributing to his greatness. The comment seems even more appropriate today with the diversity of recreational activities and the other trappings of modern life. With so many distractions at his disposal it seems unlikely that any budding billiard champion would be able to isolate himself and develop the single-minded dedication that is essential to carry him through the long, long hours of practice. When Lindrum was in his youth in the early part of this century, the lifestyle was conducive to the single-minded pursuit of sporting excellence. There was a comparitively limited range of recreations to choose from and many people could not afford to indulge in the activities that were available.

With billiards now superseded by snooker it is more likely that any budding champion would be dedicated to the 22-ball game. It is generally accepted that there are vast differences between the type of training and practice involved in snooker and billiards. The three-ball game demands hours of practice when the player can develop and refine his game and obtain knowledge of the multitude of strokes. It is only through practice that a player can develop the store of knowledge that is a necessary preliminary to any appreciable improvement in his standard of play. It is not feasible for the billiard player to attempt to master the game in the environment of match play. A billiardist has to serve a long apprenticeship — up to twenty years — before he has, by regular practice and competition, developed his game to its potential. Conversely, it is generally agreed that a snooker player who shows an aptitude for the game can be developed into a quality player in two or three years. Although it is also necessary for the aspiring snooker player to devote many hours to practice he is more able to benefit from active competition than the billiards player.

With the current popularity of snooker there has been an influx of good players into the professional ranks. There seems to have been a rise in the standard of play with the new brigade, headed by Steve Davis who is acclaimed as the most promising player seen for several years, making it more difficult for the old brigade — the Reardons, the Spencers, the Charltons — to maintain a standing. Despite the current high standard of play the consensus of opinion is that few of the professionals would have stood much chance if pitted against the legendary Joe Davis. This view seems to support the theory that life in the early decades of this century was conducive to the development of this sporting ability. Indeed Joe Davis admitted that his horizons were very limited. He saw his choice of a career as being either a professional cueist or a coal-miner.

In the present snooker boom a player does not have to be a top notch professional to make a reasonable living. That is his good fortune and is a consequence of this age of sponsorship and television which has been of great benefit to so many sports. The point is, though, that the modern snooker professional does not have to strive, as Lindrum, Davis and the others did, to be number one in the game. While he may be hungry for success, the modern professional is not so reliant on that success for his survival. For example, when Joe Davis held the world titles for both snooker and billiards he was still living an austere existence. His hunger for success as a cueist was partly fed by his hunger for survival. Certainly he was far hungrier in these terms than the modern day counterpart. Having experienced the hardship and hunger of those battling years, Davis would never have forgotten it. The memory would have served to carry him on to greater proficiency. In a similar way Walter Lindrum was spurred on to greater heights, partly as a means of ensuring his very survival. Although Lindrum was never mercenary in his approach to life he, of course, needed a certain amount of money for survival.

It can thus be seen that there were a multitude of factors that led to Walter Lindrum being the greatest billiard player of all time. His obsession for greatness provided the stimulus. Lindrum's obsession and the nature of his upbringing both contributed to the single-mindedness of his concentration. The development of his physical armoury — the cultivation of his touch and stroke play — was facilitated by his genius and perfectionist attitudes. His physical strength, so essential in the compilation of large breaks, had been developed to a high level, during the long hours of practice. The end result of these interrelated factors was that Walter Lindrum became the closest thing imaginable to a human scoring machine.

No chapter on Lindrum's greatness would be complete without some reference to his snooker ability. Even though snooker was always a secondary consideration, Lindrum did play a moderate amount of the 22-ball game, especially in his exhibitions during World War II. It was because of snooker's increasing popularity that Lindrum felt obliged to play more of the game during exhibitions in his later years. There was no other factor stimulating his interest in the game. There are very few statistics available on Lindrum's snooker. At the time of the publication of his book, *Billiards and Snooker,* in 1940, Lindrum's best snooker breaks were listed as 139, 135, 133, 129 and

128. Lindrum added considerably to this list during the war years, although it is not known if he ever exceeded his 139 break. In the Melbourne billiard match with Fred Lindrum junior in May–June of 1941 Walter made two breaks of 135 in the frames of snooker played at the end of the sessions. On 23 September that year, Walter made a snooker break of 137 during an exhibition for the Silver Wings Auxiliary Ambulance Fund. Incidentally, the 137 break was immediately preceded by a break of 1087 at billiards. Walter Lindrum seldom, if ever, attempted to make the maximum break of 147 at snooker. During his exhibitions he was more intent on entertaining the spectators than pursuing records. For example, as a means of providing variety, Lindrum preferred to screw down the table after potting a red, take a lower colour, and then screw back up the table for the next red.

During his visits to England in the 1929–33 period Lindrum participated in very few snooker events. The biggest snooker event in which Lindrum played was in the 1930–31 season, during the staging of the International Tourney — the biggest billiard event ever staged. At the end of each billiard session, which ran for one-and-three-quarter hours, one frame of snooker was played. Thus during the 24 sessions of each match there were 24 frames of snooker played. With the International Tourney being conducted over two rounds each two players were opposed for a total of 48 frames of snooker. It must have been on the basis of these frames of snooker, and perhaps a few other even smaller events, that Joe Davis later claimed in his book, *Advanced Snooker* (1954): "For instance, it is well known that Walter Lindrum, who had my measure by a touch when we met at billiards up to 1934, was my inferior at snooker to the extent of two blacks and more."

Davis attributed this vast difference to a weakness in Lindrum's cue action. He stated that because Lindrum's left elbow was tilted slightly backwards, into his back, instead of being truly perpendicular, he could not have been a 'great' at snooker without some adjustment to his action. Although Davis must be respected as an eminent authority on snooker his judgement of other players seemed to place too much emphasis on correct style. It was the correctness of the style of first Rex Williams and later Eddie Charlton that prompted Davis to predict that both would become world snooker champions. Davis has been amiss in both these predictions. On the basis of style Davis would have dismissed Ray Reardon's prospects of winning a world title. Reardon has been a giant of snooker, winning six world championships with a cue action that has been subject to adverse comment. Thus it was insufficient for Davis to dismiss Walter Lindrum's ability because of his cue action alone. In making his assessment of Lindrum's snooker Davis could have been misled by Lindrum's performances. For example, in the International Tourney of 1930–31 Lindrum was conceding 7000 start to Davis, Newman and McConachy at billiards. It was a stupendous task to overcome such a start and one which had Lindrum totally embraced during each and every session of play. When he was so pre-occupied in the one-and-three-quarter hours of billiards it would not have been surprising if Lindrum did not treat the following frame of snooker too seriously. That is not saying that Lindrum was not trying. It is simply suggesting that he would not have played the frame of snooker with the same determination that he had applied to the preceding period of billiards. Additionally, Lindrum was, on average, occupying well over half the time allotted to billiards. It seems feasible to suggest that he would have been the more-fatigued of the two players at the end of the billiard session. These factors all point to Lindrum not performing at his top in the snooker frames. Joe Davis may not have considered these points when claiming that he was at least two blacks superior to Lindrum.

Indeed, there were several other authorities in the billiard and snooker world who disagreed with Davis' claim. Tom Newman, in his column in the *News of the World*, (27 December, 1931) said: "I sometimes wonder how good Walter is at the 22-ball game. A 'needle' match at snooker between Lindrum and Davis would be worth going a long way to see."

Horace Lindrum was, in 1946, putting in many hours of practice at his Saloon in Pitt Street, Sydney, prior to departing for England where he hoped to wrest the world title off his old foe, Joe Davis. Horace had met Davis in two previous finals but had failed to dislodge the champion. Several of the young players who frequented the Lindrum Parlour were convinced that 1946 was to be Horace's year for championship honours. One of Horace's keenest fans was Les Wheeler, who later rose to a prominent position on the *Sydney Morning Herald*. Wheeler enthusiastically declared: "Why, Horace, if you beat Davis you will be the greatest snooker player in the world". Came the reply from Horace Lindrum, without the slightest hesitation: "Well, not quite. If Uncle Walter wanted to play snooker, he would be".

Another who believed that Lindrum's snooker potential was not to be underestimated was Richard Holt, editor of the English magazine, the *Billiard Player*. In 1960, following Lindrum's death, Holt said, of Lindrum and his billiards: "He was a master of every class of the game, and it is hard to believe he would not have excelled equally well at snooker had he given his mind to it". These comments by Tom Newman, Horace Lindrum and Richard Holt carry a similar theme. The one thing which stood between Walter Lindrum and snooker greatness was motivation. Walter Lindrum simply had no passion for snooker. He found the 22-ball game lacked the charm, the elegance, the fascination and the challenge of billiards. There can be no doubt that there is much more involved in the mastery of billiards than in snooker. Walter Lindrum was adamant in this view. He believed that snooker was merely one aspect of billiards — the potting aspect. Lindrum found no challenge in conquering snooker, a game which he regarded as inferior to billiards. Having already scaled the Everest of the billiard table Walter Lindrum was totally indifferent to climbing a lesser peak.

It may be an academic matter to ponder over what Lindrum could have achieved at snooker, if he had really wanted to. Life involves the realities of the situation, not the 'ifs' and 'buts'. In terms of the record books there is no question that Joe Davis was the greatest snooker player of his time, and possibly of all time. There is, though, no question of Lindrum's ability at snooker, latent as it may have been. The final word on Lindrum's snooker came from none other than Joe Davis. The comment was made in 1960, some months after Walter Lindrum's death. What prompted Davis to make the comment is unknown. It certainly was different from the impression Davis had conveyed in *Advanced Snooker*. Davis' tribute to Lindrum appeared in the *Sporting Globe*: "Walter Lindrum was the greatest billiard player there has ever been or is likely to be. And if he had taken to snooker, he would have been the greatest snooker player the world ever knew". (14 January, 1961.) This from the man who held the World Snooker Championship for 20 consecutive years, is statement enough.

15 Epilogue

Lindrum was, simply, a genius who conquered his sport more thoroughly than any other player has ever conquered any other.

The Story of Billiards and Snooker by Clive Everton

The funeral service for Walter Albert Lindrum was conducted at St Paul's Cathedral, Melbourne, on the afternoon of Tuesday, 2 August 1960. Almost 2000 people representing sports, charities, business and civic groups crowded the cathedral for the service. The Reverend L. Llewelyn Elliot of St Silas' Church, Albert Park, and a close friend of Walter for more than twenty years, gave the funeral address. He said:

> Walter Lindrum's success in raising huge amounts for charity lay as much in the candour and simplicity of his character as in his consummate skill with the billiard cue.
>
> Self-denial is generally associated with the aesthetic and austere way of life, but Mr. Lindrum was a good living man who loved the society of others and who was a great sportsman and a fine gentleman. He in fact, walked with kings, but never lost that common touch which endeared him to thousands.
>
> Walter Lindrum was honoured by the Queen with the Order of the British Empire in recognition of his services to charity.
>
> I feel that it should be stressed that there was an element of self-denial in Mr Lindrum's living which is not appreciated unless one considers the immense sums that he could have gained for his own personal use had he chosen to commercialise his talents for personal gain. He was a man who not only gave of himself but of his substance.

The pall-bearers were: The Acting Chief Secretary, Mr Thompson (representing the State government); the State Opposition leader, Mr Stoneham; the senior vice-president of the Sportsmen's Association of Australia, Mr Lou Abrahams; and other sporting identities, Mr Bill Dooley, Mr Jack Pearce, Mr Alan Lechte, Mr Ted Hayes, Mr Jack Green. A guard of honour at the service consisted of the following sporting identities: Mr Harry Hopman (tennis), Doug Bachli and Ossie Pickworth (golf), Ted Rippon and John Coleman (football), Frank Williams and Les Roche (billiards), George Oke (boxing), Harold Matthews (coursing), the secretary of the Sportsmen's Association, Jack Callanan, and the treasurer, Bruce Fordham. Other sportsmen included Fred Tupper, Gordon Blackburn, Keith Lynch, Jack Lynch, Jock Sturrock, Theo Lewis, Richard Capper, Lou Richards, Laurie Nash and Frank Sedgman.

Amongst the mourners were the Lord Mayor of Melbourne, Cr Evans; President of the Lawn Tennis Association of Australia, R. N. Vroland; Chairman of the Victoria Racing Club, Sir Chester Manifold; president of the Royal Children's Hospital, Lady Murdoch; the secretary of the

Australian Board of Cricket Control, Jack Ledward, president of the Victorian Football League, Ken Luke, and many others. As the funeral left St Paul's the traffic in the centre of Melbourne ground to a halt. Crowds lined the streets as the cortège moved on its way to the Melbourne General Cemetery. The Masonic service at the graveside was read by the chaplain of the Crimea Lodge, Philip Joseph.

Of the many tributes which flowed in after Lindrum's death, perhaps the greatest came from the Prime Minister. An urgent cabinet meeting had detained Menzies in Canberra and prevented him from attending the funeral. Menzies forwarded a wreath and was represented at the funeral by Mr Hubert Opperman (later Sir Hubert). Menzies' tribute read as follows:

> Walter Lindrum was the greatest player of billiards the world has ever known. He was further ahead of any rival than the champion of any other game.
>
> He achieved this position not only by a remarkable innate talent but an infinite capacity for practice and self-discipline.
>
> For many years he employed his gifts most generously in the service of the nation. No good cause ever applied to him in vain. He raised by exhibition games enormous sums of money for public and charitable ends. He was, for all these reasons, a great sportsman and a most patriotic citizen. But for me he was more than this. He was a great gentleman and a great friend.
>
> He was, on occasions, my guest at Canberra. I visited him in his own home. He had an engaging personal modesty and charm. He was himself in any company. I had a deep affection for him. My only regret was that the pressure of affairs made our contacts and conversation relatively rare. Walter was a good man in every way. His death, which came too soon, was a personal grief to thousands of us.

Some months after Lindrum's death an appeal was launched to perpetuate his name. It was known as the 'Walter Lindrum Memorial Fund'. The *Herald & Weekly Times* Limited, which opened the Appeal with a donation of £1000, accepted the donations, which came from people such as Prime Minister Menzies, Opposition Leader, A. A. Caldwell, John Wren junior, Ken Luke, Lord Mayor Evans, H. E. Bolte. Contributions were received from sporting personalities, including Scobie Breasley, Jack Pearce, Theo Lewis, George Oke and dozens of others. After six weeks the Fund totalled £7099/6/6 — a fine tribute to Walter Lindrum. The money was used to establish an annual scholarship directed to technical education. Every year since 1961 a scholarship has been awarded to a student of a technical college.

On the first anniversary of Walter Lindrum's death members of the Sportsmen's Association made a pilgrimage to his grave. The members were disturbed that there was no gravestone to mark the resting place of the man who had done so much for others. The Sportsmen's Association decided to pay for the erection of a suitable monument. The result was a marble-topped billiard table, complete with a cue and three brass billiard balls — a very fine tribute indeed. In 1963 the Sportsmen's Association members established a further tribute to the man who had been their foundation president. They instigated the 'Lindy Award', a trophy which is given annually for outstanding sporting achievement by an Australian sportsman or sportswoman. This prestigious award has been won by some household names in Australian sport, including Betty Cuthbert, Ron Clark, Heather McKay (three times), Margaret Court and Shane Gould.

The one other reminder that Melburnians have of Walter Lindrum is the Billiard Saloon, run by Walter's niece, Dolly. The Saloon is now located at 26 Flinders Street, adjoining The *Herald & Weekly Times* Ltd. The Flinders Lane room closed in 1973 after more than fifty years of operation.

The life of Walter Lindrum remains an inspiration to all budding champions, regardless of their field of endeavour. His performances epitomised the absolute in dedication and perfection that should be the goal of any aspiring champion. The name of Walter Lindrum remains a perpetual monument in the transient world of sporting champions.

During the 1933 World Billiards Championship in London the referee, Arthur Goundrill was walking down Haymarket with Joe Davis. Goundrill asked Davis: "Will there ever be another player like Walter?"

"Could there be, Arthur?" was the prompt reply from Davis. (*Sporting Globe*, 28 January, 1961.)

This reference to Lindrum the billiard player, applies equally well to Lindrum, the man. He was a very human character who had his share of foibles, of which he was aware. These foibles were the source of Lindrum's great strengths for, instead of allowing them to destroy his life, he turned them into a positive means by which he could help his fellow man. That was the 'luverly bloke', the little man who never allowed the Walter Lindrum legend to affect his modest nature. And therein lies a message for us all.

16 Some Statistics

Results of the more important matches of Walter Lindrum's career.

Year

1914	W. Lindrum (received 4000) 322 break	18 000	beat	F. Lindrum junior	15 831
1915	*W. Lindrum 434	15 271	lost to	F. Lindrum junior 461	16 000
1916	*W. Lindrum	13 285	lost to	F. Lindrum junior 532	14 000
	W. Lindrum 785, 785, 766, 704	18 002	beat	C. McConachy 601	12 469
	W. Lindrum	18 000	beat	C. McConachy	16 587
	**W. Lindrum 463	16 000	beat	F. Lindrum junior	14 802
	W. Lindrum	16 000	beat	C. McConachy	12 543
1922	W. Lindrum 1417	16 002	beat	H. W. Stevenson	6545
1929	W. Lindrum 732, 644, 614, 763	24 234	beat	W. Smith 1058, 731, 720, 709, 703	22 147
	W. Lindrum 1434, 1090	22 317	lost to	W. Smith 1383, 1028	23 446
	W. Lindrum 2002 in 102 minutes	21 431	led	W. Smith 646, 770, 743, 645.	19 308

(Match abandoned owing to the death of Mrs Walter Lindrum).

1929–30 English Season

	W. Lindrum 1083, 1330	22 694	beat	C. McConachy	21 200
	W. Lindrum 1110, 1721	23 400	beat	W. Smith 991, 924	22 039
	W. Lindrum 8 x 1000, including 1925 and 1228 made on one day	28 333	beat	W. Smith	20 350

*Both these matches were for the Australian Championship.
**After victory in this non-Championship match Walter Lindrum issued no further challenges for a title match with Fred Lindrum junior.

| W. Lindrum | 28 003 beat | W. Smith | 21 962 |
| 6 x 1000 | | 1490 | |

(including 3262 — world record)

| W. Lindrum | 22 884 lost to | W. Smith | 23 985 |
| 1231, 1812 | | | |

| W. Lindrum | 24 147 lost to | W. Smith | 24 719 |
| 6 x 1000 | | 4 x 1000 | |

(including 2140 — Scottish record)

| W. Lindrum | 19 781 beat | W. Leigh | 10 080 |
| 4 x 1000 | | (received 7000) | |

| W. Lindrum | 29 056 beat | J. Davis | 26 172 |
| 5 x 1000 | | | |

(The aggregate of both players scores, 55 228, was a record).

| W. Lindrum | 30 817 beat | W. Smith | 19 344 |
| 10 x 1000 including 2419 | | | |

(228 match average — record)

| W. Lindrum | 23 387 lost to | C. McConachy | 24 224 |
| 4 x 1000 | | | |

| W. Lindrum | 28 722 beat | T. Newman | 24 090 |
| 3 x 1000 | | | |

(including 2053 made in one session — record,
sessional average of 2664 — record)

| W. Lindrum | 36 256 beat | W. Smith | 14 971 |
| 11 x 1000 | | | |

(including 1978 and 1824 made in one day,
also 4815 points in two sessions,
262 match average — all records)

| W. Lindrum | 15 157 beat | T. Newman | 9783 |
| 3 x 1000 | | | |

(including 1531 — Irish Record)

| W. Lindrum | 13 955 lost to | T. Newman | 14 145 |
| 1006 | | | |

During the 1929–30 English Season Walter Lindrum made 67 breaks in excess of 1000 (more than any other player had made in a lifetime.)

1930–31 English Season

The major event of the 1930-31 season was the International Gold Cup Tourney in which Walter Lindrum conceded 7000 start to each of his opponents. The Tourney is regarded as the greatest billiard event ever staged and the performances of Lindrum to win the tourney were probably the most remarkable of his career. For these reasons the complete results of the tournament are given.

Results of the International Gold Cup Tourney

29 September	W. Lindrum	24 883 beat	T. Newman	23 699
to	3 x 1000		(received 7000)	
12 October	J. Davis	24 863 beat	C. McConachy	22 689
	(both players off 7000)			

13 October to 26 October	T. Newman (received 7000) J. Davis	24 086 beat 28 219 beat	W. Lindrum 4 x 1000 C. McConachy	23 006 23 737

13 October   T. Newman   24 086 beat   W. Lindrum   23 006
to   (received 7000)   4 x 1000
26 October   J. Davis   28 219 beat   C. McConachy   23 737
                (both players off 7000)

27 October   W. Lindrum   29 276 beat   J. Davis   24 775
to   8 x 1000, incl. 2063   (received 7000)
9 November   T. Newman   29 204 beat   C. McConachy   20 851
                (both players off 7000)

10 November   W. Lindrum   29 554 beat   C. McConachy   16 867
to   7 x 1000   (received 7000)
23 November   J. Davis   30 394 beat   T. Newman   25 804
                (both players off 7000)

24 November   J. Davis   24 613 beat   W. Lindrum   23 867
to   (received 7000)   5 x 1000
7 December   T. Newman   36 230 beat   C. McConachy   19 374
                7 x 1000 (both players off 7000)

8 December   W. Lindrum   27 907 beat   C. McConachy   21 431
to   5 x 1000, incl. 2331   (received 7000)
                and 3905 (record)
21 December   T. Newman   26 859 beat   J. Davis   26 402
                (both players off 7000)

After the completion of the above heats Lindrum, Davis and Newman had each recorded four wins. A play-off was necessary. Lindrum drew the bye, with Davis and Newman meeting to decide the other finalist.

Results of Play-Off

5 January 1931.   T. Newman 30 663 beat J. Davis 25 515
        to   (both players off 7000)
18 January

Results of Final

1 February   W. Lindrum 25 807 beat T. Newman 24 436
        to   7 x 1000, incl. 2853   (received 7000)
14 February   and 2583
                        average: 248.1   average: 169.3
                        (Newman's lead during the match was,
                                at the end of the 7th session : 9177
                                                10th session : 7429
                                                12th session : 3780
                                                15th session : 1590
                                                16th session : 2439
                                                20th session : 2974
                                                21st session : 971

Lindrum caught Newman at 23 355 and led at the end of the 22nd session by 248 points.

Other Matches of the 1930–31 Season

1930   W. Lindrum   28 799 beat   C. Falkiner   19 523
        1108   (received 8000), 1130 break

1931	W. Lindrum 5 x 1000	23 801	beat	C. McConachy (received 7000)	19 383
	W. Lindrum 5 x 1000	25 625	beat	J. Davis (received 7000)	24 014
	W. Lindrum 1082	6641	lost to	C. McConachy (received 3500)	10 362
	W. Lindrum	16 223	beat	C. McConachy (received 3500)	10 829
	W. Lindrum 4 x 1000	11 123	lost to	T. Newman (received 3500)	11 957
	W. Lindrum 2 x 1000	11 418	lost to	T. Newman (received 3500)	12 599
	W. Lindrum 4 x 1000	24 521	lost to	J. Davis (received 7000)	27 555
	W. Lindrum	6155	lost to	T. Newman	8747
	Breaks of 750 plus counted			breaks of 500 plus counted	

During the 1930–31 English Season Walter Lindrum made 65 breaks in excess of 1000.

1931–32 English Season

1931	W. Lindrum 6 x 1000	19 008	lost to	T. Newman (received 5000)	19 930
	W. Lindrum 1082	12 435	beat	J. Davis (received 3500), 1524 break	11 754
1932	W. Lindrum 3 x 1000	23 208	lost to	T. Newman (received 7000), 1374 break	24 430
	W. Lindrum 5 x 1000 (including 4137 — record)	26 162	lost to	J. Davis (received 7000) 1424, 1276, 1247	27 413
	W. Lindrum 1372, 1218	12 332	beat	T. Newman	10 583

These were the only matches of the 1931–32 season that Lindrum played in England. He spent part of the season on a tour of the U.S.A. and Canada.

1932–33 English Season

1932	W. Lindrum 570	9462	beat	T. Newman (received 2500)	9383
	W. Lindrum 869	9833	lost to	T. Newman (received 3000)	10 416
	W. Lindrum 732	19 008	beat	J. Davis (received 3500)	18 531

The above three matches were played under the 100-point baulk-line rule. At this point the rule was altered to require a crossing once in every 200 points.

	W. Lindrum 4 x 1000	21 459	beat	C. McConachy (received 6000), 1119 break	18 949
	W. Lindrum	9720	lost to	C. McConachy (received 3000)	10 119
	W. Lindrum	12 700	beat	C. Falkiner	11 683

'Test Match'

	Australasia	28 644	beat	England	25 348
	(Lindrum and			(Davis and	
	McConachy)			Newman)	
				Davis — 1009 break	
1933	W. Lindrum	11 225	lost to	J. Davis	11 676
				(received 3000)	

Gold Cup Tourney

W. Lindrum	17 440	lost to	C. McConachy	20 520
			(received 6000)	
W. Lindrum	23 262	lost to	T. Newman	24 066
1020			(received 6000)	
W. Lindrum	24 007	lost to	J. Davis	24 758
1164, 1041			(received 6000)	
W. Lindrum	10 852	beat	T. Newman	10 255
			(received 3000)	
W. Lindrum	8739	lost to	T. Newman	9700
			(received 3000)	
W. Lindrum	9393	beat	J. Davis	8780
			(received 2000)	
W. Lindrum	8936	lost to	T. Newman	9285
			(received 2000)	

1933 World Championship

W. Lindrum	21 470	beat	T. Newman	20 252
1578, 984, 707			877, 805, 754	
J. Davis	20 136	beat	C. McConachy	16 110
995, 605				
W. Lindrum	21 815	beat	J. Davis	21 121
1492, 1272, 1013			792	

1933 : South Africa.

W. Lindrum	39 195	beat	F. Ferraro	33 523
7 x 1000, incl 2269			(received 25 000)	

1934 : Australia.

W. Lindrum	21 691	lost to	J. Davis	22 269
1212, 1591			4 x1000	
W. Lindrum	19 520	beat	J. Davis	18 523
957				
W. Lindrum	20 807	lost to	J. Davis	21 731
1909			1395	

Facing page: *The South East Asian tour of 1957. From left: Pat Neubronner, Cliff Nowland (marker), Wong Kwok-Leong, Walter Lindrum, Beryl Lindrum, Bill Hughes (manager), unknown, George Foong, unknown, Tan Seck Kay. (W. W. Hughes, copyright Lim Koy Yen, Kuala Lumpur)*

Overleaf: *Members of the Sportsmen's Association proudly displaying their trophies. From left: Jock Sturrock (yachting), Peter Thomson (golf), Doug Bachli (amateur golf) and Walter Lindrum. (Melbourne* Age)

The marble billiards table, complete with brass cue and balls, erected by the Sportsmen's Association in memory of Walter Lindrum. (Dolly Lindrum)

Preceding page: *Everybody was willing to coach Sabrina in the art of bowling when it was announced that she would bowl the first ball in an International match between England and an Australian Eleven. The match was organised by the Sportsmen's Association in aid of the Red Cross. Sabrina is getting some advice from former Australian Captain, Ian Johnston, supported by England's Len Hutton, Walter Lindrum, President of the Sportsmen's Association (left) and the Secretary, Maurie Fleming, look on. (Central Press Photos Ltd. London)*

1934 World Championship.

W. Lindrum	21 903	beat	C. McConachy	20 795
1065, 807			892, 829	
W. Lindrum	23 553	beat	J. Davis	22 678
1474, 1353, 1013			824, 728	

1938 : Australia.

W. Lindrum   18 349   beat   C. McConachy   14 121

This match marked the last occasion on which Lindrum played against others of the 'Big Four' of billiards (McConachy, Lindrum, Newman and Davis).

The Evolution of Walter Lindrum's Break Record
322 v. Fred Lindrum junior (May 1914)
434 v. Fred Lindrum junior (May 1915)
785 v. Clark McConachy (May 1916)
802 v. Fred Lindrum junior (May 1920)
1237 v. T. Thompson (January 1922)
1417 v. H. W. Stevenson (May 1922) red-ball break
1879 v. Claude Falkiner (September 1925) red-ball break.
1953 v. Horace Lindrum (March 1929)
2002 v. Willie Smith (August 1929)
3262 v. Willie Smith (December 1929) World Record
3905 v. Clark McConachy (December 1930) World Record
4137 v. Joe Davis (January 1932) World Record

National Break Records Held by Walter Lindrum
England: 4137 (January 1932)
Scotland: 2140 (January 1930)
Ireland: 1531 (March 1930)
U.S.A.: 2711 (April 1932)
South Africa: 2269 (September(?) 1933)
India: 983 (October(?) 1933)
Australia: 2609 (July 1931)

Other Notable Breaks by Walter Lindrum
3361 v. Fred Lindrum junior, 31 July 1940
3735 v. Fred Lindrum junior, 15–16 May 1941
3752 v. Fred Lindrum junior, 31 May 1941
3612 v. Fred Lindrum junior, 4 December 1941
All made under the revised baulk-line rule.

Cannon Sequences
253 consecutive cannons in September 1924, v. Claude Falkiner
273 consecutive cannons in April 1931, v. Tom Newman
529 consecutive cannons in March 1933, v. Joe Davis, under 200 point baulk-line rule.

Lindrum's Fast Scoring
1011 in 30 minutes at Manchester, February 1930
998 in 29 minutes at London, March 1930
663 in 15 minutes at London, 1930
346 in 8 minutes at Melbourne, 1934

100 in 46 seconds at Sydney, March 1941 (official)
100 in 27.5 seconds, 1952 (unofficial)

Lindrum's Breaks Over 1000
When the book *Billiards and Snooker* by Walter Lindrum was released in 1940 it accredited him with the following breaks:
711 breaks over 1000
 29 breaks over 2000
  2 breaks over 3000
  1 break over 4000
Lindrum added to this record during the years of World War II. For example in a match with Fred Lindrum junior, spread over five weeks in May and June of 1941, Walter Lindrum made 31 breaks over 1000. It is reasonable to estimate that the total of thousand-breaks which Walter Lindrum scored was well in excess of 800.

Appendix: A General Introduction to Billiards

This section is included for the benefit of those readers who are unfamiliar with the fundamentals of billiards. It has been kindly provided by Mr. J. S. (Jim) Collins A.M., former President of the Billiards and Snooker Association of N.S.W. and former Billiards Champion of N.S.W.

This brief appraisal of the game of billiards is offered to assist the relatively uninformed to a greater appreciation of this book. It will serve also as a mark of gratitude from one of the many who were influenced by the magic of Walter Lindrum, who were privileged to know him, however briefly, and perhaps enjoy the honour of holding the other cue, or receive advice from the maestro.

The Equipment
A full-sized billiard table has a slate surface, or bed, measuring 12' x 6'1½" and standing 2'10" (plus or minus one half inch) above the floor. The

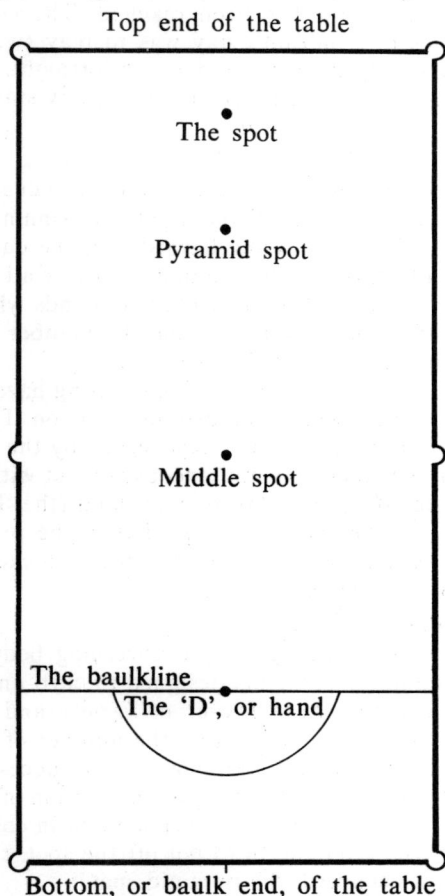

Top end of the table

The spot

Pyramid spot

Middle spot

The baulkline

The 'D', or hand

Bottom, or baulk end, of the table

table bed and the surrounding cushions are covered with a green cloth, often described as baize, which is in fact a fine Merino wool of short length. To qualify as a 'Standard Table' its four corner and two centre pockets must comply with templates authorised by the governing body. Spots are located on the longitudinal centreline of the table at 12¾" from the face of the top cushion (The Spot), the exact centre (The Centre Spot), midway between the centre spot and the top cushion (The Pyramid Spot), and on the middle of the baulkline. The baulkline is 29" from the face of the bottom cushion, and the semicircular 'D' is 11½" radius, centred on the middle of the baulkline. Balls are approximately 2 1/16" diameter. Cues are required to be not less than 3 feet long and show no substantial departure from the traditional shape and form.

Commencement and Duration of Play
A game commences after the players toss a coin or string (play the ball to the top cushion and return it as close as possible to the bottom cushion). The player winning the toss or string has choice of balls (spot or plain white) and choice of break (playing the first stroke from hand, the red ball being placed on the spot). The players have alternate turns, or visits, at the table until the specific time or points limit has been reached. The common practice in professional matches of Lindrum's day was to play two daily sessions, of either 1¾ or 2 hours, usually over a period of a fortnight. A time limit is still in favour for professional and amateur events of any standing, and a points limit is more common in lesser events.

Scoring
A scoring stroke is made when, after contact between cueball and object ball (or balls), (a) object ball is pocketed ('pot' or winning hazard), (b) the cueball is pocketed ('in-off' or losing hazard), (c) the cueball contacts both object balls (cannon) or, (d) a combination of any or all of these. A 'break' is an unbroken succession of scoring strokes, and ends when the striker fails to make a scoring stroke or commits any one of a number of foul strokes. The other player then becomes the striker.

Three points are scored for each winning or losing hazard off the red ball, two points if off the object white, and two for a cannon. The value of a losing hazard in combination with a cannon is governed by the first contact of the cueball, or two points if there is simultaneous contact with both object balls. The cueball if pocketed is next played from hand (the 'D'). The red ball if pocketed is placed on the spot, if occupied then the pyramid spot, if also occupied then the centre spot. The object white if pocketed remains out of play for the rest of the break.

Sequence Limitations
Throughout the history of the game the governing body has introduced a succession of rules and amendments designed to curb undue exploitation of repetitive scoring techniques, in favour of variety and spectator interest. Currently the rules place a limitation on the number of successive hazards (15), cannons (75) and pots off the spot (3). A succession of hazards or cannons is ended by one of the other, or a combination of both. A succession of pots off the spot is ended with any other score or in combination with any other score. Otherwise, after the third pot off the spot, the red is placed on the centre spot or, if occupied, the pyramid spot.

During the Lindrum era, and for many years after, pots off the spot were limited to two. This later became 15, then 5, and now 3. Billiards purists tend to deplore this undue licence given modern players and would prefer the old 2-pot rule as encouraging greater variety and expertise in top-of-the-table play. Other restraints imposed in the Lindrum era required an indirect cannon (ball-cushion-ball) after 35 successive direct cannons, and later, that the cueball cross the baulkline at certain intervals during a break (originally once each 100 points, then once every 200 points and finally once every 180-200 points). Neither requirement now survives which is a reflection on the comparitive standards of play. The indirect cannon rule caused no problems to Lindrum & Co. The baulkline rule did reduce the size of the breaks being made but the professionals soon adapted their play and so reduced the impact of the rule.

The Half-Ball Shot

Indisputably, the 'half-ball' or 'natural angle' stroke is the basic shot in billiards. It is achieved by aiming through the centre of the cueball to the approximate outside edge of an object ball and striking normally. (A 'normal' stroke is obtained when the cueball is struck at moderate pace just above centre to induce a moderate degree of forward propulsion). This will produce a delightfully constant angle of deflection of the cueball off the object ball. It represents the widest angle of deflection obtainable without the use of expedients such as side, screw, stun or force (which are described below). When the contact between the cueball and object ball is thicker or thinner than a half-ball contact, the result is a narrower, and less predictable, angle of deflection.

When properly exploited the half-ball shot played normally, or sometimes with the judicious use of other expedients, can produce the bulk of the points in a break, in terms of losing hazards and cannons. The half-ball shot is also used to create position for the execution of the more-advanced scoring methods, such as top-of-the-table play, and even nursery cannons, if such is the player's skill.

Common Expedients

A little about those expedients, and for this purpose we will take the word contact to mean contact of the cueball and the object ball. If the cueball is struck towards the top it will accentuate forward propulsion and induce 'follow through' effect after contact. Striking (briskly) dead centre, at short range, will cause 'stun' effect and limit cueball travel after contact. Striking (briskly) well below centre will cause 'screw' effect and widen the angle of deflection, in varying degrees depending on the thickness of contact. If applied to a full contact the cueball will 'screw back' or recoil in reverse after contact. 'Check side' is imparted when the cueball is struck on the side nearest the desired point of contact, 'running side' when struck on the side furthest from that point. Generally speaking, check side has an arresting effect on the cueball after contact, and narrows the angle of deflection. Running side has quite the opposite effect, and widens the angle of deflection. In certain circumstances the effects of side may change dramatically when, after contact, the cueball touches a cushion. Force is a factor to be used with caution but has value in some difficult circumstances where other expedients are inadequate by themselves.

By combining expedients the difficulty of certain shots is greatly reduced.

Special Expedients

Other expedients, not so commonly used, include the swerve and massé. The swerve employs side and forward propulsion in combination, imparted to the cueball from a partly elevated cue position and, if properly executed, the cueball makes a shallow arc. Greater expertise is required to execute a massé, which is played with the cue held vertically, or nearly so, and impact is made at an elected point on the cueball as viewed from above, depending on the nature and degree of arc it is desired to achieve. Very deep arcs are possible with the massé and, properly executed, it is the most spectacular of shots.

Methods of Play

Hazard Play

Early exponents of the game relied heavily on the various forms of hazard play. It was not long before a limitation was placed on the 'spot' stroke, to restrict those who sought to exploit the relatively simple routine of potting reds off the spot with great continuity. Thereafter there was much more emphasis placed on the ability to play losing hazards (mostly from hand) since, with reasonable command, it offered excellent break-building potential, interspersed with the occasional pot or cannon. With players generally striving to master this technique, some became so successful that a limit on successive hazards was also introduced. Nevertheless with the rules as they now stand there is ample opportunity for the occasional cannon in between sequences of hazards. Less experienced players will certainly rely on hazards to provide the bulk of points achieved in their typical 'all-round' play.

Top-of-The-Table Play

This technique involves all three balls being grouped in close proximity at the top end of the table and scoring with a succession of short range pots and cannons. A typical starting point is with the red placed on its spot, object white on or near the centreline somewhere between the spot and the top cushion, and the cueball poised nearby to pot the red or make a gentle cannon. If the pot, then it should be played so as to leave the cueball in good position for the next shot. If the cannon, then the purpose is to disturb the object white as little as possible and finish clear to pot the red which has been left near the corner pocket. Then in potting the red the cueball must again be left in good position for the next shot, and so on. This form of play makes it possible to compile really big breaks in relatively short time, but requires a great deal of practice and fine touch to control effectively the movements of all three balls. In the 'postman's knock' concept, the object white is manoeuvred into a hard-up position, dead on the centreline, and kept there as long as possible. In the 'floating white' concept it is manoeuvred back fron the cushion towards the spot by doubling or rear contact, but is not allowed to stay against the cushion.

Since the balls will rarely 'happen' into top of the table position it is normally contrived by one of two common methods. The most reliable method is to place the object white into position above the spot off a losing hazard into a centre pocket, then pocket the red into a centre pocket so that the cueball follows up the table to the desired position. The other method is to first place an object ball into position off a losing hazard and then play a cannon from the other object ball, 'dropping' onto the first ball, to leave the three balls closely grouped in the region of the spot, or with the red near the corner pocket. Less common methods are sometimes suggested by the inherited table situation.

Nursery Cannons
The very ultimate in cuemanship is the ability to 'nurse' the balls along a cushion in a succession of very delicate cannons, turn them around corner pockets, and 'feel' past centre pockets. Lindrum was able to play these nursery cannons with consummate ease, and on occasions continue on to circumnavigate the table, rules of the time permitting. Though not the originator of nursery cannons, Lindrum perfected them as a match-winning factor, and forced contemporaries into efforts to follow. A small few had some success.

No attempt should be made here to describe the many different shots that occur in a nursery cannon sequence. Many appear similar, but no two are identical except as to type. Some require the use of side, others do not. Strength and thickness of contact are also variable. Position for nurseries is usually obtained by a gathering cannon assisted by cushion rebound of the first object ball struck, to group with the others (also near a cushion). If anything, it has to be negotiated with even more care and expertise than is required for the nurseries themselves.

It seems a matter for regret that at the time of this biography, some twenty-two years after Walter Lindrum's death, professional standards should have declined so markedly, and that so very few can demonstrate nursery cannons at all, let alone employ them as a match-winning factor.

Bibliography

Alcock, Henry Upton, *The Alcock Book of Billiards,* 5th ed., Alcock & Co., Melbourne, 1901.

Bennett, Joseph, *Billiards,* 5th ed., Thos. De La Rue & Co., London, 1889.

Buggy, Hugh, *The Real John Wren,* Widescope International, Camberwell, 1977.

Carroll, Brian, *From Barton to Fraser,* Cassell, Melbourne, 1978.

Cashman, Richard and Michael McKernan (Eds.), *Sport in History,* University of Queensland Press, Brisbane, 1979.

Cleary, Tom, "Memoirs" (unpublished).

Daly, Fred, *From Curtin to Kerr,* Sun Books and Macmillan (simultaneously published), Melbourne, 1977.

Davis, Joe, *Advanced Snooker,* Country Life, London, 1954.

Davis, Joe, *The Breaks Came My Way,* W. H. Allen, London, 1976.

Dunstan, Keith, *Sports,* Cassell, Melbourne, 1973.

Everton, Clive, *The Story of Billiards and Snooker,* Cassell, London, 1979.

Gray, George, *Red Ball Play,* Cassell, London, 1911.

Kentfield, Edwin, *The Game of Billiards,* 6th ed., Alfred Boot & Son, London, 1886.

Levi, Riso, *Billiards For All Time,* R. Levi, Cheshire, 1935.

Lindrum, Horace, *Snooker Billiards and Pool,* Paul Hamlyn, Sydney, 1974.

Lindrum, Walter, *Billiards,* Methuen, London, 1930.

Opperman, Sir Hubert, *Pedals, Politics and People,* Haldane Publishing, Sydney, 1977.

Reece, Tom and W. G. Clifford, *Billiards,* A. & C. Black, London, 1915.

Rosenwater, Irving, *Sir Donald Bradman,* B. T. Batsford, London, 1978.

The *Sporting Globe,* A series of articles on Walter Lindrum, 18 June – 22 October, 1938.

Thurston & Co. Ltd, *The Noble Game of Billiards,* (Booklet, first printed 1908).

Whitington, R. S., *Great Moments in Australian Sport,* Macmillan, Melbourne, 1974.

Index